Sport Beyond Television

The Internet, Digital Media and the Rise of Networked Media Sport

Brett Hutchins and David Rowe

Routledge
Taylor & Francis Group
NEW YORK   LONDON

First published 2012
by Routledge
711 Third Avenue, New York, NY 10017

Simultaneously published in the UK
by Routledge
2 Park Square, Milton Park, Abingdon, Oxon OX14 4RN

*Routledge is an imprint of the Taylor & Francis Group,
an informa business*

Library of Congress Cataloging-in-Publication Data
Hutchins, Brett, 1973–
   Sport beyond television : the internet, digital media and the rise of
networked media sport / by Brett Hutchins and David Rowe.
      p. cm. — (Routledge research in cultural and media studies ; 40)
   Includes bibliographical references and index.
   1. Mass media and sports. 2. Social media. 3. Communication in
sports. 4. Sports—Social aspects. I. Rowe, David. II. Title.
   GV742.H88 2012
   070.4'49796—dc23
   2011048018
First issued in paperback in 2013
ISBN13: 978-0-415-73420-2 (pbk)
ISBN13: 978-0-415-88718-2 (hbk)
ISBN13: 978-0-203-12041-5 (ebk)
Typeset in Sabon by IBT Global.

For Janine and Rowan. We're still standing tall.

For Dan and Maddy, and to the living memory of Patrick.

Contents

Figures and Tables

FIGURES

TABLES

Abbreviations

AAA	Australian Athletes' Alliance
AAP	Australian Associated Press
ABC	Australian Broadcasting Corporation
ACA	Australian Cricketers' Association
ACCC	Australian Competition and Consumer Commission
AFL	Australian Football League
AFP	Agence France-Presse
ANZLA	Australian and New Zealand Sports Law Association
AOC	Australian Olympic Committee
AP	Associated Press
APCS	Association for the Protection of Copyright in Sport
ASC	Australian Sports Commission
ASTRA	Australian Subscription Television and Radio Association
BBC	British Broadcasting Corporation
BOCOG	Beijing Organizing Committee for the Olympic Games
CA	Cricket Australia
COMPS	Confederation of Major Professional Sports
DRM	Digital Rights Management
EA	Electronic Arts
EPL	English Premier League
EU	European Union
FA	Football Association
FFA	Football Federation Australia
FIFA	Fédération Internationale de Football Association
GPS	Global Positioning System
IAAF	International Association of Athletics Federations
ICC	International Cricket Council
IFNA	International Federation of Netball Associations
IOC	International Olympic Committee
IPL	Indian Premier League
IPTV	Internet Protocol Television
IRB	International Rugby Board
IRC	Internet Relay Chat

ISP	Internet Service Provider
Mbps	Megabits per second
MEAA	Media, Entertainment and Arts Alliance
MFC	MyFootballClub
MLB	Major League Baseball
MLS	Major League Soccer (North America)
MMOG	Massively Multiplayer Online Game
MPAA	Motion Picture Association of America
NASCAR	National Association for Stock Car Auto Racing
NBA	National Basketball Association
NBN	National Broadband Network
NCAA	National Collegiate Athletic Association
NFL	National Football League
NGO	Non-Governmental Organization
NHL	National Hockey League
NMC	News Media Coalition
NRL	National Rugby League
OECD	Organisation for Economic Co-operation and Development
PANPA	Pacific Area Newspaper Publishers' Association
PGA	Professional Golfers' Association
PMG	Premier Media Group
RWC	Rugby World Cup
SANEF	South African National Editors' Forum
SBS	Special Broadcasting Service
SMP	Sports Media Publishing
SROC	Sports Rights Owners Coalition
UFC	Ultimate Fighting Championship
VPN	Virtual Private Network
VRC	Victorian Racing Club
WAN	World Association of Newspapers
WCG	World Cyber Games
WTO	World Trade Organization

Acknowledgments

This book is the outcome of over three years research made possible by an Australian Research Council (ARC) grant for the project, 'Struggling for Possession: The Control and Use of Online Media Sport (DP0877777)'. We would like to thank Janine Mikosza for her excellent research assistance over the course of the entire project, particularly in relation to analysis of the interview data and the Web metrics presented in this book. Her direct input is evident in the analysis of blogging and the Olympics presented in Chapter 4. Thanks also to Genna Burrows, Callum Gilmour, and Vibha Bhattarai Upadhyay for their capable and professional research assistance at different points of the project. Rebecca Steinberg's polished editing skills were of immense assistance in delivering the final product. We are grateful to our colleague and friend, Andy Ruddock, who moved from verbal sparring partner to valued collaborator on articles related to the ARC project. His influence is most obvious in Chapter 5 and its discussion of MyFootballClub. Brett would like to thank his family and the people who have offered many forms of direct help and related support over the course of the research and writing for this book, including Libby Lester, Shane Homan, Kevin Foster, Peter Murphy, Simone Murray, Gerard Goggin, Michelle Cook, Toby Miller, Simon Cottle, Graeme Turner, and Philip Smith. David would like to express his usual appreciation for his nearest and dearest in Australia, Wales, and the West Country, and to record his gratitude on this page to Michelle Kelly and Christy Nguy for their valued assistance and forbearance in the workplace, and to James Curran, Paul Jones, and Rod Tiffen for their sustaining academic camaraderie. We also thank our colleagues in the School of English, Communications and Performance Studies, Monash University (Brett), and in the Institute for Culture and Society, University of Western Sydney (David) for their support over the course of the project on which this book is based.

A debt of gratitude is due to those professionals working in the sports and media industries who agreed to be interviewed during the project and generously gave of their time. Of course, while many people have made this book possible, ultimate responsibility for the arguments presented is solely attributable to the authors.

Our thinking about the issues examined in this book developed over the course of several writing projects. Small sections of this book were published in earlier articles and have since been fully updated. These publications are Hutchins, B. & Rowe, D. (2009) 'From Broadcast Rationing to Digital Plenitude: The Changing Dynamics of the Media Sport Content Economy', *Television & New Media*, 10(4), pp. 354–70, Sage; Hutchins, B., Rowe, D. & Ruddock, A. (2009) '"It's Fantasy Football Made Real": Networked Media Sport, the Internet, and the Hybrid Reality of MyFootballClub', *Sociology of Sport*, 26(1), pp. 89–106, Human Kinetics; Ruddock, A., Hutchins, B. & Rowe, D. (2010) 'Contradictions in Media Sport Culture: The Reinscription of Football Supporter Traditions through Online Media,' *European Journal of Cultural Studies*, 13(3), pp. 323–39, Sage; Hutchins, B. (2010) 'The Acceleration of Media Sport Culture: Twitter, Telepresence and Online Messaging,' *Information, Communication & Society*, 14(2), pp. 237–57, Sage; Hutchins, B. & Mikosza, J. (2010) 'The Web 2.0 Olympics: Athlete Blogging, Social Networking and Policy Contradictions at the 2008 Beijing Games,' *Convergence*, 16(3), pp. 279–97, Sage; Hutchins, B. & Rowe, D. (2010) 'Reconfiguring Media Sport for the Online World: An Inquiry Into "Sports News and Digital Media"', *International Journal of Communication*, vol. 4, pp. 696–718. Thank you to the journals and editors for allowing us to extend our ideas in this volume.

1 Introduction
Fishing for Eyeballs

Television is dead. Long live television. This was the message of the Sports Broadcasting Summit, a media industry event held in 2010 at a plush harborside hotel in Sydney, the picturesque host city of the 2000 Olympic Games. With registration costing AUD$2,000, this was an exclusive two-day event that, according to the event organizer, guaranteed opportunities to meet a range of 'top level decision makers as they collectively discuss the evolving sports media landscape' (Informa 2010). High-profile speakers included Australian media and advertising doyen, Harold Mitchell, and Peter Holmes à Court, the multi-millionaire entrepreneur and co-owner of the South Sydney football club with Sydney-based Hollywood star, Russell Crowe. Holmes à Court declared that his club was in the broadcasting business, despite spending much of his time detailing the merits of websites and digital media in the engagement of fans or customers. The type of 'broadcasting' of most interest to Holmes à Court and many other presenters was not terrestrial free-to-air, satellite, or cable television, but primarily Web-based (e.g., Web and mobile 'TV'). This malleability of definition and meaning was reflected in the overall event program, with half of the presentations focused specifically on the challenges and opportunities of the Internet and digital media. Other presenters emphasized developments in advertising, marketing, and free-to-air and pay-for-view television.

Observing proceedings from the auditorium and conversing with delegates over lunch at the Summit revealed that, contrary to the projection of public confidence, there is deep anxiety among the traditional 'power players' of the allied media sport industries—leagues, clubs, and media organizations. These interests have enjoyed several decades of relatively prosperous and unchallenged dominance in the commercial media marketplace, but are not enjoying the current period of change. Over the last 40 years or so, a stable compact had been established between television broadcasters and sports leagues selling tightly controlled and lucrative exclusive coverage rights to mass audiences. The pattern of these arrangements has varied across the globe, but in mature media sport markets there has been a relatively orderly trade in broadcast rights. The financial security and certainty afforded by this compact is under threat. The advent, expanding activity, and growing popularity of specialist digital media companies and telecommunications operators in sports coverage and reportage have cast doubt on the viability of this established business model, particularly with the growth of Web-based audiovisual streaming services, Internet Protocol television (IPTV), [1] and wireless communications.

The varied and loose deployment of the term broadcasting by speakers underlined an acute uncertainty arising from this situation, and invoked an altogether different meaning for the second half of broad*casting*. Media operators, big and small, old and new, are metaphorically fishing for audiences in the midst of rapid social and technological change. Multiple lines are cast by a growing number of media sport operators into a sea of convergent media platforms and technologies. The likelihood of catching sports-loving 'eyeballs' reliably and in plentiful numbers is, however, difficult to guarantee at a time of changing industry practices, and of shifts in viewer and user behavior. Broadband Internet, webcasting, social networking, user-generated content, mobile television, 'smart' television sets, and a host of other digital media technologies are the baited hooks signaling that the analogue-broadcast era is passing into history. Digital-convergent media are playing an ever-increasing role in the production, presentation, and consumption of media sport, although, as will be shown in the following chapters, this does not mean that large-scale corporate media influence is set to dissipate anytime soon. Instead, patterns of media use and communication are changing in a multimodal, multichannel, and multiplatform environment (Castells 2009). Only 15 years ago, when TV almost always referred to a broadcast receiver located in a living room and dial-up Internet was still widely in use, a Sports Broadcasting Summit would have been a very different experience. For some delegates at least, there was evident longing for an age when broadcasting was less suggestive of an audience fishing expedition than of the assertion of comfortable market dominance. Yet, as our analysis demonstrates, time and tide wait for no one in the 21st century media sport environment.

SPORT ON MULTIPLE SCREENS

This book investigates and analyzes the widespread and transformative media developments discussed by speakers at the Broadcasting Summit. For half a century, sports fans and viewers saw television as the most immediate and appealing means by which entertainment, spectacle, and news was delivered to their lounge-room or favorite bar. This long-established media and leisure arrangement is undergoing a fundamental shift as broadcast media, and the global media industry structures associated with them, are challenged by the increasing pervasiveness of online media via the Internet and World Wide Web. The function and meaning of television is complicated by its interaction with online audiovisual platforms, viewing practices such as time-shifting, and the emergence of dedicated online audiences, especially among younger users. These changes are a source of market unease because of uncertainty about the longevity of emergent structures, technologies, and practices. Table 1.1 summarizes the challenges faced by the range of media sport institutions and actors discussed throughout this volume.

Table 1.1 Challenges Faced by Members of the Media Sport Industry

Sports Organizations	Broadcasters	News Media Outlets	Digital Media and Tele-communications Companies	Fans, Viewers, and Users
• Maintain or improve the value of broadcast rights and contracts. • Deal with the potential devaluing of broadcast rights by online media. • Establish alternative business models and strategies designed for online media, and develop their own broadcast, online, and mobile media content. • Circumvent or prevent online piracy and unauthorized content reproduction. • Accommodate online feedback, criticism, and independent content reproduction by fans and consumers. • For minor sports, explore opportunities for exposure and revenue generation through the Internet and Web. • Where possible, build successful and profitable partnerships with computer game developers and publishers.	• Establish complementary and attractive online sites and distribution points for viewers. • Compete with new online market entrants, including telecommunications providers. • Adjust to an altered advertising market. • Circumvent or prevent online piracy and unauthorized content reproduction. • Accommodate online feedback, criticism, and content reproduction by fans and consumers. • Deal with regulatory uncertainty in a fast changing communications environment.	• Establish viable business models that identify profitable linkages between print and/or broadcast and online and mobile media. • Compete with or limit the activities of online content aggregators. • Deal with changing viewer, listener, and reader habits and practices. • Confront new online competitors for users and 'eyeballs', including 'official' Web portals that distribute sports news and information. • Adjust to an altered advertising market.	• Break the stranglehold of broadcasters over coverage rights to popular sport. • Establish profitable business models for online sport. • Obtain and package reliable 'premium content' to attract users. • Cope with regulatory uncertainty in a fast changing communications environment. • Consistently profit in an aggressively competitive and changing marketplace. • Establish viable and affordable technology offerings that change the consumption patterns of sports consumers (e.g., IPTV and mobile media). • Develop profitable and appealing sport related digital applications and services, including downloadable apps, and specialist mobile news and highlights packages.	• Access quality sports news and information in the face of plentiful online choice. • Decide which sites, voices, and sources can be 'trusted' to provide accurate, timely, and reliable content. • Deal with increased expectations of 'pay-for-view' or access online. • Decide how to access sports content (e.g., online and/or mobile and/or broadcast and/or print), as well as how much and how often in a '24/7' media environment. • Choose whether to pay, or try to access (perhaps illegally) sports content for free. • Decide whether to exercise the ability to create fan-produced or modified content. • Choose from a growing range of sport related products and services, including downloadable apps, fantasy sports, and computer games.

Source: Hutchins and Rowe (2010)

The number of Internet users worldwide has grown by an estimated 480 percent since the year 2000 to over two billion people (*Internet World Stats* 2011).[2] A rough 'guesstimate' of the world's total digital content produced the figure of 500 billion gigabytes in 2009. Monthly global Internet traffic is thought to be around 21 exabytes in total. Oceans of data and an abundance of applications reveal that the Internet is best understood as several different intersecting 'media' that foster clusters of social and cultural communication and activity (Benkler 2006, p. 372). Sport is a pivotal cluster online, particularly with the burgeoning popularity of online video. Industry and news media estimates display a consistent picture and should be noted in spite of their sometimes exaggerated and self-serving nature. Internet users in the US and UK are currently watching an average of 17 hours of online video per month. Users in Australia are quickly catching up, averaging around 10 hours a month (Frost & Sullivan 2011). Presently sitting at 40 percent, Internet video is likely to constitute 62 percent of consumer Internet traffic by the end of 2015 (excluding video exchanged by peer-to-peer file sharing) (Cisco 2011). Arguably the world's largest ever sports mega-event (Roche 2000) to date, the 2008 Beijing Olympiad, reported impressive online coverage and viewing statistics. Live broadband streaming accounted for 2,200 of the estimated 3,600 total hours shown by the American NBC-Universal networks (NBC 2008). While broadcast television is still a prime attraction for audiences (Rowe 2011a), these figures and estimates are evidence of a rich and popular second screen experience for fans and viewers, with mobile phones and devices evidence of a third screen (Lotz 2007, p. 68; Goggin 2006, pp. 180–81).[3] When people talk of the screen that delivers them footage of their favorite professional sport, many are talking about desktop, laptop, and tablet computer screens as well as television, with the distinction between screens blurred by technologies such as IPTV and video on-demand services.

While public pronouncements about communications and media technology innovation are often little more than facile 'cyberbole' (Woolgar 2002) and digital myth-making (Mosco 2004; Carey & Quirk 1992) proffered by boosterist entrepreneurs and would-be digital prophets, we argue that the last decade does represent an important shift in the history of sport and media. The birth of a new media sport order is being experienced that is not dissimilar to that of the 1950s and 1960s when television began its ascent as the dominant medium delivering sport to viewers and advertisers. This progress altered the role of radio but, importantly, did not signal the redundancy and demise of radio for sports coverage and reportage. In other words, both television and radio continued to cover sport, but the economics, administration, and form of professional sport changed forever with the coming of live television (Rowe 2004a). The new broadcast order then produced further effects as it evolved in relation to audience tastes, commercial decisions, advertising markets, and technological developments, such as the introduction of FM radio, and international satellite and cable television. A parallel readjustment of the media sport industries and cultures is occurring following the uptake of personal computing, expansion of the Web, introduction of broadband and wireless communications, growth in mobile media use, and the upsurge in popularity of services and platforms such as Facebook, Twitter, Google+, LinkedIn, WordPress, Tumblr, and YouTube.

The aim of our book is to explain how and why contemporary media sport is changing. This is achieved by identifying features of the marketplace, communications technology, and uses of media that explain the appearance and operation of media sport in the digital age, or, as we conceive and name it, *networked media sport*. We analyze why sports content is valuable and significant, connecting its production, consumption, and commercialization to the conditions that have facilitated the advent and expansion of 'the network society' (Castells 2000a).[4] The application and attempted control of the network and of networking logic have been investigated at every level of experience, including work, education, crime, politics and government, markets, gender, religion, and environmental activism. Given the social, cultural, and economic significance of sport, it is important to account for its role in the operation of media markets, communication flows, and digital media technologies (Rowe 2011b).

Particular attention is paid to the mechanisms and processes by which media sport relations are presently negotiated among leagues, clubs, athletes, fans, news media companies, broadcasters, and telecommunications providers. With a nod to television studies scholarship (Lotz 2007, 2009a; Ross 2008; Spigel & Olsson 2004; Turner & Tay 2009), the title of this volume intimates that the transition under examination is from broadcast to broadband and digital media. As will become apparent, it signifies a challenge to the hegemony of television, which can be alternatively bypassed, undercut, and complemented by online media. Television is, in effect, no longer the only medium that matters when it comes to the exercise of major economic and cultural power in media sport. There are many valuable studies available that deal with analogue and broadcast media sport, outlining how a widely accepted economic, cultural, and social relationship between professional sport, television, and commercial media became naturalized over the decades since the mid-20th century (for example, Boyle & Haynes 2000; Brookes 2002; Chandler 1988; Goldlust 1987; Rowe 2004a; Wenner 1998; Whannel 1992). By contrast, full-length books on the Internet, digital media, and sport are few and far between, with some notable exceptions like Raymond Boyle and Richard Haynes' *Football in the New Media Age* (2004); a valuable work that, as the title indicates, focuses on soccer (association football) in the UK and Europe.

Sport Beyond Television provides up-to-date findings and an extended analytical and empirical focus. Original evidence is presented from 45 in-depth interviews with industry professionals working for digital technology companies, major and minor national sports organizations, clubs and teams, telecommunications operators, news media, and industry regulators, in addition to legal experts, athletes, bloggers, and fans.[5] It is surprising that so little attention has been paid to such sources given the role of sport in slowly maturing digital media and telecommunications markets. By way of comparison, much has been published on the interaction between convergent media technologies and the global music economy, the publishing industry, television production and consumption, online video and computer gaming, digital storytelling, and film (see, for example, Bruns 2008; Castronova 2005; Hellekson & Busse 2006; Jenkins 2006a, 2006b). This imbalance has continued despite a proclamation 15 years ago by Rupert Murdoch, the head of the global News Corporation 'empire': 'sport absolutely overpowers film and everything else in the entertainment genre' (Quoted in Eckersley & Benton 2002, p. 20; see also Arsenault & Castells 2008). Murdoch's opinion is notable for more than its hyperbolic tone. He has acted on his belief through the strategic, if not always successful investment in both sport and sport related media properties in the UK, US, Europe, the Middle East, South America, the Asia-Pacific, and Australasia (Andrews 2006; Rowe 2011b). Divisions of Murdoch's media operations have also acquired online properties such as the sports news and Web portal Scout.com, the fantasy sports site WhatIfSports, the sports news and blog network Yardbarker, and a share of SportingPulse (see Chapter 3) as part of a digital media expansion strategy. Sport is central to the structure and function of media markets and cultures, and our book gives proper recognition of this development in the digital age.

The impetus for this study also relates to changes in the adoption and use of new communications technologies. The supplementation, augmentation, or replacement of broadcast sport with online coverage is a 'generational time bomb' (Ball cited in Boyle & Haynes 2004, p. 150). Children and teenagers are growing up with digital technologies (as so-called 'digital natives') and assimilating them into their everyday lives, meaning that sports content and information is increasingly accessed via networked communications technologies as part of daily media consumption habits. This often-advanced claim is consistent with the results of a number of Internet user surveys, including those completed by the Pew Internet & American Life Project. Adults born between 1977 and 1990—labeled the 'Net Generation'—represent the biggest percentage of the online population (30 percent), with numbers dropping for each pre-1977 generation (Jones & Fox 2009). Alongside teenagers, the Net Generation is the most likely to use the Internet for entertainment, although older generations are also said to be engaged in more activities online than ever before. Jay Scherer (2007) explains how sports advertisers and marketers were among the first professionals to understand that traditional and clichéd distinctions between sport lovers—'jocks'—and those interested in computing and technology—'geeks'—are no longer sustainable (if they ever were). This situation is indicated by the experience of those running digital media sport businesses, with an older male manager reflecting on how the creative process in his workplace unfolds:

> We were sitting around talking the other day about staff, and the staff member that comes up with the most ideas about what we do is 19 years of age. I don't even know how he started here, but he's like a programmer. He's the one that goes into the programmer's office more often than not and says, 'Have we thought about this? We've got to get into this space'. People his age are the ones actually using modern technology. (Interview with author)

A globally profitable conjunction between technology and sport can be witnessed in high-profile international industry conferences such as 'Sport & Technology' and the contents of widely read trade magazines like *Sport Business International*. Adidas is responsible for the neologism that signals the normalization of this relationship: 'jeeks'. These are defined as male, computer-literate sports fans (Scherer 2007, pp. 476–77). That the apparently 'aware' creative professionals working at Adidas could not see their way clear to imagine females as part of this new formulation shows, however, that not everything has changed following the growth of online media and digital culture. Young males remain a difficult market segment to generate sustained loyalty from over time. Yet, the frantic pursuit of their attention and money continues, as they match the description of new consumer technology 'early adopters' *and* sports fans (Boyle 2004). Sitting within this equation is a firmly entrenched gender bias that has pervaded sport since well before the invention of the World Wide Web, but which continues to be perpetuated online (cf. McKay, Messner, & Sabo 2000; Messner 2007; Plymire & Forman 2000; Mean 2010). This gender order in media sport, we argue, should be challenged on social equity and cultural inclusion grounds, but also in response to simple market principles. As the television industry learned over two decades ago, halving the potential population of viewers, users, and participants makes little economic sense even in the absence of appropriate cultural and political sensitivity (Miller 2001).

CONCEPTUALIZING SPORT BEYOND TELEVISION

The arguments presented in this book are guided by theories and concepts from media studies, cultural studies, and sociology. The employment of these interdisciplinary analytical tools assists with the difficult challenge of tracing the impact of fast moving social and technological change, which can lend itself to over-excitement or cynicism. The excitement and 'thrill of the new' felt by many people when using shiny, sleek digital devices like the Apple iPhone is typically countered by curmudgeonly commentaries

declaring that new media technologies are contributing to shortened attention spans and social isolation. Neither utopian nor dystopian prognoses
capture the complexity of technological innovation and diffusion (Spigel
& Olsson 2004, pp. 11–19; Turner 2009, pp. 150–56). This point is well
understood by the more astute media sport industry 'insiders' charged
with balancing the interrelated value of broadcast and online platforms
when making investment and operational decisions. For instance, the following comment was offered by an influential media manager (who was
paraphrasing the words of physician-geneticist and leader of the Human
Genome Project, Francis Collins): 'When it comes to new technologies, we
tend to overestimate their impact in the short-term and underestimate it in
the long-term'. The effects of near- and long-sightedness can be avoided by
the use of concepts and theories that supply proven and reliable analytical frames to evaluate the evolution of communications and media. These
frames are then critiqued and developed in accordance with new problems,
events, and evidence covered in this book.

A key concept drawn upon is the *media sports cultural complex* (Rowe
2004a), which, in building on the earlier concepts of Sut Jhally (1984) and
Joseph Maguire (1999), is used to encapsulate the intricate interrelation-
ship between sport, cultural symbols, and the social formations of which
they are a part. In describing the operation of media sport, it helps to build
understanding of

> . . . the extent to which the great engine of signs and myths itself symbol-
> ises and helps create our current 'being in the world'. By gaining a better
> knowledge and understanding of how media sports texts are produced
> and what they might mean, it is possible to learn more about societies
> in which 'grounded' and 'mediated' experience intermesh in ever more
> insidious and seemingly seamless ways. (Rowe 2004a, p. 35)

As a prominent form of popular culture, media sport is embedded deeply
within political, institutional, economic, and social relations. These relations are evident throughout elite-level and community sport, in media representations, and by the use of sporting metaphors throughout the business
world and everyday life (i.e., 'staying ahead of the pack', 'thinking like
a winner', 'overcoming hurdles', and so on). Largely absent so far from
discussion of this complex has been the role of digital communications
technologies in the mediation of these relations, both opening up and con-
straining particular possibilities for action by leagues, governing bodies,
fans, and media operators. Rather than adopting a technologically deter-
minist position, our case proposes that media and sport develop symbiotically following the emergence, uptake, and commercialization of different
media and technologies in response to prevailing cultural tastes and social
behavior. This pattern can be observed throughout the historical development of both sport and media during the eras of the commercial printing

press, telegraph, radio, television, and satellite communications (cf. Boyle & Haynes 2000; Elias & Dunning 1986; Gruneau & Whitson 1993; Holt 1989; Oriard 1993; Rowe 2004a; Whannel 1992). The Internet, Web, and digital media technologies represent the most far-reaching ensemble of changes to the media sport cultural complex since the introduction of television, situating sport as a pleasurable and widely accessed feature of online communication in the new millennium.

A related concept deployed frequently throughout the following chapters is the *media sport content economy*, which describes a fundamental shift in relations of media production from 'broadcast scarcity' to 'digital plenitude' (Hutchins & Rowe 2009a). The exclusivity of rights to cover popular spectator sport on television has ensured their economic value throughout the broadcast era, with sport offering reliable, appealing, and lucrative content for networks to attract viewers and advertisers. As a media agency director explained recently, this arrangement is still enormously attractive to broadcasters:

> You cannot underestimate the importance of exclusivity in the mindset of pay-television companies when they are acquiring rights. The kind of absolute exclusivity which rights-holders can currently offer allows them to sleep soundly at night, knowing their investment is protected. Any reduction in that exclusivity will affect what they're prepared to pay for it. (Quoted in Dunne 2011a)

Exclusivity has been protected for many decades by various barriers to entry, including the expense of setting up and maintaining broadcast technology infrastructure, the limited supply of and access to broadcast spectrum, state regulation, and concentrated market competition. This is an economic order that has stimulated demand by guaranteeing a restricted range of distribution channels for high-quality, popular sports content. Only a limited number of television networks (public and private, free-to-air, and subscription) possessed the production and distribution capacity and capital to broadcast major leagues, championships, tournaments, and events. Value for stakeholders in the broadcast model also proved resistant to erosion by non-rights-holders and consumers, with unauthorized video dubbing and illegal pirating of cable television channels having a relatively minor impact on success and failure in the media market.

Online content distribution mechanisms, particularly broadband video streaming and download technologies, are restructuring the media sport content economy. Digital plenitude prevails where once there was comparative scarcity in terms of quality content and channels of communication. Significantly lower barriers of access and cost have multiplied the number of media companies, leagues, clubs, and even individual athletes that can produce and distribute content for online consumption. Lower barriers have also allowed large numbers of users to access, appropriate, and share live sports footage (see Chapter 2). These arrangements are challenging the control of television networks and major sports organizations over the distribution of popular media sport content. New attitudes and practices are demanded from executives, administrators, and fans drawn into the orbit of an online gift economy, social networking, and a 'do-it-yourself' digital media culture that produces unanticipated ways of relating to and using media content. At stake are the ownership and control of valuable and celebrated media sport properties, especially regarding the ownership and regulation of Internet transmission rights. For instance, one estimate suggests that market revenues for IPTV worldwide will swell from US$12 billion in 2009 to US$38 billion in 2013 (International Television Expert Group 2009), as a range of companies offering IPTV services, including 'now' (Hong Kong), France Telecom's Orange, Verizon (US), British Tele-com, and Telstra (Australia), become integral components of the global media sport industry.

This realignment of the media landscape connects with another theme of this book, which appears less regularly but implicitly informs much of what follows. The theme involves a conceptual transition that deliberately challenges the reader to think about the *extent* that information technology, digital media, and media conglomerates actively constitute the material reality and experience of sport. It is time to think less in terms of the longstanding relationship between sport *and* media, and more about *sport as media*, given the increasing interpenetration of digital media content, sport, and networked information and communications technologies (Hutchins 2008; Hutchins, Rowe & Ruddock 2009). This case dovetails with Mark Deuze's (2007, 2009, 2011) provocative argument about a 'media life'-based ontology of contemporary reality—we now live *in*, rather than *with*, media. For those people living in developed economies with sufficient resources, pervasive and ubiquitous media are the 'invisible interlocutor' of their lives, experiences, and habits (Deuze 2011, p. 139) and, for better or worse, everyday life is mediated 'more than ever before' (Livingstone 2009, p. 7). It is imperative to begin considering the ways in which digitally mediated connection and interconnection are threaded through the fabric of sport, defining its touch, feel, and look (cf. Silverstone 2007, pp. 26–27, 110–11). This approach demands that attention first be drawn to the intervening media, technologies, and corporations that perceptually and materially underpin its experience and practice.

Professional sport has become reliant on a digital 'nervous system' (cf. Castells 2002, p. 65) that is making the form of sport indivisible from that of media. Examples of this phenomenon include IBM's provision of a massive data, real-time statistic, and presentational 'backbone' for Grand Slam tennis tournaments such as Wimbledon, including the event website, which annually reports over 10 million unique visitors. Another case in point is the influence of Electronic Arts (EA) in the creation of vivid sport computer games for players who, as Chapter 7 demonstrates, include fans and athletes. This global computer game developer and publisher releases online-enabled console games for Sony, Microsoft, and Nintendo that interact in real-time with 'real-world' sporting fixtures and weather conditions. These games are licensed by many international governing bodies, including the Fédération Internationale de Football Association (FIFA—the international governing body of soccer), National Football League (NFL), National Basketball Association (NBA), and National Hockey League (NHL). It is no surprise that the International Olympic Committee (IOC) has made an official recommendation

> . . . to strengthen its partnership with the computer game industry in order to explore opportunities to encourage physical activity and the practice and understanding of sport among the diverse population of computer game users. (IOC 2009a, p. 19)

The terrain mapped here is one where ubiquitous computing or information processing, integrated almost imperceptibly into the rhythms and background of social life, are routine features of sporting spectacle and engagement. For example, in professional leagues across the globe, large-scale live statistic and player movement tracking occurs for the benefit of team coaching staff, broadcasters, and fantasy sports websites. This surveillance is complemented by sport science tools like biofeedback devices monitoring the physical performance of athletes (e.g., heart-rate and breathing), and GPS-based (Global Positioning System) systems to trace the distances covered by players, their speed in performing a range of tasks, and the measurement of the g-forces that occur during collisions in body-contact sport. Sections of the data generated by these instruments that colonize the athletic body are now a feature of television and online commentary and coverage.[6] The exact speed of every pitch or serve and length of each throw or drive are now made available as commonplace knowledge for those watching. These techniques are used to enrich the visual and auditory field of the viewer and to provide expert commentators with quasi-scientific diagrams and numbers to discuss as contests progress. The affordability of many of these technologies is also seeping down to recreational activities like running. Inexpensive GPS-enabled applications (apps) for smartphones such as Runkeeper, MapMyRun, and MiCoach are examples of 'locative media' (Farman 2010) that allow runners to map courses, monitor distances covered, maintain pace via audio prompts triggered by calculation, and upload times and data to the Web. These types of innovation speak to the growing techno-social materiality of sport and leisure, which is increasingly hard to separate from representation and experience.

A deceptively compelling example that emphasizes how digital technology experimentation is spreading to almost *every* imaginable aspect of media sport presentation is the 'eCoinToss' (Figure 1.1) used at US college football's Liberty Bowl. Here digital movement sensors are inserted into the coin used for the toss by the referee prior to the match, which determines the team that will kick-off. A customized and, most notably, sponsored digital image of the coin is projected onto the electronic scoreboard, accurately reproducing 'the motion, flight and spin rate' (eCoinToss Sports Display 2010) of the physical coin as it turns in the air. This mechanism focuses the attention of millions of spectators, viewers, and users onto a pre-match ritual that once attracted minimal direct attention. Prior to this time, only those people directly involved in the toss were close enough to see on which side the coin landed.[7]

The eCoinToss indicates that the sophisticated application of digital technology is seeping into the very foundations of media sport. This trend can be exciting and disquieting at the same time, providing amusing diversions for those watching, and an excess of opportunities for advertising, sponsorship, and fan engagement. Networked communications and digital media are, in effect, central to physical competition, spectator experience, and fan interaction, as well as to an increasing range of leisure activities like gaming and betting.

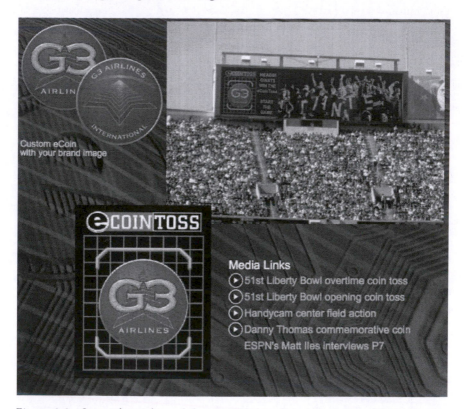

Figure 1.1 Screenshot taken of the eCoinToss website. Courtesy of P7 Technologies, LLC, and eCoinToss.com

Various developments highlight the interrelation of sport and media over the last 30 years, including the escalating commercialization and mediatization of the Olympics, the soccer World Cup, and the NFL (Guttmann 2002; Sugden 2002; Tomlinson & Young 2006; Whitson 1998).[8] In its various permutations and empirical complexities, sport as media represents a logical—but nonetheless radical—extension of this process, incrementally integrating the organizational, physical, and technological bases of sport, and contributing to a broader pluralization and problematization of the boundaries between technology and human bodies, nature and society, and science and culture (Beck & Lau 2005; Latour 1993, 1999). It is difficult for many sport followers to feel anything but ambivalent about this situation, given that it offers novel media experiences *and* additional opportunities for the commodification of sport. Even in its most nostalgic of forms, elite sport is an unavoidably mediated affair that is reliant upon media frames, technologies, corporations, and institutions (Ruddock, Hutchins & Rowe 2010).

Other concepts are introduced throughout the following chapters in order to explain and contextualize the evidence discussed. Borrowing from and critically adapting the work of key social and cultural theorists and media commentators, these concepts include *transmedia sport experience, media flow, digital media sport divide, information accidents, online crowds, remediation,* and *attention multiplier.* Taken together, they are a suite of ideas used to help understand developments in media sport over time, which will continue to offer insight even as websites, brand names, and consumer digital technologies change in the coming years. Attention now turns briefly to the research approach that informs our analysis.

MAKING SENSE OF FAST MOVING CHANGE

The approach taken in this study combines theoretical and conceptual analysis and empirical evidence in an effort to make sense of media conditions and relations characterized by uncertainty and change. Achieving an appropriate perspective under these conditions is difficult, not least because rapid change acts to obscure points of continuity. This difficulty is exacerbated by a constant bombardment of news and media reports announcing the latest technology products and the 'next big thing' or 'killer application'. At the time of writing, for example, much of the hype is centered on the iPad, ultrabook computers, Foursquare and cloud computing, whereas only a few years earlier the 'buzz' surrounded netbooks, MySpace, and Nokia mobile phone handsets. Then there are the entrepreneurs hawking their products in the hope of reaching stratospheric heights of online popularity. The CEO of Tout, a new video-based social media platform, boldly promised that 'we will be much bigger than Twitter' after the NBA's Shaquille O'Neal used Tout to announce his retirement from professional basketball

(Harvell 2011). As with other constituents of the culture industries, sport is affected by fads that, perhaps paradoxically, are signs of a collective effort to articulate the features and consequences of longer-term structural transformation in media systems. In other words, the latest media technologies regularly come to symbolize major shifts in the condition of social experience. For example, a now obsolete personal media device, the Sony Walkman, received a book-length treatment as a technological artifact signifying a shift in the experience of urban life (du Gay, Hall, Janes, Mackay & Negus 1997).

The struggle to understand change is most obvious in media commentaries that discuss how new online platforms are set to replace or co-exist with broadcast and print media. Moreover, each of these opinions and predictions may be at least partly correct depending on which of the innumerable media contexts, content forms, and technologies is under discussion. There can be no doubt, however, that the speed with which new products, platforms, and upgrades are released is giddying, as is indicated by this observation from a manager at a global consulting firm about the state of the media market just five years earlier:

> Think back to 2002–03—the first iPod had only just been released. Most people had never heard of 'social networking', let alone MySpace or Facebook. Even a digital stalwart like Amazon was yet to make a full year profit. (Tony Singh, Spectrum Value Partners, quoted in *Sport and Technology* 2008)

Since the time of Singh's comments, technological and market convergence has proceeded swiftly, and the expanding capacity of 3G mobile devices to access the Internet and perform many personal computing functions has transformed once-novel communication capabilities into ordinary media use habits:

> There can be some things that appear very new, such as mobile, for instance, that appear very distinct and different from other forms of new media, that after a short time really become part of the general landscape. The difference is mainly because of their newness and not because of the fact that, in the longer term, they have any real distinguishing factors. Anybody who has a Blackberry or a Windows mobile device will know that you can access virtually any Internet site using those devices. The fact that it is mobile is really incidental to the site; it is just another way of accessing it. (Dominic Young, News Media Coalition, Proof Committee Hansard, 15 April, 2009, p. 4)

A protean communications environment has led influential social theorist Scott Lash (2002) to reassess the possibility of considered critical reflection when digital media culture and global information flows move so fast that 'immanence' becomes a primary experiential motif. Thus, it is suggested that the capability of a detached, contemplative perspective is diminished. Whilst not subscribing to Lash's diagnosis for coping with this predicament, which is to write in an 'informational mode' that accepts immanence as an inescapable condition of thought (see also Gane 2004, 2006), his point concerning the disconcerting speed of the informational order is important and demands a careful response.

This study applies an orthodox social research methodology involving in-depth interviews with sport and media industry representatives, and extensive use of case studies and examples.[9] These techniques are informed by an historical awareness of the development of broadcast sport that grounds the analysis and avoids, as far as is possible, hyperbole and baseless 'futurist' speculations. This approach is modeled on the research of Leyshon, Webb, French, Thrift & Crewe (2005) on the Internet music economy. Much has been written about the impact of networked file sharing and music downloading on the entertainment and music industries. Instead of outlining these effects 'after the fact', the contribution of Leyshon *et al.* (2005) has been to identify major developments *currently under way* within the industry in response to emergent, dynamic practices through semi-structured interviews with industry informants. The effect of this strategy is to invest both arguments and conclusions with a tenable degree of relevance and longevity. In addition to extensive online and text-based research, the 45 interviews completed for this book enable examination of the ways in which networked digital media technologies are actively changing media sport production and consumption. Rather than treating industry actors as if they possess the keys to unlock the mysteries of media sport development, we regard them as having to negotiate uncertain circumstances over which they strive to give the appearance of control. Most crucially, this method supplies difficult-to-find background information and analysis that rarely appears in news and technology media sources, and enables discussion of emerging issues that require consideration from user, industry, and regulatory perspectives. Underpinning this claim is an anthropologically informed sensibility (cf. Askew & Wilk 2002) that asks critical media researchers deliberately positioned 'outside' an industry sphere to enter into dialogue with informants working on the 'inside'. While gaining access to informants is difficult and time consuming, such engagement provides valuable insight into the motivations, thinking, and decisions helping to structure the media sport industries, as well as the sources of tension and disagreement in different parts of the sector.

The next step in making sense of changing media sport relations is to use judiciously selected case studies and examples. The tracking of specific events is detailed in many of the chapters that follow, including the use of blogs and Twitter by athletes at the Olympics, the difficulties of amateur and lower-tier sports organizations as they administer websites, and the experiences of moderators on fan-run online message boards and discussion forums. The selection of examples appearing throughout this book was not predetermined. Rather, cases appeared during the three-and-a-half years of research completed for this study, or were raised repeatedly during research interviews. Addressing these phenomena serves to crystallize sources of tension, disjunction, uncertainty, and emerging consensus among those working in the media sport industries. That conflicts are occurring frequently demonstrates that, while the precise technological forms and uses of sport are far from settled in the movement from analogue-broadcast to digital-convergent media, the *dynamics of change* are identifiable,and in need of concrete examples and information to make them comprehensible (Lotz 2007).

The examples presented are drawn from a host of sports and events in North and South America, the UK, Europe, and Asia, including soccer, rugby, tennis, basketball, baseball, motor racing, golf, yachting, the Olympic Games, and cricket. All of the interview data are Australian in origin, although many of the interviewees work for sports and media organizations with substantial international reach and/or have experience of working across several different countries. Australia, we observe, is an ideal context in which to collect evidence of this type. Regarded as one of the world's most crowded sporting markets, the significance of sport in Australian cultural and social life is widely acknowledged, with Donald Horne (1964, p. 40) claiming in his seminal work of cultural critique, *The Lucky Country*, that 'Sport to many Australians is life and the rest a shadow. To many it is considered a sign of degeneracy not to be interested in it'. Whether viewed positively, negatively, or neutrally, sport has long been a key feature of nationalistic representations and mythologies, a situation that prevailed even prior to federation in 1901 among the colonies that would later comprise the Australian state (Cashman 2010; Mandle 1976). Sport has also been central to the historical and contemporary development of the media industries in Australia and elsewhere, providing both appealing routine content and spectacular media events, such as the 1956 and 2000 Olympic Games in, respectively, Melbourne and Sydney. These events helped to instantiate the nation through live free-to-air television broadcasts of itself in competition with other nations. Sports coverage has also fuelled two of the most publicized and expensive disputes in the history of the Australian media industries, the impact of which was felt internationally: the Kerry Packer-led one-day cricket 'revolution' of the late 1970s (Haigh 1993) and the attempted takeover of Australian rugby league by Rupert Murdoch's News Limited in the mid-1990s through the Super League concept (Miller, Lawrence, McKay & Rowe 2001). Furthermore, just as in other nations around the globe, the delicate balance between respect for national cultural specificity and local competitions, and the strong desire for transnational market penetration, is negotiated strategically by sport and media organizations in Australia (Rowe 2011b). Built into these challenges of the national and the global are strengths and weaknesses when it comes to online media. Highly localized codes such as Australian rules football are presented with a different set of challenges than globally dominant codes such as soccer. The former can exercise a reasonable level of control over online match footage and advertising in Australia given the limited popularity of the code overseas, but also has difficulty leveraging the global reach of the Internet due to this lack of international appeal. In comparison, the latter can and does use the Internet to cultivate and reach massive international audiences, but is also vulnerable to unauthorized streaming of live events sourced in multiple territories (see Chapter 2), and the undercutting of associated intellectual property rights on independent websites, blogs, and bulletin boards. In differing levels of detail, both of these scenarios are covered in the following chapters.

THE STRUCTURE OF THE BOOK

The chapters of this book reveal that the evolution of networked media sport pivots on the ongoing *intensification* of content production, *acceleration* of information flows, and *expansion* of networked communications capacity. The Internet reached 50 million users in the US in five years once it was made widely available to consumers. Television took around 13 years to reach this mark and radio 38 years (Flew 2005, p. 7). However, as we make clear in the following chapters, the significance of online communication goes far beyond raw numbers, and relates to transformations in the practices, cultures, and economies that deliver sport to audiences and users.

The next chapter outlines the continuities and discontinuities concerning broadcast sport and networked digital media. Our analysis describes the digital plenitude characterizing the media sport content economy, as demonstrated by the ascent of specialist online providers such as Google. These new providers are joined by the operators of illicit Internet streams of live sport, much to the frustration of leagues and broadcasters. However, it is also clear that television networks are prepared to meet the challenges presented by Google and online 'pirates' aggressively, responding with the exercise of commercial power in the marketplace, the supply of their own online program offerings, and the lobbying of legislators in pursuit of favorable regulatory and competition conditions.

Chapter 3 surveys the operation of networked media sport, examining how leagues and media companies attempt to measure the activities of online users and commodify website metrics. The opportunities offered by websites and independent online media activities are also shown to create difficulties for leagues and clubs, each of which is attempting to manage and distribute its own content. These initiatives can upset the 'competitive balance' in the media sport market. Furthermore, online media platforms present different challenges for both high-profile and lower-tier sports. A contribution of this chapter is the investigation of the potentially lucrative market in contracts to manage the websites of national sports associations that run community sport and recreation. Millions of people play sport away from cameras and commentators, and the chance to collect and mine the data provided by their online registration and activities is an attractive prospect for many digital media companies.

Chapter 4 details the impact of 'social software' on sport, with a particular emphasis on blogs, Facebook, and Twitter. These online platforms and their associated media practices are causing long-established broadcast media and planned publicity strategies to collide with the unpredictability of user-driven communication in participatory media environments. Attention is paid to the IOC's formal athlete blogging and social networking media policy, which thus far exhibits a contradictory combination of internal inconsistency and proven effectiveness in managing the risks of unwanted online disclosures and comments by athletes. Other issues covered in this chapter include the spread of fake athlete profiles on Facebook, scandals resulting from injudicious comments on Twitter, and the consequent promotion and defense of athletes' projected images and personae.

The ability of fans to produce their own sport related content and commentary poses difficult questions for sports organizations. Chapter 5 provides examples of sports and clubs that embrace fan input, as well as those that have sought to censor or shut down online message boards offering criticism. The interplay between these two responses reveals much about how the open and affective character of online fan communication clashes with the proprietorial and controlled character of sports branding and marketing. A case study presented in this chapter is that of 'MyFootballClub' (MFC), an online experiment that has seen a fan collective purchase an English semi-professional soccer club and attempt to run it via a website under the motto, 'Own the club, pick the team'. MFC twins the idealistic belief that fans are the 'true owners of the game' with the widespread recognition that users can also be producers of content and experiences in convergent media environments. Variations on this theme run throughout much online fan activity, including the appropriation of fan labor by clubs in monitoring the off-field behavior of athletes (Sanderson 2009a).

Pressing debates in the field of sports journalism are connected to those being actively pursued in journalism in general (Allan 2006, 2010). Chapter 6 demonstrates that these discussions register the emergence of *convergent sports journalism*. This mode of professional practice requires journalists to produce and repurpose stories for online, print, and/or broadcast platforms, often with great alacrity. Extensive evidence drawn from interviews with journalists highlights the complicated and onerous labor demands involved in producing stories for multiple platforms. This content is then 'creatively cannibalized' (Curran 2011) by other professional journalists, bloggers, and online aggregators, producing heated arguments over the rightful ownership of intellectual property. Details of the first-hand experiences of journalists confronted by the challenges of technological change in the workplace are contextualized within the wider institutional, legal, and commercial conflicts occurring between sports organizations and news media over the ownership and control of content.

The networking capacity of the Internet and Web are not only changing sports coverage and content, but consumption and leisure. The global popularity of Internet-enabled sports games and fantasy sports for computer, console, and handheld platforms are the most obvious manifestation of this development. Chapter 7 argues that for sports fans, gamers, and even athletes, the production and playing of these games 'remediate' (Bolter & Grusin 1999) the experience and understanding of sport. The use of 'physical technologies' (Francombe 2010) such as the Nintendo Wii and Microsoft Kinect are also discussed in this context. Other evidence of a remediation process is the emergence and success of popular e-sport computer gaming tournaments such as the World Cyber Games (WCG), which is modeled on the Olympic Games. These tournaments are shown to be public affirmations of the link between sport and technology in the perpetuation of masculine hegemony.

We conclude *Sport Beyond Television* by looking to the future, assessing coverage rights deals and events that structure how media sport will be accessed and experienced over the next decade. The control of online distribution mechanisms, coverage, and transmission rights is of most concern, particularly as broadband Internet capacity grows and significant amounts of content are controlled by wealthy broadcasters and telecommunications operators. The issue of public access to sport is set to become a pivotal issue in the politics of media use and the marketplace, which helps to explain why media sport matters in the evolution of the network society.

2 Television and the Internet

> If you can't control the arteries, what you do is get control of the blood.
>
> Graeme Samuel, Chairman of the Australian Competition and Consumer Commission (ACCC; Quoted in Kruger 2005)

> Content is not just king, it is the emperor of all things digital.
>
> Rupert Murdoch (Quoted in Lee, J. 2010)

The 'blood' referred to by Samuel is media content that will attract consistently large numbers of viewers, users, paying subscribers, and advertisers. As opposed to the era of mass media, power in the market is no longer principally a question of controlling the 'arteries', or capital-intensive mechanisms of distribution such as broadcast spectrum, large-scale printing presses, and specialist production facilities. Built on a foundation of comparatively cost-effective, portable, and user-friendly computing technologies and the Internet, an expanded range of providers can now supply 'first-run' or retransmitted sports footage and information to anyone with the ability to access it. This means that 'premium content' (Goggin & Spurgeon 2007; Evens, Lefever, Valcke, Schuurman & De Marez 2011)—the most popular live sport, highlights, and up-to-date news and information—is a highly valued asset in the media sport content economy. As the prefatory quotations above indicate, this is a point well understood by figures as diverse as the head of a national competition authority charged with maintaining fairness in the marketplace, and a media mogul who has demonstrated no compunction about testing the outer limits of market influence in multiple regions and territories around the globe. Samuel and Murdoch both know that sport holds the key to attaining dominance in convergent media environments where television, online, and mobile media overlap, interact, and compete. Samuel has long contended that sport is one of only two forms of 'compelling content' available online alongside films (ACCC 2006, p. 18), announcing just prior to his mid-2011 retirement that content is the 'paramount' consideration in the operation of the 'new media' market (Yeates 2011). Samuel's position is shared by industry regulators in Europe dealing with media companies determined to control coverage rights for elite-level soccer on a range of platforms (Nicita & Rossi 2008).

The intensity of competition for rights to media sport is matched by commercial anxieties about the exercise of tight control over content distributed via the Internet. The abiding concern is that people will not pay for content, despite survey results suggesting that two-thirds of Internet users willingly pay for selected online experiences and services, including music, games, and software (Jansen 2010). The problem for producers and providers is twofold: those users consistently unwilling to pay are concentrated in younger age groups, and both commercial and non-commercial operators can retransmit digital content easily without authorization. Even where this practice is demonstrably not occurring, interviews with professionals working for major sport and media organizations reveal the *fear* that it might, especially in relation to content aggregation, user-generated platforms, and online piracy. This anxiety points to a disjunction in the content supply chain delivering sport to fans. The impetus for media companies to own and control networked media sport conflicts with worries about their ability to control and profit from its supply and distribution. In other words, the open and networked logic of online communication clashes with a desire to create closed, centrally controlled models of content production and distribution characteristic of the analogue-broadcast era. The contradictions, uncertainties, and innovations produced by these contending media logics are the focus of this chapter, which also stresses the intricate continuities and discontinuities existing in contemporary media systems and markets.

The value of media sport resides in the attractive unscripted drama of live competition, and the demand for up-to-the-moment match and event results by fans. Sport is a 'perishable product', making the purchase of exclusive rights to first-run sporting events an attractive proposition for broadcasters. Live sports, which features regular intervals in play, is well suited to the placement of extensive advertising at a time when on-demand consumption is seeing viewers skip advertisements and promotional messages in other program genres with the help of personal video recorders and online viewing platforms. A founding executive at Fox Sports Media Group, Ed Goren, explained that the attractiveness of sport is its immutability as a broadcast form in a changing media industry:

> We invested billions of dollars in sports rights . . . with the belief that, as we move forward with more [viewing] options for people, and as the television universe gets more and more diverse, the one segment of network television that would continue to be must-see TV and would continue to deliver large audiences would be the major sports events because that's where the water-cooler talk will be. (Cited in Johnson 2009, p. 114)

The market value of sports rights is built upon the immediacy of fixtures. On the one hand, this makes live television broadcasts vulnerable to illicit

Internet streaming, a practice examined later in the chapter. On the other hand, the clear preference of fans and viewers for live sports guarantees a level of popularity and commercial protection for rights-holders. Events and matches attract a sizable and attentive audience while a result is in the balance. The appeal of most events then erodes significantly once the outcome is known, making them much less susceptible to myriad post-event duplication and replay options that occur in relation to film, music, and many fictional genre television programs. Unlike the textually interventionist and productive fan communities that have formed around *Star Trek*, *Star Wars*, and *Doctor Who* (Hills 2002; Jenkins 1992; Tulloch & Jenkins 1995), only a handful of supporters will watch the same world cup or league final dozens of times, or copy and share past programs among a large community of users.[1] Also, as any sports fan can attest, the timeliness of sports news and information works against the practice of time-shifting unless the viewer can avoid hearing or reading about the outcome of a match, which can be a challenging task given the range of media and news sources available in both private and public spaces.

The relative resistance of live sports content to devaluation is consolidated by the difficulty of substantially disrupting established chains of production that deliver enthralling athletic spectacle. The putative collapse of distinctions between professional and amateur ('pro/am') media observable in online knowledge production and sharing—exemplified by Wikipedia, digital storytelling, and interactive game 'modding' (Bruns 2008; Nieborg & van der Graaf 2008; Ferriter 2009)—cannot be replicated in soccer or basketball at the level of event staging, content provision, and athletic labor (the case of sports journalism is discussed in Chapter 6).[2] Only a handful of wealthy organizing bodies and leagues such as FIFA, the NBA, and the IOC are able to attract and afford the highest quality athletes who can deliver mesmerizing athleticism on a consistent basis. As lower-level sport worldwide shows, dedicated amateurs are welcome to play and contribute their energies, but the number of people watching online and live is small at best because the skill and competition on display pales in comparison to top-flight sport. As will be shown in Chapter 4, another dimension of this situation is the realization by the best professional athletes that they can promote themselves heavily online, thereby undercutting the overall level of media control exercised by leagues and competitions.

In industry parlance, sport is a rare source of 'must-see' content for millions of people in a world of multiplying digital communications technologies, fragmenting audiences, and proliferating Web-based special interest communities. In addition to complicating claims made about the extent of user productivity in online 'participatory media cultures' (Jenkins 2006a; Kreiss, Finn & Turner 2011), this capacity places sport in a unique position to influence how online media markets will function once the current period of industry volatility recedes. While the features of networked digital media are new in many respects, similarly unsettled periods of change have been experienced since the introduction of the telegraph in the 19th century (Carey 2005; Winston 1998). Market and social disruption are observable following the invention, suppression, and eventual diffusion of almost every socially useful and commercially exploitable communications technology. It is worth recalling that the telephone was once used as a tool for public address, including relaying sports news and concert performances, before its unanticipated acceptance as a mode of private one-to-one communication (Marvin 1988). Just as with the telephone, Internet and Web-based media are gradually fade 'into the woodwork' of everyday life (Mosco 2004, p. 127), signaling a collective forgetting that obscures the upheavals that travel with communications technology innovation, market adjustment, and social adaptation.

A common approach to analyzing transitions in media and communications is to first examine the prototypes and iterations of a technology that help to explain its subsequent usage. Our perspective reverses this order of thinking, contemplating how the coverage and delivery of a specific form of media content—sport—is helping to mold the use of digital media technologies and market structures from a range of possibilities. A previous example of this pattern can be seen in the way that British public service television producers responded to the popularity of sports broadcasts among audiences from the late 1930s. The technical requirements of delivering outside broadcasts—remote signal relays, camera design, lens types—helped to 'define what television actually was' in the minds of those running the British Broadcasting Corporation (BBC) (Chandler 1988; Haynes 1998, p. 212; Whannel 1992; Boyle & Whannel 2010a, p. 259). This feedback loop stabilized the meanings and uses of television for those controlling programming decisions and the millions of people attracted to watch. A variation on this pattern occurred from the mid-1990s in India when cricket coverage shaped the satellite television market as this broadcast technology spread across the subcontinent (Haigh 2010; Majumdar 2011). The following sections demonstrate that a similar process is at work in relation to networked media sport, particularly in terms of deciding how the Internet, Web, and mobile media interact with or serve as television (or, more accurately, a variety of *televisions*). Broadcaster responses to the entry of digital media operators into the market for coverage rights are then analyzed, as well as the tactics used to combat online sports piracy. As will be discussed in the concluding comments, the interplay between broadcast and networked media sport is ultimately characterized by contested norms of access and control. In the evolution of a digital-convergent media system, each of these issues is worked out in practice, which is why it is important to acknowledge the voices of media and sports professionals who make decisions and respond to these conditions.

IT'S TELEVISION BUT NOT AS WE KNOW IT

A curious feature of the network society is that the Internet is said to form the very 'fabric of our lives' (Castells 2002, p. 1), yet somehow there are more types of television than ever before. The proliferation of IPTV, Web TV, Internet TV, mobile TV, 3D TV, cable and satellite TV, pay TV, free-to-air TV, digital TV and 'smart' Internet-enabled TV sets is an affirmation of the conceptual, material, and commercial significance of television. It continues to announce itself, adapting, mutating, and reintegrating (Andrejevic 2009) at the same time as Internet and Web-based media continue their march into almost every dimension of social life in developed economies. There is no contradiction in this situation, but a multi-layered reality that makes any attempt to declare a life after television or the advent of a post-broadcast age debatable and demanding of careful qualification and explanation (Miller, T. 2009).[3] Amanda Lotz, writing in her perceptive book, *The Television Will Be Revolutionized* (2007), describes the conditions that see the continued dominance of 'television' as the label applied to screen-based practices of viewing despite the emergence of new modes of delivery: 'We may continue to watch television, but the new technologies available to us require new rituals of use' (p. 2).

Television sport is now best thought of as a *multi*media and/or transmedia phenomenon (see Chapter 4, this volume), available through different platforms, devices, and services. This scenario accords with the comments of industry representatives interviewed for this book, and a clear message from these professionals is that television is still the 'main game'. Their confusion arises in discerning which *types* of television matter the most as reliable sources of coverage rights income, particularly when media content is digitized and transmitted through different television platforms. Competing and complementary business models deliver content through broadcast spectrum, satellite technology, cable systems, and wireless and broadband Internet. As Web TV or Internet TV operators like YouTube and Metacafe attest, what was once clearly a broadcast technology is also a networked communications technology, with the categorical coherence of television held together by the experience of watching. Television is not so much superseded by the Internet and Web, as repositioned and redefined by its relationship to the Internet, Web, and mobile media (Lotz 2007, p. 6). This realignment extends beyond technology to institutional and organizational realignment given the different strategic and commercial responses of influential broadcasters such as the BBC (Born 2004) and the US networks (Wolf 1999).

IPTV is a major telecommunications policy and media market issue in Organisation for Economic Co-operation and Development (OECD) countries throughout North America, Asia and Europe (OECD 2007; ACMA 2010). This technology offers a useful illustration of continuities and discontinuities in television delivery and reception relations. While the means by which programs are delivered to the viewer differ from a traditional broadcast signal sent over the airwaves, the *experience* of IPTV for the viewer is, according to one high-ranking industry professional, not markedly different to any other type of television accessed through a set-top box (see Marshall 2009, pp. 44–45). As 'long as it works' and 'the football isn't interrupted', he believes:

> The average punter won't know anything different between having pay television or an IPTV set-top box. It'll sit in the same position, it'll record, it'll do all those things, you'll be able to download movies, all those things which you can currently do . . . it's just a different pipe for sending audiovisual down. (Interview with author)

Although valid in its own terms, this assessment omits the conspicuous disruptions occurring as once-successful broadcast business models are challenged by online and digital media, of which the viewer may be happily unaware. These models are emerging in relation to different habits of use, including IPTV's tendency to offer a greater range of international programming, the increased ability of the viewer to access different kinds of on-demand content, and the capacity to record two different channels while watching another.

Sport plays a vital role in this context as a reservoir of market value in a media landscape where reliably profitable content is difficult to locate for producers, and may, in some instances, be drying up. In addition to its capacity to draw large audiences, the immediacy of live sports and the unremitting demand for fresh news and results act to protect durable notions of 'appointment TV' and 'the network schedule' (Lotz 2007, p. 149; Lotz 2009b, p. 8), even when the TV in question is delivering footage via networked digital communications technologies. Unlike genres such as drama, comedy, and documentary, which in most cases can be watched at any time and shared in various ways, quality live sports acts as a bulwark against the displacement of programmers as authorities over time and content provision. Indeed, other genres of television, including 'reality', game, and music/dance contest forms, employ a sport-like format to draw live audiences (Rowe 2011a).

Uncertainty about how to deal with changing categories of television is widespread throughout the media sport industries. Leagues and competitions are experiencing difficulty in accurately valuing their rights packages and in separating them into coherent 'parcels' (for example, free-to-air, pay, online, IPTV, and mobile for various territories). On the other side of the equation, media companies seeking to purchase coverage rights and access to sports information and data are faced by the same challenge—how to value each rights package in relation to the others that are available. Rights-holders are also required to assess the likelihood of erosion of exclusivity and value by commercial competitors, content aggregators, unauthorized online operators, and new consumer technologies. At present, in addition to free-to-air and pay television, radio, DVD releases, and video games, a growing array of digital rights are discussed by sport business and technology commentators, including:

> Live Web Video—Game TV broadcast. Available streaming becoming more viable as broadband capacity increases.
> Live Web Audio—Live game coverage streaming. With many radio stations now streaming, some sports are putting a price on these rights.
> Web Hosting—Web development & advertising outsourced for sports in return for a web site & cash.
> Mobile—new developing area that can include video & audio as above, as well as 'official' apps for smartphones like iPhone, Blackberry & Android. (*Sports Geek* 2010a)

To this list can be added the rights to control and operate the online audiovisual archives of competitions and tournaments such as Major League Baseball (MLB) and the Olympics.[4] While archives lag well behind live content, highlights, and behind-the-scenes footage in terms of value, noteworthy sums are paid for footage featuring momentous events and famous victories in the history of a sport. These treasured moments can be used for promotional purposes, edited packages, on-demand services, and advertisements.

The valuation and organization of rights packages are problematic because separate digital platforms can quickly become difficult to distinguish when new digital consumer products are released. Obvious examples here are 3G and 4G mobile devices, with smartphones and tablet computers performing what were clearly personal computing functions only a few years ago, including accessing, downloading, and streaming from the Internet. The Apple iPhone brought this development into bold relief when, in late 2008, a modest market for mobile video and data rapidly expanded, with audiovisual sports highlights and news proving attractive to many mobile users (cf. Goggin 2011, pp. 139–56). Apple reported sales of over 6.8 million units in the fourth quarter of 2008, compared to only 1.1 million in the corresponding quarter of 2007 (Apple 2008). Sales momentum since this time has been maintained, with over 100 million iPhones having been sold. The range of rights available, and devices showing the same or similar images, make it difficult to know when separate rights packages aligned with a particular technology will clash with another platform, be eroded by a different supplier, or simply prove less valuable than initially anticipated. For instance, contrary to expectations, the popularity of mobile handsets has not consistently translated into larger mobile rights contracts for the English Premier League (EPL) soccer and other competitions in the UK and Europe (Bignall 2009; Evens & Lefever 2011).

The proliferation of assorted types of television and rights packages connects with Richard Lanham's (2006) engaging explanation of the economics of attention that underpins the information economy. Lanham notes that there has been an historical transition in the means of production. The industrial processing of physical raw materials and the production of 'stuff' have given way to an information economy based on the production, manipulation, and ownership of 'weightless' data. Attention is now the prized commodity for cultural producers. He identifies that a media environment dominated by digital screens is characterized by 'an economics of plenty' that allows direct competition between previously discrete word, image, and sound-based media (p. 20), meaning that competition for the attention of users and audiences has become 'stiffer than ever before' (p. 264).

Lanham pinpoints an experiential dimension of a market defined by the capture and allocation of attention. The cornucopia of digital media options and information overwhelm the individual and collective capacity to consume all the content and information related to specific domains of social and cultural activity: 'our range of choices has become so plenteous that plenitude itself seems to present a problem' (p. 264). The production and availability of digital media sport exceeds the capacity of fans to pay attention to all that might interest them. This mismatch between an excess of content and the time to attend to it means that the specific ways in which people can be induced to pay attention, and for how long, become the primary units of value for rights sellers and purchasers. The competition among different types of television then occurs at the level of assessing which are accessed the most, how often, and at which pivotal moments. The commodity in this formulation is the quality and quantity of attention directed by users at a particular device or platform that can be commercialized by means of advertising, subscription fees, user plans, and 'predictive' consumer behavior. But this is where difficulties arise in negotiations between rights sellers and purchasers—a significantly expanded range of delivery options for the same or similar content means that consensual valuation of coverage rights are hard to establish.

Exactly how much each of the different rights packages and the intellectual property attached to them are worth is the subject of volatile debate, disagreement, and variation. For example, the market dominant telecommunications company in Australia, Telstra, spent approximately AUD$170 million in 2006–07 to secure Internet and mobile rights to a number of major sports for a five-year period, including the Australian Football League (AFL). These purchases elicited the following assessment from an expert observer involved in the coverage rights market:

> A lot of sports certainly undervalued [their online and mobile rights] in the last round, and they have 'clicked' onto this fact. I'll probably use the AFL as a bit of a benchmark. I think if you looked at the first rights

deal that they did a few years back, it was overvalued. The deal after that one [2006–07] was undervalued, and I think we've seen quite a dramatic shift in the last 18 months. (Interview with author)

Valuing the unpredictable flow and direction of audience-user attention in relation to changing viewing options is an unenviable task. The variability of market conditions produces different strategic responses from sport and media organizations, including alternately conservative and highly optimistic value estimates for rights to mobile and online video, as well as a cautious strategy of delayed response in other quarters. A club media manager explained that his organization, after extensive deliberation, ultimately decided not to sell their digital rights, keeping control of them in-house. The club wanted to avoid undervaluing the mechanism that controls the distribution of attention in media markets—their intellectual property—particularly when the market value of online rights fluctuates from year to year. While other sporting groups 'basically sold all their IP [intellectual property] off . . . being the new frontier, we just weren't sure what it was worth and we decided to opt out for that reason'. (Interview with author)

A gradually emerging response to the conditions described so far has been the development of platform neutral rights. In avoiding the temptation to separate different platform rights into ever-multiplying and crosscutting packages, this arrangement is seen by many influential media sport executives as the most effective way of proceeding. This approach accepts the multiplication of television forms and the inescapable gravitational pull of media convergence. ESPN Star Sports, for example, purchased the rights to television, Internet, mobile, and radio across 24 Asian territories for Formula One motor racing (Fry 2008a), while Italian Serie A soccer also decided to sell its 2012–13 season rights on a platform neutral basis (Dunne 2011b). Such arrangements shift the burden onto the rights-purchaser, who then has to decide how and/or whether platform-specific rights should be on-sold to other content providers. Sport administrators are relieved of the need to predict whether platforms will stay separate or clash in the short- to medium-term. These advantages are leading many leagues to countenance or adopt a platform neutral approach, even in smaller markets.

There is a potential disadvantage in platform neutral arrangements for users and audiences. If wealthy television companies control all the available content packages, they can then 'warehouse' those digital media rights that are seen to threaten their proven broadcast business model (Evens *et al.* 2011, p. 34). This is a likely outcome in markets where the state, either directly or through industry regulators, is unable or unwilling to intervene in the media sport market. An online business manager for a major sport confirmed that the warehousing of rights does occur:

That's why you tend to see really big companies typically acquire broadband, mobile, and broadcast rights. And then they will just sit on the broadband rights, and they are doing it to protect their television business . . . we've almost got a monopolistic scenario happening when it comes to rights for major sports anyway. (Interview with author)

By purchasing rights that they have little interest in using or exploiting fully, broadcasters reduce the range of digital content available to new market entrants, including online and mobile operators, and suppress the development of digital media markets. This determination to preserve market power shapes the media sport content economy in tandem with technological innovation, which, as the next section argues, informs how television networks are dealing with problems presented by online behemoths like Google.

OFFENSE, DEFENSE, AND THE GOOGLE THREAT

The nervousness of broadcast television networks about the possible loss of audience share to other forms of digital TV and the Internet has been exacerbated by the entry of specialist digital media companies into the market for live coverage rights. Flexing its financial muscle, Google announced in the *New York Times* that it intended to purchase rights to 'more live events and live sports' after having 'new conversations with lots of folks' (Timmons 2010). Google's potential strength in the media sport market is emphasized by annual revenue of over US$13 billion, quarterly profits exceeding US$1 billion, operation of an estimated 450,000 servers in about 25 locations, and the provision of 159 country-specific portals (Kumar 2010, p. 159; Cubitt, Hassan & Volkmer 2011, pp. 150–53). Utilizing its YouTube platform (acquired in 2006 for US$1.65 billion), Google had already purchased the online rights to Indian Premier League (IPL) cricket, successfully carrying the 2010 tournament's 60 matches live to an estimated 50 million viewers. Facilitated by the 2009 financial collapse of IPL broadcast rights-holder Setanta Sports, YouTube's coverage attracted high-profile advertisers, including Coca-Cola and Hewlett-Packard. Coverage of the IPL contributed to a 25 percent increase in YouTube's unique visitors in India for 2010 compared to the previous year (*Sport Business International* 2011a). While nowhere near the reach of live broadcast television, the size of the IPL's international Web audience suggests that a workable Internet business model is emerging, particularly when forged by a company with enough resources to sustain initial losses in its establishment. YouTube has since streamed the 2011 Copa America football championship live from Argentina to 50 countries (Cutler 2011a), and had discussions with the NBA and soccer leagues in Europe about live coverage arrangements (Ehrlich 2011). The Google TV platform service is further evidence of a determined challenge to the broadcast order that has dominated sport for over half a century. The publicity generated by Google's media sport initiatives announced the existing and prospective value of worldwide Internet rights. In a show of faith for a tournament that had become badly mired in scandal and accusations of mismanagement, Times Internet (part of the Times of India group) then led a consortium that paid AUD$58 million for the 2011–14 online, mobile, and radio rights to the IPL (Hiscock 2011). Another major online media sport operator, the Perform Group, announced in early 2011 that it intended to float approximately 25 percent of its equity on the London Stock Exchange, which would see it valued at around £500 million. Started in the UK in 2007, Perform soon had contracts with over 200 leagues internationally, and streamed more than 25,000 live events during 2010 (Sweney 2011).[5] Targeting the needs of local markets in particular, the decision to embark on a public share offering was based on the company's 'first mover advantage in distribution and monetizing digital sports content' (Clark 2011).

Live webcasts are proving popular. The Ukraine-versus-England FIFA World Cup qualifying match in September 2009 was available live only on the Internet for the first time ever, attracting approximately 250,000 subscribers and 500,000 viewers (Gilmour 2009). While the sequence of events leading up to this match again involved the financial collapse of Setanta, the pay-for-view online experiment received substantial industry and fan attention. This game is estimated to have generated over £1 million in revenue and a profit for its backers. Philipp Grothe of Kentaro, the sports rights agency handling the match, stated, 'I have received a lot of calls from people around the globe who are looking into this. It's not a one-off trial here' (Gibson 2009a). The globally popular and unusually violent Ultimate Fighting Championship (UFC) has pioneered the use of Facebook to give fans free access to selected fights in an effort to connect with its audience. Promoting the use of a social networking platform for live streaming, UFC's Dana White proclaimed that 'everything is moving towards the Internet' as it is 'where the next generation of fans is going for news and entertainment' (*Sport Business International* 2011b, p. 22). Following the example of UFC, a partnership between the Football Association (FA) in England and a sponsor, Budweiser, has seen a qualifying-round fixture for the FA Cup between Ascot United and Wembley FC streamed live on Facebook (Bagchi 2011). There is also ample evidence of online viewing innovations that focus attention on once-ignored or hard-to-access 'side-events' attached to major international tournaments, such as the qualifying event to enter the main draw of the Australian Open tennis tournament (*Viocorp* 2009).

In a pattern reminiscent of record companies responding to threats posed by the Internet music economy (Leyshon *et al.* 2005), sport broadcasters are reacting both offensively and defensively to contain competition from new digital operators. Offensively, broadcasters are providing their own online and 'catch-up' television services (e.g., ESPN Player, Hulu, and the

BBC's iPlayer) that counter the activities of online-only operators, as well as using the additional distribution capacity offered by the Internet to show events that are unavailable on their main broadcast channels.[6] ESPN3 is an example of such a specialist sports service, operating in a manner resembling an ESPN cable channel for paid subscribers, and using the reach of the Internet to attract North American and international users. This live and archived streaming service shows a range of sports, including men's and women's basketball, American football, motor racing, golf, Grand Slam tennis, Champions League soccer, and Australian rules football. Operating as a supplement to the global ESPN network of broadcast channels, its attraction to users is the reliability of its content streaming service (minimal buffering, freezing, and dropouts) and the quality of the footage, which exceeds that of most unofficial or unauthorized Internet streams. For a monthly user fee, Fox Soccer also webcasts major soccer and rugby union fixtures into the US and extends the audience for competitions broadcast by Fox Sports around the world. These services demonstrate that, rather than allowing digital media providers free reign online, broadcasters are attempting to create their own Internet business models.

Another maneuver in response to the 'Google threat' is to set up authorized YouTube channels for club- and event-based footage, highlights, interviews, and news. Operating in conjunction with the video content offered on official sports websites, YouTube channels are available for competitions like the NBA, North America's Major League Soccer (MLS), the Wimbledon tennis open, the National Rugby League (NRL), and the AFL. In addition to supplying minor income streams, these initiatives increase the likelihood that fans will follow hyperlinks that transport them back to official sports websites. By appropriating potential online spaces of transgression for their own purposes, these channels counter the posting of unauthorized footage on YouTube by fans and reduce the determination of leagues to issue takedown notices, track individual users, and threaten legal action.

Existing alongside these offensive moves are aggressively defensive actions intended to curb the activities of digital operators and to maximize the exclusivity of the broadcast rights that have been expensively acquired. A much publicized and ultimately unsuccessful US$1 billion lawsuit for copyright infringement launched by media conglomerate Viacom against Google and YouTube (Liedtke 2010) was matched by an equally fruitless class action by the EPL against the same targets. Both actions commenced in the US court system and concluded in roughly the same period (2007–10). The EPL alleged widespread copyright violations by YouTube following the uploading of match footage. Other international sports organizations joined the case, including the Scottish Premier League, Rugby Football League, Finnish Football League Association, French Tennis Federation, and French Football League (Church-Sanders 2008). The crux of these court decisions is that YouTube is shielded from copyright infringement providing that the offending content is removed after they receive notification from rights owners. According to the presiding judge in the latter case, YouTube 'need not monitor or seek out facts indicating such activity' (Quoted in McCullagh 2010). A system that aims to flag copyright infringement at the point of posting on YouTube does, however, assist in this task. An intriguing statistic identified in the ruling was that over 24 hours of video content is uploaded to YouTube every minute. By comparison, the 24-hour time scale used by television schedule programmers is strikingly sparse (although the production quality of the content on YouTube is highly variable). Contending distinctions and commonalities between broadcast footage and Internet video are central to these legal actions that, whatever their merits, see broadcasters risk the alienation of sports fans increasingly accustomed to Web environments characterized by a 'participatory *habitus*' that encourages the sharing of content (Song 2010).

The risk of alienating fans has not prevented public complaints by prominent broadcast sport figures. The Chairman of the Fox Sports Media Group in the US, David Hill, has deplored the increased streaming of sports footage on the official websites of the NFL, NBA, and the National Association for Stock Car Auto Racing (NASCAR) (Ourand 2010). All of these competitions are telecast on Fox in some form, and an increase in streams elicited a clear warning to North American leagues that Fox may negotiate less valuable broadcast rights contracts if they continue to multiply their digital distribution mechanisms. Hill predicted:

> The leagues [will] kill the goose that lays the golden egg . . . If they keep slicing and dicing, one morning we're going to wake up and say, 'This doesn't work for us'. (Ourand 2010)

For those sports that are travelling fast towards the digital frontier, Hill's statement is a blunt message that they should not stray too far from the exclusive ethos of free-to-air and subscription television contracts.

Threats by broadcasters to reduce the value of rights contracts are arguably a more effective defensive tactic than legal action in suppressing the growth and potential of digital media sport operators. Whether implicit or explicit, warnings of this type help to explain the sometimes modest online activities of leagues that are heavily reliant on the income generated by broadcast deals. The fact that those professionals running sport know that broadband Internet and digital devices offer the opportunity for experimentation and innovation does not mean that they are willing to take a vanguard role in the use of them. A director of league marketing and communication explained the following:

> We have always taken a fairly conservative view of technology. We don't think it is our responsibility to be at the leading edge of technology, but we think we should be fast followers where it is appropriate. (Interview with author)

An inability or lack of desire to break the hold of reliable broadcast income informs this attitude, especially given the uncertainties produced by contested online user measurement systems (which are discussed in the next chapter), fluctuations in the advertising market, and multiplying television formats and digital products.

Hill's admonition is matched by complaints about the Internet and competition regulation from other parts of the News Corporation cable television empire (Hutchins & Rowe 2009a, pp. 361–62). The (then) CEO of Australian-based Foxtel (home of the Fox Sports channels), Kim Williams, has declared that competition between broadcast and online operators is potentially unfair. Internet operators are not bound by conditions contained in Australia's *Broadcasting Services Act 1992* (as amended). This means that there is no regulatory impediment to a broadband Internet provider exercising exclusive rights over an entire sport. An example of a prospective provider that expressed interest in the rights to a Fox Sports staple, AFL matches, is Fetch TV, which delivers subscription television through broadband Internet.[7] The entry of new companies such as Fetch into the media sport sector increases the range of competitors for rights and poses a problem for incumbent rights-holders, particularly if they drive up the cost of exclusive coverage. Importantly, Williams' comments are an open acknowledgement that broadband 'television channels' are directly competing for the time and attention of sports fans, thereby blurring the distinction between broadcast and online as content markets and media sectors. His position represents a shift from Foxtel's (and News Corporation's) more familiar harping about government over-regulation and, in particular, federally legislated anti-siphoning provisions ensuring that many major sports events remain on free-to-air television (under Section 115 of the Act). Rather than putting the case for further media industry deregulation and the purported free play of the market, Williams is in effect lobbying for a new set of regulations that limits the power of online content providers in order to protect Foxtel's financial and market position.

Despite manifold technological change, industry conflict, lobbying efforts, and legal action, a note of caution is needed here to prevent premature predictions of broadcast television's demise. The digital plenitude that has forever changed the content distribution and communication mechanisms of media sport is offset by the heavy concentration of ownership, capital, and power in broadcast markets. In the US, for instance, approximately 90 percent of the major cable networks are owned by just five conglomerates, with comparable levels of oligopolistic control observable in other countries and continents (Miller 2007, 2010a). This supremacy is a particularly acute problem in nations (like the US) that lack a strong public service broadcasting sector. For instance, the NFL attracts a phenomenal US$4 billion in multi-year television coverage contracts from CBS, ESPN, Fox, NBC, and DirecTV (Wilner 2009). NBC-Universal paid US$4.38 billion for the US broadcast rights for the Olympics between 2014 and

2020 (*Sport Business International* 2011c). This remarkable level of invest-ment, which outstrips the money presently paid for Internet and mobile rights, perpetuates deeply embedded television network promotional strat-egies built around 'big event sport' as a staple for audiences. This impos-ing financial and symbolic media power has been buttressed by 30 years of market deregulation and neoliberal governance (Harvey 2005; Couldry 2010), and half-a-century of an entrenched and mutually beneficial rela-tionship between sport and television (Rowe 2004a). Sports organizations and leagues have become dependent on the regular injection of substantial broadcast rights revenue for their survival and operation. While the wealth of the television networks and the global advertising support that follows them persist, broadcasters will offensively and defensively exert influence whenever and wherever possible.

It is necessary at this point to reiterate an important point made ear-lier—television is not being replaced by the Web and digital media, but repositioned and redefined by them (Lotz 2007, p. 6). As the rise of Google, webcasts, and online audiovisual streaming demonstrates, the stranglehold of broadcast networks over the transmission of media sport is loosening, but it is not yet broken. The offensive and defensive strategies of broadcast-ers continue to resist the undermining of a profitable and resilient business model that they wish to protect and prolong for as long as possible. The following section analyzes another issue demanding a resource intensive response from sports organizations and television broadcasters—unau-thorized Internet streams of live telecasts.

DIGITAL PIRACY

Sport is rarely mentioned in the media piracy literature despite the fact broadcasters have dealt with this issue for many decades. In 1944, a coali-tion of British sports organizations formed the Association for the Protec-tion of Copyright in Sport (APCS) that was dedicated to preventing the 're-diffusion' of live telecasts in public places (Haynes 1998, p. 215). The 1950s proved a fertile time for the 'pinching' of footage by rival newsreel companies at live events in England. Cameras were smuggled into stadia and scaffolds erected outside grounds, while exasperated rights-holders occasionally employed balloon barriers and spotlights to blind cameramen (Boyle & Haynes 2000, pp. 32–33). As mentioned in the opening chapter of the book, unauthorized video dubbing and illegal access to cable and satel-lite television channels have been evident since at least the 1970s.

Credible arguments can be presented both in favor of and against lib-eralized approaches to the sharing and modification of media content and computer code on the Internet (Lessig 2005; Epstein 2005; Cammaerts 2011). Our critique laments the difficulty of meaningful open debate about online piracy when industry propaganda and suspect claims of damage in the marketplace dominate the public messages in circulation. These factors coalesce to obscure the actual impact of media piracy, the complex elements contributing to it, and the varying experiences of it within different sectors. A range of scholars have skillfully dissected the rhetorical strategies and moral pedagogy deployed by the 'global copyright [or culture] industries' in relation to film, television, music, and software (see Gillespie 2007, 2009; Yar 2005, 2008; Sundaram 2010; Karaganis 2011a; Gates 2006; Nissenbaum 2004; Mirghani 2011). Indeed, the widespread deployment of the term 'piracy' and its historical relationship with seafaring illegality is part of this pedagogy. Directed at preventing unauthorized downloading and copying, these strategies loudly assert the legitimacy of national and global corporate control over popular media content. Efforts at establishing the legitimacy and public acceptance of this control encompass legal, policy, and cultural issues. One common tactic is to denounce file sharers and those who distribute commercial content outside the framework of the market as digital 'folk devils' (Cohen 1980). This characterization is perpetuated by sophisticated public relations campaigns, propagandistic education programs in classrooms and workplaces, the lobbying of governments to influence legislation, and law enforcement activities. These efforts increasingly criminalize once-acceptable forms of online behavior and spawn moral panics about the extent of illicit online practices.

A principal historical architect of industry-led anti-piracy campaigns was Jack Valenti (1921–2007), ex-bomber pilot and President of the Motion Picture Association of America (MPAA) for 38 years until 2004. Valenti's 'shock and awe' rhetoric saw media piracy added to the language of global fear alongside organized crime, pornography, and terrorism (Gillespie 2007, pp. 105–35; Mirghani 2011). Cinemagoers and DVD watchers are routinely exposed to anti-piracy advertising featuring images of a devil and scenes of shoplifting and motor vehicle theft.[8] These so-called public education advertisements are accompanied by copyright warnings shown before programs (including sports broadcasts) that, depending on their content, have questionable legal validity and fail to acknowledge the intermittent difficulties of distinguishing between fair 'dealing'/use and copyright infringement (Anderson 2010; deZwart 2009; Tushnet 2007).

Advertisements and announcements are part of a well-funded long-term campaign characterized by the elision of facts, blending of half-truths, and over-statement of financial impact. Their purpose has been to ensure that, as much as possible, active Internet users adopt the preferred position of supine consumers (Gates 2006). Harsh punishments handed down by the court system to hackers reinforce the message that 'netizens' should exercise scrupulous self-discipline in their online activities (Nissenbaum 2004, p. 206). Piracy campaigns are supported by opaque or flawed methodologies that frequently possess a 'very loose' and ambiguous relationship to evidence (Karaganis 2011c, p. 2; Dyer-Witheford & de Peuter 2009, p. 207). Such campaigns embellish the financial expense of media piracy and construct alarming images of 'epidemics' or 'crises' demanding immediate intervention by state authorities (Yar 2005, pp. 689–90; Eltham 2011). The unspoken truth across a range of industry-sponsored arguments is a refusal to concede a legitimate role for the existence of non-market, informal, or encrypted peer networks dedicated to popular media content on the Internet. These campaigns represent an unusually aggressive defensive tactic designed to maintain audience reliance on established and profitable media distribution mechanisms such as broadcast television, cinemas, retailers, video stores, and industry-backed online services.

Recent years have seen major sports leagues and free-to-air and subscription broadcasters join the anti-piracy fray. As the speed and carrying capacity of consumer broadband Internet connections have improved, so has the quality of the images that can be streamed in real-time to Internet users. The limited data plans and download speeds for households that once served as a protective layer for broadcasters against online piracy are now falling away, which is a worrying development according to Kim Williams:

> What we have had in our favour is the large file size of a TV show or movie which makes it harder to download, but clearly as technology gets better you reduce the complexity of piracy. (Cited in Bingemann and Chessell 2010)

Sports events are most vulnerable to *live* unicast and peer-to-peer streaming, as opposed to distribution after the point of release through file sharing protocols like BitTorrent and file locker sites. As already outlined, it is the commercial value and popular appeal of live sports events that explains the vulnerability of television broadcasts to online streams. Although illicit streaming services are regularly taken down, directories and sites can be located by users through online searches and fan bulletin boards where URLs are circulated via posts, live chat, or private messages exchanged between users.[9] Accessing these sites involves little more than pointing and clicking and, occasionally, registering as a member of the relevant website. The technology required to retransmit a live television broadcast online is also readily accessible through most home computers with the addition of software that is easily downloaded and a TV tuner card, which can be purchased from most high-street or mail-order computer stores. The challenge from the perspective of sport and television executives is how to combat downloadable software, cheap off-the-shelf hardware, and Internet users searching for free access to telecasts. This combination compromises exclusive broadcaster control over who has access to live television sport in different territories (domestic and various international markets) and by what means (for example, free-to-air, pay-for-view, or official streaming services).

Digital piracy of live sports broadcasts has not so far reached the scale of music peer-to-peer file sharing through the likes of Kazaa, Grokster,

Napster, and Limewire in the early-to-mid-2000s (Crawford 2005; Leyshon *et al.* 2005). Nor has sports piracy received the news media attention generated by the legal action taken against the operators of music download sites. General awareness is, however, growing among sports fans, with soccer leagues peculiarly vulnerable because of the sport's global following and year-round competition schedules (Giulianotti & Robertson 2009). A notable event announcing this development in Australia was the keenly anticipated 2007 Grand Final of the national competition, the A-League, between Melbourne Victory and Adelaide United. The match underscored the spread of rogue Internet streams and the difficulty of stopping them. This incident affected a pay television operator reliant on a combination of subscriptions and advertising for profitability. The game was meant to be shown exclusively on Fox Sports, which had paid Football Federation Australia (FFA) the relatively modest sum of AUD$120 million over seven years for exclusive rights to A-League matches. But, for those households without access to pay television (approximately 65 percent in Australia), a US-based streaming website, channelsurfing.net, offered a free stream of the Grand Final and the extraordinary five-goal performance of Victory's Archie Thompson. Despite knowledge of the pending stream in the lead-up to the game and instructing lawyers to issue a cease-and-desist order to the operators of the website, both FFA and Fox Sports were powerless to stop it. The Chief Operating Officer of Fox Sports Australia, John Marquard, was reported to be furious at the actions of those individuals running channelsurfing.net (Heinrichs 2007). This outcome was all the more upsetting for Fox Sports because knowledge of the stream was circulating in popular online forums at least five days prior to the Grand Final.

The difficulties outlined here have accelerated since 2007, affecting the world's wealthiest sports leagues and events. The EPL, despite reporting combined club annual revenue of over £2 billion, has called for UK Government assistance in convincing Internet users that piracy is not a 'victimless crime' (McCullagh 2009a). Internet streams motivated the EPL to issue over 700 cease-and-desist letters to website operators worldwide over the course of the 2008–09 playing season, producing an 87 percent success rate in takedowns (Gibson 2009b). Officials are particularly perturbed by the experience of the global music industry, as well as focus group research revealing provocations from respondents such as, 'Pirating isn't a crime, it's a lifestyle' (McCullagh 2009a). (This comment can be read as a sardonic retort to the alarmist images depicted in many anti-piracy advertising campaigns.) Threats of legal action by the EPL have been made against the website, Justin.tv, accompanied by suggestions that more than one million users access some live streams (Birmingham & David 2011). The owner of UFC, American sports promotion company Zuffa, has also filed a lawsuit against Justin.tv for repeated infringement of pay-for-view cage fights, and promises to aggressively pursue anyone 'who steals our content' (*Sport Business International* 2011b, p. 23). The available literature and online observational analysis suggests that audiences for the most popular streams are measured in the thousands or tens of thousands, but very few secure audiences of such magnitude at present.[10] The stance of the EPL and UFC is consistent with that of other leagues and competitions, with the NFL, NBA, and MLB each implementing measures to address unsanctioned online viewing. MLB has appointed three full-time employees to monitor streams (Gibson 2009b), while the UFC hired a third-party contractor to undertake the same task. Tennis Australia has complained to a parliamentary inquiry about '59 sites offering unauthorized streams or sites linking to these streams' during the Australian Tennis Open (Tennis Australia 2009, p. 9). Illicit transmission of this Grand Slam event is of concern to event organizers because it threatens the value of existing and forthcoming broadcast contracts, as well as being time consuming and costly to stop:

> [t]he reality is that attempting to use the legal system to police unauthorized delivery of content is at best slow, cumbersome and costly, and at worst almost entirely ineffective. (Tennis Australia 2009, p. 9)

The IOC has, however, experienced a modicum of success in this area. Through a combination of ample resources and China's extensive Internet security infrastructure, the IOC praised the 2008 Beijing Olympics organizers for detecting 4,066 cases of unauthorized live Internet streaming into the US, Europe, South America, Australia, Vietnam, and China (Xinhua 2008). However, neither the IOC nor the Beijing Organizing Committee for the Olympic Games (BOCOG) (via Chinese state authorities) could prevent peer-to-peer file sharing of the spectacular Beijing Opening Ceremony. According to Marshall, Walker & Russo (2010, p. 271), the IOC became so irritated at the frequency of the ceremony's redistribution on the Stockholm-based Pirate Bay that it launched a fruitless appeal to the Swedish Government for assistance in the matter.

The reactions of media sport professionals to the 'piracy problem' during our research interviews ranged from mild irritation to alarm. The uploading and replay of highlights on video sites such as YouTube and Daily Motion (Stauff 2009), and the file sharing of game replays, were considered little more than a distraction for Australian informants as there is a 'limited audience for that content' (Interview with author). Interviews revealed that letters or takedown notices sent to the operators of user-generated content sites are, in the main, acted upon. However, the discussion of streamed live events saw the expression of hard-line opinions because it is precisely this activity that, if demonstrated at significant levels, erodes the exclusivity of broadcast coverage rights. A director of a media company confirmed this situation when asked about the reproduction of his company's intellectual property without permission. He stared, paused and offered a sharp, 'We don't tolerate it' (Interview with author). In contrast, a sport communications director appeared calmly resigned to the intractability of online piracy, but found the hydra-headed abilities of website operators frustrating:

> Proliferation of online media means you might manage to shut down one part, one pirate. But there's a lack of consistent legislation across the world, so one might be shut down but can then just freely open up in another market . . . so piracy is a big issue. (Interview with author)

The media manager of another prominent sports organization confirmed the difficulty of battling 'fast-moving technologies and mutating networks' (Sundaram 2010, p. 132), explaining that considerable time and effort were expended tracing the location of site operators:

> We're battling. There's one service out there right now that we're trying to shut down. They'll continue to pop-up these peer-to-peer streaming services, and we haven't got deep enough to work out where this one is being operated from. But they're very easy to create and very difficult to shut down. (Interview with author)

Contributing to this exasperation is the fact that the 'digital armor' (Mosco 2004, p. 157) meant to protect content producers and providers against piracy are effective mainly against casual infringers. Digital rights management (DRM) tools (see Gillespie 2007, pp. 50–64) like encryption algorithms and watermarking of footage are of questionable use in consistently preventing streaming of live events, while proxy servers and virtual private networks (VPNs) circumvent geo-blocking measures that limit access to websites in specified geographical territories. These problems are unsurprising given that DRM measures are trying to combat the very practices that the Internet and Web are designed for—sharing and communicating in a decentralized fashion.

Conventional legal action against piracy is difficult to execute successfully because of jurisdictional issues and the financial resources required. Prosecuting individuals that access sites is costly and time consuming because they are hard to identify, and this course of action is likely to produce minimal change unless severe punishment has a demonstrably deterrent effect. Prosecuting users also involves a public relations risk for the sport, which can be seen as victimizing loyal fans if the news media reports the story.[11] Similarly, pursuing website operators and issuing takedown notices to Internet Service Providers (ISPs) confronts complicated matters of territory, jurisdiction, and the parameters of relevant laws. Jack Birmingham and Matthew David (2011) explain that proving 'contributory copyright infringement' against the music service, Napster, was possible because it was shown the operators knowingly failed to purge infringing materials from their servers, which made them liable when users downloaded songs.

But live sports content is comparatively transient. An infringement notice sent to Justin.tv is 'unlikely to be effectively acted upon until the event has finished, and the stream terminated anyway' (Birmingham and David 2011, p. 74). Using the dual-use defense, site hosts can defend themselves by stating they do not encourage or condone unauthorized streams and, unless they are specifically reported, remain unaware of their existence at the time of their transmission. Coordinated lobbying of search engines like Google in order to limit the appearance of pirated materials in results pages has produced some change (*BBC* 2010). Again, this course of action tends to affect casual users rather than those who might systematically and materially benefit from piracy.

The problems discussed here explain the continuing appeal of broadcast television coverage to sports organizations. Broadcasting offers reasonably consistent financial returns and prompts longing for the pre-Internet era when sport was much easier to protect against illicit transmission. In the internal cultures of sports leagues that occupy prominent space in broadcast schedules, television is positioned as a 'good' or 'reliable' media technology, whereas the Internet and Web tend to be viewed as 'risky', 'challenging', or, in an optimistic guise, 'exciting'. Accepted media industry discourses around Internet piracy contribute to the framing of these technologies, reinforced by the knowledge that it is difficult—and probably undesirable—to orchestrate completely foolproof blocking, filtering, and censoring of online sites. As the next section shows, however, the captains of global media sport are not about to meekly surrender to the so-called pirates.

PRESERVING THE BROADCAST BUSINESS MODEL

Lessons from the political lobbying, education campaigns, and intelligence-gathering activities of copyright industry coalitions like the International Intellectual Property Alliance, International Anti-Counterfeiting Coalition, and the Alliance Against IP Theft have been absorbed by the media sport sector. The Sports Rights Owners Coalition (SROC) can now be added to a long list of industry-financed organizations operating in this area. SROC members include some of the world's biggest sports bodies, including FIFA, the International Cricket Council (ICC), International Association of Athletics Federations (IAAF), International Rugby Board (IRB), Formula One, International Federation of Netball Associations (IFNA), and the World Marathon Majors.[12] The SROC seeks to influence broadcast and intellectual property policy development, making representations to the European Union (EU) and the World Trade Organization (WTO), and commenting publicly on matters under consideration by the French Parliament. The SROC-sponsored *Background Report on Digital Piracy of Sporting Events* (NetResult 2008) recalls the moral pedagogy of the music, film, and software industries. In order to encourage government and law enforcement intervention, professional sports are positioned as the hapless victims of 'digital piracy', which is 'an *extraordinarily difficult challenge to which they are ill-equipped to respond* given the current legal and technical means at their disposal' (p. 3; original emphasis). Combating online pirates is said to be an increasingly expensive activity, with four sports organizations and a broadcast rights-holder reported to have spent over €1.3 million in a single year on dealing with unauthorized streams (NetResult 2008, p. 15). No detailed indication of how this figure was calculated is contained in the report.

Standing alongside SROC is Copyright Integrity International, a private consultancy headquartered in India that operates under a title suggesting a public interest mission. This company has been hired by 13 national and international cricket-governing bodies to send cease-and-desist letters to websites, and to track and shut down streams where possible. Dr. Clinton Free of Copyright Integrity International has commented in the Australian news media that the volume of 'pirate consumption reduces paid consumption by 3.5 to 20 per cent' and results in 'losses in the millions of dollars to rights holders' (Sinclair 2010). This statement was made after Cricket Australia (CA) stated that a broadcaster had withdrawn from negotiations for coverage rights in the US market because 'pirated Internet feeds' had devalued them. Free's use of a percentage figure is a departure from the common industry tactic of referring to the number of streams detected, which produces a larger number that better suits the discursive construction of an epidemic (for example, 177 different sites, 941 individual sites, 3,200 unauthorized live broadcasts).

A recurrent pattern of user recalcitrance, financial injury claims by industry, unrelenting lobbying of government and regulators, and dissemination of anti-piracy propaganda has taken hold. This situation continues to construct piracy as a product of enforcement debates, and prevents an accurate description of specific online behavior and its impact (Karaganis 2011b, p. 2). Any countervailing benefits that might flow from piracy in terms of market penetration and product awareness are overlooked.[13] Prevailing counter-piracy tactics betray a yearning by many media industry leaders for the replication of a closed analogue-broadcast system on the Internet, enabling tight control over content distribution and quality. This way of thinking will continue until outdated notions of property law based on physical goods are jettisoned and the complexities of user activities and cultures on the Internet are confronted (cf. Coombe 1998; Dyer-Witheford & de Peuter 2009). Tarleton Gillespie describes the outlook preventing the acceptance of alternative or adjusted approaches to content distribution that display greater resistance to, or tolerance of, online sharing and live streaming:

> It seems safer to preserve an existing business model than be forced into the riskier alternative, that is, having to renovate that business model, with no guarantee that it will succeed, in order to compete against more innovative [or illicit] challengers. (2007, p. 105)

Affordable and high-quality official live sports Internet services are appearing slowly, but are unevenly spread and display inconsistent levels of accessibility depending on where a user is located. An exception is MLB.TV, which employs online blackouts in the geographical area covered by a club's local television market. This site is estimated to have generated US$500 million in revenue during 2010 (McCullagh 2011). The National Collegiate Athletic Association (NCAA) also streams the Men's Division I 'March Madness' Basketball Championship live on computer and mobile platforms. Other sports appear willing to stream into overseas territories, but provide limited or non-existent services at home. Yet the longer that sports organizations and broadcasters persevere with a protectionist mindset by failing to invest seriously in reliable and widely accessible authorized services, the more likely it is that online word-of-mouth among users will continue to expand the audience for illicit streams (see Birmingham & David 2011, pp. 76–77).

There are few encouraging signs that a collective rethink about sports piracy is imminent or that the propaganda campaigns based on folk devils and moral panics will be discarded. Statements by Chairman and Chief Executive of News Corporation in Asia and Europe, James Murdoch (the now infamous son of News Corporation Chairman and Chief Executive, Rupert Murdoch), display a trenchant refusal to accept changing norms and practices of digital content circulation. His attitude is supported by several legal cases against small online television companies accused of stealing News Corporation content. A noticeably irritated Murdoch revealed his punitive attitude at the 2010 Abu Dhabi Media Summit:

> These are basic property rights. There is no difference from going into a store and stealing a packet of Pringles or a handbag, and stealing something online. Right? And the idea that there is this new consumer class that somehow are thieves, but we call them consumers, and we say we have to be customer friendly when they're stealing stuff is lunacy. Right? The basic condition for investment and economic growth is some level of sanctity around property rights, whether it's my house or a movie I've made. OK? And there's no difference. I think it's crazy frankly, people say, 'Oh, it's different, these kids, you know, these crazy kids'. No, punish them. (Background Briefing 2010a)

In a style reminiscent of the late Jack Valenti, Murdoch conflates material goods (a brand of potato crisps, a handbag, and his house) with immaterial goods or data (a movie, online data), ignoring that no material goes missing when a user accesses a live peer-to-peer stream (Lanham 2006, p. 12). The other feature of Murdoch's speech is the assertion that tolerance of this online behavior is 'lunacy' and 'crazy', thereby rhetorically denying a capacity for reason by those who countenance an alternative approach. However, Murdoch's polemic has not been able to silence those individuals and groups who pose difficult, unavoidable questions about the relationship between intellectual property regimes and the Internet. An Australian lawyer responded immediately to Murdoch from the floor of the Abu Dhabi conference, countering that a law that is neither respected nor enforced cannot be considered a law. This challenge connects with the suggestion that any law broken by very large numbers of people should at least be reconsidered (Gillespie 2007, p. 121).[14] These counterpoints emphasize the picture that emerges from the evidence presented in this section: the copyright industries complain loudly of piracy and declare an epidemic whenever and wherever groups of users do not pay for content or fail to access a designated content source. In the case of sport, the curious dimension of this apparent economic self-interest is that the value of television coverage deals worldwide shows few signs of collapse and audience numbers remain healthy.

THE INTERSECTION OF ACCESS AND CONTENT

Broadcasters and sports leagues are attempting to adapt effectively to the changes posed by online media and the vicissitudes of digital television formats and devices, to use the advantage of incumbency against new media sport operators, and to protect the economic value contained in the live broadcast event. These are conditions of continuity and discontinuity that are variously accompanied by moods of fear, uncertainty, indifference, defiance, belligerence, and opportunism. Judging by the materials that we have collected and analyzed, the most fascinating feature of these shifting, structurally induced moods is that they revolve around positioning for the future, what *might* happen, and the need to capitalize on a digital 'revolution' that is still unfolding in front of those who aspire to exploit it. The uncertainty accompanying this mindset positions the Internet and the Web as a problem for sports broadcasters and leagues that have come to rely on a profitable but restrictive compact to sustain their operations and public profile. CA, the organization responsible for running 'the national game' of cricket in Australia, spelt out the situation during the formal parliamentary inquiry mentioned earlier (also see Chapter 6):

- Digital media are available 24 hours, seven days per week [unlike live-to-air broadcast platforms].
- Platforms and applications are constantly evolving.
- New technologies are being developed every day.
- Time offers no bounds.
- Geographical reach and storage capacity are unlimited.
- The public can access with ease.
- Updating of material is possible at any time and as often as desired.
- Aggregation of material is easy and possible by anyone, not just 'news' organisations. (Cricket Australia 2009, p. 11)

While excited by digital media and the 'fabulous opportunities' that the Internet offers, CA also bemoaned the fact that 'traditional media business models' founded upon 'selling media rights based on exclusivity' are under challenge in 'the digital age' (Cricket Australia 2009, p. 11). A celebration of consumer choice, therefore, connects to a complaint about the challenge to the broadcast business model that has served elite sport so well.

There is a need to move beyond the defensive positions adopted by CA and many other sports leagues and organizations if we are to identify the specific causes of anxiety present in the media sport content economy, and the conditions driving change in the media sports cultural complex as a whole. Digital plenitude provides part of the answer to such questions, provoking changes in how sports content is produced and experienced, who can provide it, and what is presented. But plenitude alone does not explain how the mechanisms of power and control over content are changing with adequate precision. While we have adapted it specifically for the purposes of our analysis, Ben Goldsmith (2009) and the assembled research team for the 'Outside the Box—The Future of Television' Project (Lloyd-James, Gibson, Bell, Pattinson, Goldsmith, Chandler & McKay 2009) have developed a useful heuristic tool with which to understand media transformation and the multiplication of digital platforms and devices. Their matrix (see Figure 2.1) involves plotting on an axis the two key 'critical uncertainties' of media today—'the *access perspective* and the *content perspective*' (Lloyd-James *et al.* 2009, pp. 6–8).[15] The access perspective 'refers to the potential and actual access of corporations, interest groups and individuals' to the production and distribution of content, while the content perspective is about the control of 'information and cultural content (programs, news services, live broadcasts of sport, etc.) distributed or distributable via television' and media (p. 6).

Quadrant 1 ('controlled content, closed access') represents the traditional broadcast model, and any departure from it threatens to erode the revenue streams of popular professional sports and free-to-air and pay-for-view broadcasters. It is for this reason that, as has been discussed at some length, considerable offensive and defensive energies are spent maintaining exclusive control over broadcast sport and combating the growth of new online providers. Other points of vulnerability are emerging as leagues, teams, athletes, and specialist online operators experiment with alternative business models online that stake out different positions within this matrix, sometimes involving a move towards Quadrant 3 ('controlled content, open access'). YouTube's coverage of the IPL is an example of this strategy. Lower-level and amateur sports, which are discussed in the next chapter, are often happy to provide completely open access to their content because it has little embedded commercial value, but still insist on a degree of control over it in order to minimize adverse publicity and potential legal problems that may result from its modification or supplementation. There is limited evidence of activity in Quadrant 2 ('uncontrolled content, closed access'), although membership-based online club and league websites provide partial examples when they permit the uploading of fan videos and

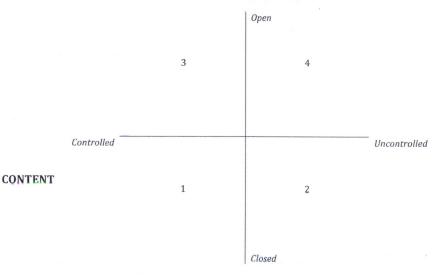

Figure 2.1   Matrix of access and content for contemporary digital content. Reproduced from Lloyd-James et al. (2009, p. 8).[16]

commentary. Almost every party with a vested interest in the media sport industries is resisting a wholesale or even limited move towards Quadrant 4 ('uncontrolled content, open access') given the difficulty of commodifying this arrangement—a point emphasized by the discussion of online piracy. Sports leagues and media companies might differ on *exactly* where they would like to locate themselves within this matrix and at which points of its axes, but they have one attitude in common. Each wishes to exert a degree of control over the distribution of content and/or the access and behavior of users and audiences. This control enables minimization of financial and operational investment risks and the pursuit of reliable revenue and profits. Media technologies and practices are changing, but the financial imperative of the global media sport industries remains constant.

In this chapter we have concentrated on how television and broadcasters have pursued strategies such as protection, reinforcement, adaptation, integration, and co-optation in an effort to establish a strong position in a networked media sport order. At the same time, we have seen how new parties and technologies have progressively moved into and disrupted what was, for around half a century, a relatively stable system of audiovisual rights exchange. In the following chapter, we investigate a developing media sport 'eco-system' in which 'television as we knew it' has a different purpose and place in the context of media structures, technologies, and habits.

3 Networked Media Sport

The 2008 Beijing Olympics represents an important moment in the evolution of the media sports cultural complex. The global appeal of the Olympics made the existing and potential value of the Internet and Web apparent, even as the relevance and role of television endured. More Internet streams were accessed in the first day of the 2008 Olympics than for the entire duration of the Athens Olympiad four years earlier (Boyle & Whannel 2010b, p. 356). A popularity threshold for online sport had been passed as growth was observed across different continents. A reported 53 million people in China watched live streaming of the Olympics on personal computers, along with 22 million users in Latin America and around 51 million in Europe. In the US, online coverage was comparatively limited, but still managed to attract approximately 18 million unique views on authorized Olympics sites.[1] These numbers compare with the estimated 894 million viewers who watched on broadcast television in the host nation alone, and a daily average audience of 30 million viewers in America at the outset of the Olympics (Marshall *et al.* 2010, pp. 268–69). While not rivaling terrestrial television, the scale of the online audience demonstrates clearly that enough users are logging on to make the Internet a major commercial and cultural concern. These developments were factored into the planning for the 2012 London Olympics, with the BBC's Roger Mosey, the executive overseeing the corporation's coverage, determined to make the Internet 'a huge part of what we do' in the delivery of a projected 5,000 hours of overall viewing (Quoted in Boyle & Whannel 2010b, p. 356; Adler 2011). In line with the IOC and the BBC, sports and media organizations around the world acknowledge that the Internet and World Wide Web occupy a key strategic position in current operations and future directions.

This chapter delineates the dynamics affecting the value of Web-based sports content and activities, although television never quite disappears from the picture. A series of decisions and claims are determining how value on websites is contested, manipulated, and measured. Like many contests that have preceded it historically, this is about the flow of media, money, and sport (Wenner 1998). Volatility results from the fact that value is almost always provisional in the current online marketplace given its immaturity and changeability relative to the established broadcast model. We aim to expand on our analysis of the operation and features of *networked media sport*, a term capturing the movement away from broadcast and print media towards digitized content distributed via networked communications technologies. The following sections examine website user metrics and the changing behavior of audiences, the inescapable tensions between the exercise of producer control and the rhetoric of consumer choice in the operation of websites and online communities, and the factors impacting upon the creation of successful online operations in amateur and semi-professional sports. The case presented leads to the conclusion that the 'digital revolution' is so far proving less than revolutionary in the context of sport. Hierarchies of popularity and media coverage, which have seen elite men's sport occupy a disproportionate amount of time and space compared to women's, disabled, and lower-tier sports for several decades, have not been dismantled online so far. There are additional opportunities for users and fans of the most popular sports to access their favorite sport in different ways, at different times, and in greater depth, but this variety does not apply to an especially wide range of sports. If anything, already dominant male football codes and major sports events are becoming more so because of human, financial, and media resource advantages. As the next section reveals, however, administrators in the elite leagues and competitions harbor their own anxieties about how the 'eyeballs' that surf their webpages should be valued and monetized.

MEASURING EYEBALLS (AT LUNCHTIME)

Contention over economic value in the media sport content economy stimulates a range of questions about how best to measure Internet and Web activity. This is a critical issue in the evolution of the online advertising market and the development of industry agreements over the valuation of user attention. As is the case with online statistics in general, estimates vary (sometimes widely), although there appears to be general agreement that the Internet is growing consistently as an advertising medium. Internet advertising revenue in the US rose by 15 percent to US$26 billion in 2010 (*Reuters* 2011), and Internet advertising was forecast to account for an estimated 14 percent of the global advertising market in 2011 (PricewaterhouseCoopers 2007). Sports website advertising is worth between US$1–2 billion globally and, while this figure lags well behind television, the value of the entire sports advertising market in the US alone is in the vicinity of US$27 billion *per annum* (Plunkett Research 2010).

Executives and administrators are acutely aware that the Web is a valuable form of media now and/or in the future, which is why so many insist on explaining (though with some variations), 'It's really important to be in the online space' (Interview with author). The difficulty is that many sports and media companies possess an organizational history and culture accustomed to the broadcast ratings system as the agreed upon 'currency' governing commercial dealings (Balnaves & O'Regan 2002, p. 30). For several decades ratings have been the accepted mechanism by which audiences are quantified and commodified. Experienced personnel accustomed to this system can sometimes view alternative systems for measuring viewer or user activity as faddish or beyond their 'core business'.[2] In another instance of the need to recognize the unique features of sport as a source of popular media content, top-level sport administrators are often former athletes or loyal officials for whom the material distinction between sporting and computer cultures was a reality for decades. Examples include the President of the IOC, Jacques Rogge, and NBA Commissioner, David Stern, who are both in their late sixties; FIFA President, Sepp Blatter, and MLB Commissioner, Bud Selig, who are in their mid-seventies; and the octogenarian Football Federation Australia Chairman, Frank Lowy. This is not an ageist argument that these men—and such leaders are almost always male—lack dynamism, are incapable of updating their knowledge and skills, or that every leading administrator is part of a gerontocratic order of power. It is that the internal cultures and practices of many sports organizations are taking considerable time to adjust to the recalibration of the media sport content economy. This is the experience of those running specialist technology companies servicing multiple domestic markets when they attempt to convince sports chiefs to invest in online media products:

> Sport almost more than any other industry is governed by someone who was involved as an athlete two to three generations ago. Typically the president of the sporting club was a club legend and he's 60. He was a club legend when he was 20. Sport honors its participants, unlike the media industry who just sack them [laughs]. Seriously. (Interview with author)

The television ratings system of value determination is still paramount in the minds of many of those running sport because of its familiarity and the fact that broadcast television is still a large source of income. Despite their acknowledged bluntness as an audience measurement tool, ratings have reliably fulfilled an institutional need to estimate who is watching what, when, and for how long (Jacka 1994; Ruddock 2001). In largely risk averse commercial settings like sport, reliable (at least in the sense of industrially accepted) guides to action and investment are only reluctantly discarded. Conservative perceptions and practices, though, cannot mask the burgeoning popularity of online distribution and consumption. As discussed in the previous chapter, this change raises urgent questions about how one medium or platform should be valued against another, particularly given the availability of a plethora of Internet metrics on consumption, such as unique browsers, average session duration, page impressions, and total sessions.

The question of how to best measure online user behavior reflects longer-term challenges in the operation of the television ratings systems. Ratings systems have moved onto an increasingly digitized footing in recent years, resulting in disagreement and controversies within the media industries themselves. Mark Balnaves and Tom O'Regan (2002) describe the trajectory of the broadcast ratings since the 1940s. Almost every new audience measurement system has been met with disputation by one or more of the following groups—networks, producers, advertisers, regulators, and media buyers. For our purposes, sports organizations can be added to this list, as they control access and rights to sports coverage. Television ratings have evolved historically from an analogue 'one size fits all' system to one that is increasingly 'customized at the individual level' and targeted at 'micro-audiences' across digitized media, including cable television, digital multichannelling, and video-on-demand (Balnaves & O'Regan 2002, p. 54). Following a steady increase in broadband Internet penetration over the past decade, Web metrics represent the latest extension and intensification of an existing preference for micro-measurement in the broadcast sector. Metrics offer access to an array of numerical indicators of user activity, thereby changing the basis for how eyeballs are measured and commodified. Recent trends in online activity measurement even extend to affective dimensions of media use. 'Sentiment analysis' involves mining online comments and conversations for commercial purposes, in an effort to assess the feelings and opinions expressed (Andrejevic 2011; Background Briefing 2010b)—although it encounters difficulties with such discursive practices as irony and juxtaposition. A sporting variation on this development is presently found in a service such as Thuuz. Using an algorithm, this website generates a real-time 'excitement measure' for major games in the US and alerts users by email or text message so they can access points of peak competition.

The challenge of this surfeit of behavioral indicators is to reach agreement across the entirety of the advertising, sports, and sports news industries about which ones are the most useful in measuring commercial value. The main trade association for online advertising in Australia, the Interactive Advertising Bureau, has engaged in the difficult process of establishing an accepted user measurement system from the dozen or more in use, including Nielsen, comScore, and Roy Morgan Research (Kermond 2010). One of the greatest difficulties is reaching agreement on a standard for measuring online video use, with the advertising displayed around video content, catch-up television, and highlights surging in value in recent years. The fact that an AUD$2 billion a year industry has struggled to agree on standards and guidelines means that sport is subject to the same uncertainty and debates affecting online media in general. This undesirable situation is exacerbated by the limited knowledge possessed by some sports and news media organizations about exactly who their users are, and why they are looking at their webpages. According to a seasoned technology commentator who has observed the operation of newsrooms and online editorial desks over the past 15 years, many professionals have a limited idea of who is reading, watching, and listening to their content:

> The human race is strange—you look around a train or you sit in a coffee shop, watch what people do. And I think part of the problem with the industry is they don't know who they're dealing with. They know them as a digit in the sense of 'we've got a hit' and they stayed on the page for a minute. Big deal. But who were they? (Interview with author)

This limitation contributes to a superficial emphasis on 'most popular article' lists on most sports and news websites that are presented as a guide to user taste preferences, wants, and needs. In reality, these lists are designed to match webpage impressions with the placement of online advertisements. They are often compiled by counting how many times an article has been viewed as opposed to how long it took someone to read an article, whether they sent it to a friend, or whether the user returned for another look at the page. The most popular reports often intersect with lurid or sensational headlines, celebrity focused stories, and major fixture results that tell editors something about user curiosity but little about meaningful in-depth engagement. Indeed, performance measures are significantly affected by prior decisions concerning story placement, headlines, and visuals, which indicates the comparative unreliability of trying to assess responses to media texts that have been enunciated and framed by the assessors themselves or their agents. As the interview comment above hints at, there is a failure to treat the Internet and Web as socially located technologies used by 'diverse people, in diverse real world locations' (Miller & Slater 2000, p. 1). An alternative approach to thinking about online media provoked a moment of dissent from a sport media manager who, contrary to the official position of his employer, thinks that unauthorized Internet streams of televised live sports are acceptable if they carry advertisements. He believes it is futile trying to direct the flow of fan attention to a single medium. The aim should instead be how to best capture the commodity of primary value to advertisers—prolonged attention:

> The way ours [rights-holders] analyze success is totally based on the traditional ratings model. But if you're taking their stream and delivering everything, including all the ads, there's value there to an advertiser. They're additional people . . . so I don't think it erodes [value]. It's the measurement system that's the problem. The way that the performance is analyzed is the issue, not so much the streaming of it. (Interview with author)

A disconnection exists, then, between how audiences and users are presently measured for advertising purposes and how people actually behave online. The necessity of filling this gap has seen Nielsen and ESPN trial alternative systems that measure cross-platform consumption, including television, (authorized) Internet, and mobile media, for the duration of major tournaments and events (Fry 2010). These measurement systems are yet to be trialed industry-wide over a full 12-month period—a length of time that matches key accounting and reporting periods. They also face resistance because of the difficulty of formulating a common cross-platform currency agreed upon by all sectors of the media sport industry, including sponsors and advertisers. The continuation of such debates leaves considerable room for website operators to make ambitious but misleading public claims about user traffic and the popularity of their sites.

Sweeping assertions of influence and appeal in the online media sport marketplace are the subject of argument and counter-argument. While a sport might like to say that it administers the 'number one' sports website in its region or country, the basis of the claim is often unclear. A declaration of this type might be based on the number of unique browsers, page impressions, total sessions, average sessions, average session duration, or a combination of two categories or more. In this sense, sports websites practice the same kind of cherry picking of audience statistics as newspapers (with different permutations of sales, circulation, weekday and weekend readerships, and reader demographics) and television stations (including prime time versus 24-hour ratings, averaging versus most popular programming, and total viewership versus targeted viewer cohorts).

The research interviews raised the possibility that a combination of smooth talking and deliberately confusing or 'tricked up' figures can make for superficially convincing claims of market power and influence. A representative of a technology provider asserted that he had managed to produce a remarkable 547 percent growth in traffic for a sports website in just one month (Interview with author). Subsequent checking revealed his statement to be factually correct, but the impression that a larger audience accessed the site was, however, misleading. Traffic—understood as simply counting 'hits' on a webpage—had increased steeply, but this improvement had been achieved by installing an automatic refresh function for live match score updates that ticked over every 60 seconds. Each refresh was then counted as a hit despite the fact that roughly the same number of users were checking scores. Thus, traffic did not equate with more eyeballs, which are the priority for advertisers and sponsors; instead, a simple technological adjustment produced the illusion of rising popularity that would only be exposed by close checking and expert knowledge.

Online metrics are extensive in range and open to substantial manipulation depending on how they are analyzed and applied. This is not to suggest that online audience measurement is entirely chaotic. Just as in the early days of the broadcast ratings system, qualified and fragile norms are slowly emerging. A commonly used tool for monitoring and measuring sports website activity is, at the time of writing, Nielsen NetRatings. A multinational ratings and media research company, Nielsen collects a range of monthly statistics for sports websites. Figure 3.1, in the form of a bar graph, was developed from data provided by Nielsen's Australian division and covers

domestic sports websites over a three-year period (2008–10). It provides a
sense of the different metrics relating to website activity, and demonstrates
that sports organizations and news companies are effectively competing in
a crowded and intensely competitive online environment. Most usefully,
Figure 3.1 reveals, as noted earlier, how the relative popularity of sites can
shift depending on the metric selected.

Two identifiable trends have surfaced in relation to the actual and putative worth attributed to particular website metrics, with each attempting
to exercise a digital governmentality (Foucault 1991) that connects metrics
and statistical calculations to commonsense notions of how online user
activity should be understood and measured. These are contested regimes of
value based on what people do individually and collectively on the Internet

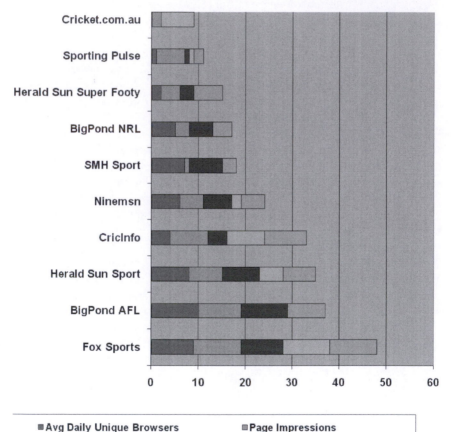

Figure 3.1 Top ten Australian sport websites January 2008—December 2010.
Source: Nielsen Netratings 2008–2010.

in relation to cultural tastes, social activities, behavioral habits, available platforms, user access, and Internet speeds.

The first trend stresses the *scale* of Internet traffic and seeks to overwhelm the media buyer, advertiser, or sponsor by highlighting the sheer amount of online activity, creating the impression that the Internet is now the 'main game' in media. Unique browsers and page impressions[3] are the metrics extracted in this formulation because they supply numbers measured in the thousands, tens of thousands, or hundreds of thousands per month that can be consolidated into commanding annual aggregate figures. As we have seen, live score updating with an automatic refresh function every 60 seconds is a technique that can be used here to bolster the number of page impressions, as are competitions, polls, photographs, and video footage. Operators of small- and medium-sized sports websites prefer these measures, as they supply an impressive raw number, though an arguably inflated sense of popularity among sports fans:

> Because the more hits [page impressions] we get, the more we get back from sponsors. So it has changed the way we have delivered the stuff because we want to get more hits. (Website operator; Interview with author)

The second trend is preferred by many larger media sport operators. This strategy stresses a combination of average daily unique browsers and, most importantly, average session duration.[4] A challenge of the Web is the notoriously short attention span of users as they flit from page to page and site to site. Advertisers want to know not only whether people are glancing at content, but also if they are actively consuming it. The longer the stay—or the more 'sticky' it is—the greater the likelihood that a user has understood and interacted meaningfully with content, and is more prone to respond positively to the suggested or implied advertising. This measure sets up a perplexing technical design challenge, as an aesthetically pleasing website with high visitor numbers does not necessarily produce a commensurate level of lasting user attention and regular return visits. This dilemma has been faced and addressed by many elite sports, including the one whose website is discussed below:

> Just to give you a snapshot, there were some quite phenomenal figures when I looked at it last year in respect of our length of stay figures. In the past 12 months, we've attracted 167,000 hours. [A competing site] attracted 78,000 hours. So we think that that is a really good indication of 'stickiness' and that we are engaging. I know we keep banging on about that word [stickiness], but that length of stay is a key engagement measure for us. (Communications director; Interview with author)

The longest average duration-of-stay for an Australian sports website in 2010 was about 10 minutes. This appears a short period of time for, say, a book, or even a broadsheet newspaper reader, but it is an eon in an online attention economy where millions of webpages are looked at for mere seconds. By way of contrast, visitors to the eighth most popular website on the Internet, the text-based Wikipedia, stay an average of five minutes and look at each page for 60 seconds (Alexa Internet 2011a). The chase for increased session durations helps to explain a number of developments in the features of sports websites worldwide that present content in ways that demand lasting attention from the user. Examples include fantasy sports leagues, match-tipping competitions, comment sections, audiovisual highlights packages, and behind-the-scenes footage.[5]

New methods of counting and harvesting eyeballs have revealed new timeslots for the consumption of media sport. People are watching, listening, reading, and interacting, but not in ways familiar to those professionals who have long deferred to the broadcast schedule and, especially, prime time as primary organizing principles. The birth and growth of lunchtime audiences for Internet content is a prominent example of change, with operators noting a considerable 'spike' in hits and durations of stay between the hours of 12 and 2pm since 2008, the year of the Beijing Olympics. This pattern was especially noted in the US and Australia during the Olympiad (Marshall *et al.* 2010, p. 270), announcing a user routine that can be exploited for commercial and news presentation purposes. Lunch hours become a significant advertising opportunity when Web metrics show people consuming sport in the middle of the day. During these hours, websites run by sports news outlets, leagues, and broadcasters are offering a variety of video services, as well as live-chat or blog sessions with famous athletes and journalists allowing fans to pose questions and offer comments. These activities intensify during peak periods of competition, including the summer and winter Olympics, the soccer World Cup, championship finals, and the NCAA's 'March Madness' basketball fixtures. Workers log on to catch up with match highlights, news, and event analysis, particularly if they live in a different time zone to where the event is hosted. These practices reveal the demise in many countries of lunch as a scheduled, shared meal in a dedicated space, with the computer replacing human lunchtime companions and the individual desk supplanting the communal dining table.

Using the example of the Internet video service ESPN360 (now ESPN3), Ethan Tussey (2009) argues that these lunchtime activities are connected to the advent of 'workspace media'. 'Technologically savvy multitaskers' are blending their work, leisure, and fandom, 'borrowing' time from their bosses, and, in the process, de-traditionalizing viewing contexts for entertainment content. Tussey (2009) suggests that fleeting online communities are formed around workspace media, especially when major sports events are taking place during conventional work hours. Populated live-chat windows running adjacent to sports footage make it easier for geographically dispersed workers united by common interest 'to follow the progress of the game (without sound) while maintaining a productive work flow', all the while keeping a keen eye out for their superiors. Tussey (2009) notes that workplace media engagement has become so common that there is now 'a feature installed into the CBS Sports viewer called the "boss button", which, when clicked, transforms the video player into a spreadsheet full of numbers and nonsense data'.

These variably transgressive activities dovetail with conjecture over the cost of social networking sites and fantasy sports leagues to workplace productivity levels and the respective rights of employers and employees regarding the surveillance of online activities (Skeels & Grudin 2009; Sprouse 2010). These issues are further complicated by computing and mobile communications that confuse the boundaries between work and leisure in the domestic environment and during so-called 'free time' (Rojek 2010; Wajcman, Bittman & Brown 2009; Gregg 2011). Utilizing now deceased infomercial salesperson Bill Mays, the promotional techniques of ESPN360 highlighted a deliberate commercial media strategy to infiltrate workspaces via networked media sport. An advertisement features a cubicle worker addressed by Mays who claims that 'watching sports at work is better than doing work at work' (Tussey 2009). This type of address to users, albeit less cheekily articulated, is observable on other sports sites where users are invited to 'join us at lunchtime' for live chat or discussion. In the ceaseless pursuit of expansion, the attempts of commercial media to infiltrate domestic and public space have moved to workspace, utilizing the enthusiasm of sports fans who spend their spare and not-so-spare time at work online. The challenge for content providers is to balance the cost of production and the purchase of rights against the need to provide compelling content at different times of the day via multiple 'monetizable' digital devices and media to cater for an array of different social and cultural spaces. As the next section shows, the desire to control and limit user movement to a provider's purpose built 'walled garden' collides with a celebration of choice in the marketing of consumer electronics, mobile communications, and Internet service provision.

CHOICE, CONTROL, AND COMPETITIVE BALANCE

A contradiction that became apparent during our investigation of networked media sport is the attempted replication of a tightly controlled broadcast model by companies and sports that, at the same time, rhetorically celebrate digital choice and consumer freedom. Amounting to little more than a cosmetic promotion of choice, media sport content providers *spruik* a range of options to sports fans and then seek to corral them into a prescribed set of service options and news sources. This rigid proprietorial mindset has not escaped the attention of sports business commentators: 'We are in the odd situation where the industry claims to be moving towards consumer choice and control, but is actually imposing restrictions on fans through its emphasis on exploitation' (Fry 2008a). Telecommunications operators, despite an historical affinity with networked communications stretching back well over a century, display a similarly proprietorial approach, having become accustomed to locking customers into fixed line telephone contracts and mobile user plans. Attempting to operate like a traditional mass media company online is, though, a flawed strategy, as user loyalty on the Web can be, at best, a temporary arrangement. The constant possibility of 'churn', with other sources trying to lure consumers by offering similar content cheaper or even at no charge, makes for an often flimsy 'contract' between provider and customer. Sports leagues are the most addicted to the continued sale of exclusive or closed platform rights and content, which is unsurprising as these rights account for anywhere between 50 and 80 percent of annual income for many national and international sports organizations.

In an attitude best described as curious in an era of convergent media, sports leagues can give the impression that broadcast contracts will both appreciate (which they mostly are at present) *and* stay safely quarantined from hopefully ever-more lucrative online and mobile markets.[6] The notion that there is an unavoidable overlap here—whereby the 'wonderful' new choices provided online must, on occasion, cut across broadcast media content and vice versa—evaded several of the industry figures interviewed for this book. Even astute, experienced professionals tended to speak contradictorily when being interviewed, caught between embracing the distribution opportunities afforded by the Internet and Web, and the rejection of the openness of user cultures that revolve around shared online content. Reflecting at length on the role of the Internet in offering fans a wide range of choices, a communications director for a leading sports organization explained:

> Anything that allows our content to be viewed by people is a positive . . . convergence is allowing those barriers to break down a bit, and our strategy is to ensure that our content is out there for people. The eyeballs and the ears need to be able to access our content. If we're not out there, someone else is in our space, so that's not a good thing. (Interview with author)

Getting 'out there' on the Internet presents problems, however, when adopting an 'unashamedly commercial, aggressive position' built around selling and managing exclusive contracts for parcels of media sports rights:

> For us it's about grey legal zones around copyright, streaming, and piracy . . . and then it's about unauthorized use of even archival material being filmed or being broadcast or the use of our logos and things like that. They're the kinds of areas that are just becoming more and

more problematic for us to protect against. There's the whole fabulous argument about online giving everybody more choice, more coverage, and that's absolutely 100 percent correct. But, on the flip side, it's opening up other areas where we have to be more vigilant in making sure that, at the same time, it's not actually just killing us. (Interview with author)

There is a fascinating disconnection in the online strategies of major sports leagues and their online media partners. The open and free market competition strongly advocated by many working in the media sport industry is not matched by a commensurate desire for user sovereignty. The consumer is offered choice and encouraged to enjoy the consumption of media sport across a range of media and devices, but only if they behave in a prescribed fashion and stay within the confines of the websites recommended by the provider.[7] Attracted by endemic 'pro-social' Internet marketing hype, providers appropriate the language of community when building and maintaining their branded, walled gardens, which are better described as closed consumption platforms. That the hierarchical structures and internal cultures of many commercial media and sports organizations are unsuited to the creation of open communities on the Web tends to be ignored (Burgess & Green 2009, p. 110). Online and offline, the fuzzily heart-warming connotations of the word community are countered by lived experiences that can just as easily prove alienating, hostile, or soulless (Bauman 2001). 'Television on the Web' is, therefore, an apt description for many media sport portals. These sites represent an exclusionary mode of centralized programming control and content provision historically associated with broadcast media, but using an open-ended communications architecture unsuited to this ethos. An attempt is then made to bridge the gap with effusive libertarian rhetoric. A principal protection for content providers (without having to resort to expensive, inefficient, and image-corrosive legal remedies) in populating and maintaining their gardens is that, when faced with seemingly infinite options, Internet users tend to display highly habituated patterns in the sites that they visit. It is ironic, then, that it is habit and inertia among users that stand between both service and content providers and the realization of the fully open market that they promote and fear. However, relying on user aversion to 'choice fatigue' (Turner 2009, p. 61) to save a business model is risky in the long-term, and vulnerable to sudden shifts of user taste and preference.

Another problem from the perspective of the sports leagues housing popular clubs and teams is that digital media offer altogether too much choice. Websites, broadband 'television' channels, podcasts, apps, and online videos give to teams, clubs, and franchises their own opportunities to connect with fans, to attract and service sponsors, and to establish independent media production facilities. Just like leagues, clubs can produce, operate, and sell their own Web, audio, mobile, and archival media content. Club-specific content, depending on the circumstances at hand, has a proven capacity to bolster, accompany, and conflict with league-wide broadcast and telecommunications media deals (Boyle & Haynes 2004). Soccer is the best contemporary example of the worldwide possibilities of 'cutting out the middle person' by going directly to fans and potential fans without reliance on external media organizations. Clubs with global pro- files like Chelsea FC and Manchester United are among the most advanced cases (Rowe 2011b) of club online operations, distributing specialist, and professionally produced audiovisual and text-based news and information. With the growth of these services—on top of already plentiful league dis- tributed and broadcaster offerings—the task becomes how to propagate and then 'slice and dice' all the available content. Prevailing market condi- tions play the determining role in how these questions are resolved in each territory and competition. Factored into these calculations is the enormous economic success of exclusive football broadcast rights sold collectively and individually (in, for example, England and Spain respectively) to major broadcasters (Horne 2006). The value of these rights are weighed against the tempting but less certain possibility of vertical integration whereby clubs own, control, and derive all the benefits from the production, mar- keting, and distribution of their media sport property.

A particularly worrying development for sports governing bodies is the self-promotion of wealthy individual clubs that openly assert their mar- ket supremacy against the 'lesser' teams with which they must compete to form a league, but from which they have largely detached in terms of power and prestige. Glasgow Celtic and Rangers, for example, possess a stranglehold on Scottish soccer that sees their bargaining power and on- field competitiveness comprehensively exceed that of their smaller compet- itors like Aberdeen and Hearts, a domination that extends to the capacity to operate sophisticated and appealing online portals. Similar imbalances exist in Italian football, where lower profile clubs earn as little as 10 per- cent of the €100 million generated annually by a leading club such as Inter Milan from media revenues alone (Giulianotti & Robertson 2009, p. 72). Spanish football clubs are able to sell their broadcast rights individually, which produces significant competitive imbalances between large clubs like Barcelona and Real Madrid, and smaller ones such as Almeria and Deportivo. FC Barcelona, for example, negotiated a broadcast agreement valued at €150 million for 2008/09, sells selected matches on a pay-per- view basis, and runs its own television channel, Barca TV (Hamil, Wal- ters & Watson 2010, p. 490). This growth in elite football market power, represented most strikingly by the English Premier League, has stimulated pressure to create a European Super League operating above the national leagues and including only the richest and most powerful football clubs in Europe.[8] Any such 'ultra-elite' competition would reflect the regional and global reach of soccer in its most highly mediated form (Giulianotti 1999; Horne 2006; Rowe 2011b).

The idea that clubs should be able to handle, commercialize, and extend their Web-based media operations independently and without interference from league authorities is, therefore, a natural and logical extension of precedents and patterns already established in the broadcast sector. This temptation also affects minor, crowded markets where the pursuit of available media and corporate capital induces a determination to extract maximum value from digital media platforms. For instance, stunning growth has seen over 500,000 apps made available in the iTunes store, making this an appealing arrangement for sports organizations even though it is based on a proprietorial platform tying them exclusively to Apple operating systems. However, such new arrangements cannot always be easily made under existing contractual agreements. For example, our research revealed that one rugby league club in Australia invested thousands of dollars in the development of its own club-specific app, only to be told by competition authorities that its release would breach a binding licensing agreement with a telecommunications provider. Despite making complaints about the restraint placed upon its business development and trade, the club reluctantly—and expensively—shelved the concept, despite the league having its own iPhone app available for purchase. These decisions and actions are symptomatic of a disrupted, uncertain media environment. As our industry interviews repeatedly found, even those supposed to be 'in the know' can find themselves compromised and confused.

The motivation for league authorities to control the online media operations of individual teams and clubs relates to the long-established 'peculiar economics of professional sports', as explained by economist and former student of Karl Polanyi, Walter C. Neale, in an essay published in 1964. Unlike commodity and service markets, where monopoly control is an ideal position for an operator to maximize profits and reduce the threat posed by would-be competitors, the success of a league demands a level of competitive balance between teams both on and off the playing field. Outcome uncertainty in sporting contests cannot be guaranteed without this balance, as it is the source of entertainment for spectators, viewers, and users. Problems arise for an overwhelmingly dominant team in the attraction of wider interest and attention when their league rivals are poorly resourced, uncompetitive, unpopular, or unknown.[9] In sport, competition is not only desirable on economic grounds; it is, almost uniquely, the foundation of economic value itself. The absence of meaningful competition on the field of play ultimately creates circumstances whereby sport has little that is compelling to sell. A recent example of these peculiar economics of sport is Serie A (the leading soccer league) in Italy. Its decision to discard the sale of individual club media rights for a competition-wide deal for the 2010–11 and 2011–12 seasons was based on the yawning income and competitiveness gap between the top and bottom clubs.[10] Nonetheless, it is likely that powerful clubs will attempt to engineer a return to individual sales if their revenue drops markedly under a collectivist arrangement (Glendinning 2009).

Neale (1964) highlights that sports success is a delicate and relative value in both economic and cultural terms. Historically, great teams and athletes are validated by their rivalries and victories over similarly talented foes. Contrary to elite sport discourses that stress winning at all costs, wealthy teams in a competition have an interest in controlled cross-subsidization of weaker competitors to ensure that opponents offer the type of reputation and resistance that guarantees an appealing spectacle. According to Neale, 'pure monopoly is a disaster':

> Suppose the [New York] Yankees used their wealth to buy up not only all the good players but also all the teams in the American League: no games, no gate receipts, no Yankees. (Neale 1964, p. 21)

Peak sport and league authorities are charged with the task of managing the ambitions of individual clubs, the competitive balance of teams, and of rationing media access to popular content to ensure healthy returns to the competition as a whole. Compared to the analogue-broadcast era, the Internet is problematic for leagues because it enables an unparalleled degree of independence for many teams and clubs that can, for the first time, become skilled independent media providers (Evens & Lefever 2011). Unrestrained pursuit of individual sporting interests using digital media technologies may prove self-destructive. But the capacity to rein in the naked ambition of clubs and franchises is made difficult for governing authorities under circumstances where the former claim the right to communicate directly with their fans.

A director of a major league explained that lessening the temptation for powerful clubs or franchises to separate themselves symbolically and operationally from the central competition website is a constant challenge. In Australasia, for example, the South Sydney Rabbitohs and New Zealand Warriors (NRL) clubs each administer independent websites outside the reach of the centralized online network used by all the other clubs in their competition. Convincing most clubs to stay centrally located is handled through the 'soft power' of dialogue and persuasion and the 'hard power' of contract law. This approach works well when clubs believe that it creates 'a better overall financial result' than going it alone, particularly as the value of Internet and mobile media rights are valued more highly when the competition as a whole is up for sale:

> The total worth has to be greater than the sum of the parts. And that's obviously the model that we're trying to develop and everyone else is trying to develop. But within that you've got to have a system whereby the club is able to keep its identity and marketing . . . so there's a challenge . . . as long as the sum of the parts argument remains the most attractive proposition, and clubs realize that individually they might be able to wedge it a bit here and there. But in the long term, we need

to convince them that it's going to be easier, less maintenance and a better overall financial result to keep building it up through the sum of the parts. And if they lose faith in that, we start to lose. (Interview with author)

Many clubs and teams are, at present, rejecting the option of 'going it alone' online because of the financial expense and risk involved. Despite expressing a desire to move in this direction, they are checked by the existing guaranteed income flowing from broadcast and other media rights contracts negotiated by league authorities. Also, while costing much less than broadcast infrastructure, running an independent website offering professionally produced and entertaining content still requires a significant initial investment and ongoing running costs. The organizations that are investing in digital media are also yet to make consistent returns. Those interviewed for this book expressed opinions that ranged from discouraged ('Revenue from the online space was supposed to be about 20 times what it actually was'), cautious ('It's a big risk. If it turns into a complete lemon, then you've wasted a lot of time and money'), and hopeful ('Ultimately, it will pay itself back'). Parallel attitudes are expressed at the amateur level of sport, the problems of which, as the next section explains, are compounded by a never-ending quest for adequate resources to sustain play on the field and operations off it.

LOWER-TIER AND MASS PARTICIPATION SPORTS

Sitting at the bottom of the sports competition pyramid are those codes and competitions with limited options in terms of broadcast, print, or online media coverage and promotion. This situation connects with the dismal amount of news and television coverage that women's sport has received for decades (Phillips 1997; Mikosza 1997; Parliament of Australia Environment, Communications, Information Technology and the Arts References Committee 2006; Lumby, Caple, & Greenwood 2009) and the struggle of athletes with disabilities to attract attention outside the Paralympics (Cashman & Darcy 2008). Historically, new media technologies that promise wider audiences and commercial opportunities for ignored and neglected sports have repeatedly delivered scant coverage, institutionalized discrimination, and stereotypical representations (Hargreaves 1994; Goggin & Newell 2000). The expansion of multichannel cable, satellite, and pay television in the 1980s offered the initial and, as it transpired, futile hope that women's and semi-professional sport would gain additional public exposure and sponsorship opportunities (Rowe 2004a, p. 89). Free-to-air television digital multichannels are presently spoken about in much the same way, with the Internet and Web thought to hold greater promise for marginalized sports than subscription television, which proved to be a considerable disappointment to them. The capacity to 'broadcast yourself', as YouTube pithily intones, suggests that anyone can now attract an audience. Almost every sports organization possesses a website providing information and news, with women's soccer, tennis, golf, and basketball at their highest levels of competition offering polished online and mobile media content. But, for the majority of lower-tier sports, a combination of limited website traffic, no or negligible television coverage, and little mainstream media news reporting is a major impediment to the attraction of sponsors, commercial development, and enhanced participation opportunities for junior and senior athletes. In effect, the hierarchy of sports funding, facilities, and overall attention that characterized the broadcast era remains substantially unaltered.

Capital reserves created out of television contracts, sponsorship, media investments, and/or state funding allow sports such as the male football codes, baseball, and cricket to support advanced and content-rich digital media operations. Those sports organizations that cannot afford the latest technology are left to administer comparatively low-tech, content-deprived websites. Barriers to access online may be much lower than those pertaining to radio and television, but resources, staffing, and the constant pressure to upgrade technology ensure that a *digital media sport divide* has taken hold (cf. Castells 2002; Servon & Pinkett 2004). Therefore, the most visited Australian sports websites over the period 2008–10 are almost entirely devoted to the major football codes, male cricket, or sports news sites with coverage heavily slanted towards these men's sports (see Figure 3.1). The only exceptions in this sample period were two sites used by surfing aficionados for swell forecasts and coastal weather conditions,[11] and a portal run by SportingPulse International (discussed later). The Chief Executive of a minor national sport expressed acute frustration with the 'false promise' of online media in generating a better public profile, especially given the amount of time and energy already expended on securing what turned out to be a derisory amount of television coverage:

> It's crazy. We can't afford an IT person. We haven't even had a marketing person for the last 12 months or 18 months, which I think is a major failure. So we don't have the expertise to develop the Web interface and develop our website properly. Our website's rubbish. (Interview with author)

Compare this predicament of a marginal sport with that of a single mid-level professional football club:

> I mean it's not Universal Studios, but we've got a company who work for us three days a week, two young men who come in here and look after all the back end. And we've recently just employed a website multimedia producer who sits inside the club and looks after a lot of our

multimedia production now. On top of that we've got a media manager and media coordinator who help populate the site. And they've all got other roles as well, but it is quite a significant job for those people to populate the website with content that's up-to-date. (General manager; Interview with author)

This informant also nominated MLB's website as worthy of emulation, identifying the resource gap between his club and the rumored 100-plus professionals contributing to mlb.com. Minor sports simply cannot compete at such an operative level, although this does not prevent their off-field leaders adopting the fashionable refrain that websites and digital media enable them to 'start a conversation' with participants and fans. But even tentative dialogue of this kind demands the production of appealing content that will elicit a response, regular updating to prevent conversational gaps, and television and news exposure to draw new interlocutors to a site. According to a communications coordinator for another minor sport, the chase for eyeballs makes it imperative to allocate scarce resources to producing audiovisual content, even if it is of inconsistent quality: 'I think you sort of get left behind if you don't' (Interview with author). This notion of being 'left behind' pinpoints the common practice of sports monitoring each other's websites for ideas and benchmarks, leading to a competitive escalation in standards that sees similarly equipped websites innovating at roughly equivalent rates.

Professional industry-standard technology and staff are the two primary factors determining whether smaller sports are able to keep pace with the major networked media sport operators. Servers, operating systems, programs, banks of computers, monitors, and bandwidth can be costly items. For those sports without the means to own or outsource this infrastructure, cheap downloadable multimedia programs and free social networking and video sites like Facebook, Twitter, and YouTube have particular appeal, as they can be customized and branded in a manner consistent with a Web homepage's style and appearance. Nonetheless, despite their affordability and adaptability, the following case demonstrates that these tools do not eliminate the time and staffing challenges involved in coordinating and monitoring Web content.[12] The board of a women's sport organization decided to think 'outside the square' in handling a human resource shortfall (that is, a shortage of paid and expert staff), according to the Marketing Coordinator (Interview with author). Fans and junior competitors were encouraged to set up fan pages for their favorite players on Facebook, only to confront an awkward and unexpected problem. The profile of one player began to attract comments that were variously risqué, lewd, or offensive from males who had little or no interest in the sport. The comments went undetected for a period as the time-poor Marketing Coordinator was also charged with uploading Web content, game-day planning, and handling intermittent general inquiries. When informed of the situation, board members were confronted by an urgent need to protect the image of the player, their inability to hire a staff member to monitor online content regularly, and a determination to keep the good will of fans who had their efforts hijacked by puerile, sexist messages. The balance between preservation of a brand and allowing the grassroots creativity of fans to flourish is a delicate one, particularly for an organization that struggles to attract and keep fans. Valuable time was spent engaging in strategy meetings and in speaking to the player in question and her teammates, with most of the profiles taken down and the necessary justification given to the fan community. Players are now encouraged to maintain their own profiles and to set them to open access if they are happy to do so. As Chapter 4 will show, transferring responsibility for maintaining profiles from the organization to the athlete still requires them to be monitored in order to prevent the appearance of embarrassing comments and photographs.

Sporadic shafts of light break through the gloom for some minor sports at the level of event coverage. In a situation unimaginable 20 years ago, digital cameras, live webcasts, and online score updates have allowed small numbers of people (from only a hundred to a few thousand) in different countries to watch competitions and week-long championships for free or a small fee. A standout example is Paralympicsport.tv and its coverage of Paralympic sports and competitions. A professionally produced site, it has benefited from the sponsorship of the worldwide Paralympic Movement by corporations such as Visa and Samsung, and claims over 11,000 'likes' on Facebook. Other initiatives of this kind include sites for various international distance running events, lawn bowls, snooker tournaments, squash, the World Wheelchair Basketball Championships, and the Cycling World Masters Championship. GB Sport TV is a new Internet channel aiming to provide sustainable exposure for a coalition of British sports, including badminton, field hockey, rowing and sailing, on a year-round basis. Women's water polo has also taken advantage of start-up companies like Rivus TV and their portable video streaming equipment to showcase competitions. These are helpful, hopeful initiatives for sports specifically targeting their participant base and existing followers. At least for the moment, however, their ability to attract broader and lasting news media and public attention remains unproven at best and unlikely at worst.

Novel deployment of networked media sport is occurring at amateur and recreational levels. Two key variables appear in the examples examined. First, minor clubs that play soccer, rugby, and cricket occasionally set up websites, customized digital media management tools, and social media profiles funded by modest proceeds from larger governing bodies, membership subscriptions, and small amounts of advertising revenue (see, for example, Read 2010). Second, amateur clubs and sports that have loyal competitors and volunteers possessing deft computing skills are able to build an effective online presence. The combination of these factors has managed to produce the occasional commercially saleable platform and small business that can then compete with established operators in the information technology sector.

An early example is Cyclingnews.com, which was formed in 1995 by an Australian cycling enthusiast wishing to share information about the sport: 'What started as a passion and hobby grew to the point that dedicated servers and high-speed data links were required—in other words, the site was caught in the Web's massive growth spurt'. By 1999 the website was sold to 'Knapp Communications Pty Limited, a Sydney-based publishing company with expertise in Web site content and production', and in 2007 to the 'British company, Future plc, publishers of Procycling, Cycling Plus, MTB UK and bikeradar.com', a company listed on the London Stock Exchange. A professional online editorial team presently produces the site (cyclingnews.com 2011).

Such developments point towards a genuinely new enterprise for sport on the Internet. Over the past five years or so, a highly competitive market in the online management and control of participant data in grassroots sport has appeared. The volunteer administrator who used to work on their kitchen table now relies on a computer, software package, database, and Internet connection to record and post results, process player registrations, and to communicate with club and team members. This change has translated into a business opportunity for so-called 'technology solution specialists' to colonize the administrative backbone of mass participation sport, as well as supply social networking style platforms for competitors to communicate, share scores and competition results, and to post pictures. The general manager of a digital technology company explained that he found himself reflecting on the connection between personal computing, accelerating Internet speeds, and the capacity of online systems to process enormous amounts of data:

> I always remember sitting there, four years ago, and you could get on the ABS [Australian Bureau of Statistics] website and work out how many people play sport, by sport, by revenue in Australia. And then we developed a financial model based on those statistics. There's 12 million sporting registrations in Australia every year. And the average sporting registration is less than $50, and then our financial model is that we take a transaction fee. So they all paid online and let's say we took 6 percent or something and you extrapolate it out, and we were going to make about $15 billion a year, which is the best business we've ever come across. And that's if you had 100 percent take-up across every sport. And so we thought, this is fantastic, and we went to the local netball club and signed them up and at the end of the first year we made $3.20 [laughs]. (Interview with author)

There are tens of millions of participants competing in organized recreational, amateur, and semi-professional sport around the world. Participants and competitors are redefined as end users in this market, each possessing a gender, age, nationality, email address, team, club, suburb, or city that can be collected, sorted, and retrieved after they register. Participants are also skewed upwards in terms of social class or socio-economic status (Coakley, Hallinan, Jackson & Mewett 2009), which makes them particularly attractive to advertisers. This unprecedented amount of detailed and valuable information is available for processing and commodification by website owners, database operators, metadata aggregators, and online advertisers (see Andrejevic 2007; Elmer 2004; Spurgeon 2008; Van Dijck 2009; Van Dijck & Nieborg 2009).

The irony of this new market is that amateur and minor sports regularly fight to survive financially while, at the same time, representing a potentially lucrative market for entrepreneurs, advertisers, and marketers in the information technology and sports business sector. Lower-level sport is considered to be one of the few online areas still 'unconquered' in sports business circles internationally (McCullagh 2009b), with a number of companies hoping to become the sporting equivalent of Google or Facebook. In Australia alone, operators offering event and competition management software, specialized websites, record-keeping, and social networking services include Pitchero, 3eep, IMG eCommerce, Interact Sport, and Bellevue IT, with many of these companies also operating in the UK, Europe, Asia, and New Zealand. Competition for clients is intense and combative in this industry, as the following comment by a company director indicates:

> We've discussed this long and hard [competition with other providers] and sometimes we've tried to sabotage deals, like a prank, you know, where we know the peak body for a sport has chosen a provider that we think sucks . . . We've been in circumstances where the peak body's chosen an alternative provider or we didn't know they were in a tender situation or they've just gone out and bought one anyway. So we'll go to clubs in that peak body's league and just try to pick them off individually. (Interview with author)

The Australian-based SportingPulse International has attracted attention for reasons that have nothing to do with sharp practice. This company shot to prominence after News Corporation (through its News Digital Media division) purchased a stake in it (Casey 2010). This move announced loudly that mass participation sport is now considered to be a serious business, a point reinforced by SportingPulse's commercial partnerships with telecommunications provider, Optus, the national retailer, Rebel Sports, and with other network partners including the Good Sports Program of the Australian Drug Foundation, National Australia Bank, and the Australian Army (*SportingPulse* 2011). Originating in a semi-professional basketball league, SportingPulse is reportedly used by 3,000 leagues and 20,000 clubs in multiple countries, and operates a business model that provides software to sports in return for marketing rights on their web-pages. It also operates the 'MySport' social network—the closest online sport platform to Facebook or MySpace that we have encountered—with 'friends', photographs, videos, and messages attached to profiles. Nielsen data demonstrate that SportingPulse is a weighty online presence, rank-ing in the top 10 Australian sports websites each month (see Figure 3.1) and attracting well over 50,000 daily unique browsers and an average session duration of just under five minutes. SportingPulse's momentum in attracting amateur leagues and clubs is attributable to its capacity to inexpensively connect weekend volunteer administrators and competitors to a sizable network of sports and people.

Not every operator in this market operates on the scale of SportingPulse, or exhibits a hard-edged competitive ethos in the pursuit of digitally driven commercial opportunities. The serendipitous conjunction of amateur play and information technology is evident on occasion, presenting a sporting inflection on romantic tales about tech-obsessed students inventing popular computer programs in their dorm rooms and garages. Cricket Australia (CA) unveiled an online management platform nationally in 2008 called 'MyCricket'. This tool supplies players, clubs, and competitions at every level across the country with a mechanism to post scores, manage playing records, and track registered junior and senior players. Yet the platform did not emerge from an established national or international technology corpo-ration. Rather, it was the needs of a local grade cricket club in Melbourne that evolved over several years that gave birth to MyCricket.[13] Two players, who later formed a small company, built a website for the club in 1999. Teammates offered suggestions and ideas for additional functionality as the playing seasons passed: 'it really just grew organically' (Interview with author). This unpaid labor saw the website mutate into a results gathering service with automated functions that proved useful to other cricket clubs and associations. Further development saw its product win a tender put out by CA. This nine-year process provides a rare example of a digital proto-type developed to suit the uniquely local needs of lower-level sport becom-ing the preferred option for a leading national sports organization.

In Australia, the federal government has considered the relationship between the Internet and lower-tier sport, with a pioneering 2009 Austra-lian parliamentary inquiry into digital sports media recounting the 'disap-pointing' outcomes for women's sport following the introduction of pay television (Parliament of Australia Senate Standing Committee 2009, p. 46). The proceedings of the inquiry, which are analyzed in Chapter 6, witnessed discussion of whether websites and digital devices can help redress the poor media coverage and financial ill health of many sports that fight, often fruitlessly, for public exposure. A formal recommendation of the inquiry was that the matter be referred to an influential full-scale federal govern-ment review of sports funding, which should then 'pay particular atten-tion to the capacity of sports to invest in digital innovation' (Parliament of

Australia Senate Standing Committee 2009, p. 49). The nationwide review subsequently produced the much discussed and controversial Crawford report—a proposed blueprint for the future funding and structure of elite and mass participation sport across the country (Australian Government Independent Sport Panel 2010). Unfortunately, businessman David Crawford and his panel of experts mostly ignored the question of investment in digital media and the potential role of the Internet in improving sponsorship opportunities and news media coverage for the less prominent sports. Administrative and running costs instead came under brief consideration, with a suggestion that the Internet may help 'create efficiencies and cost savings' if sports leagues and clubs worked collaboratively across distances (p. 23). It is this exact possibility that SportingPulse and its ilk are catering for in the pursuit of private profits generated from publicly subsidized sports organizations.

Sports either wishing to avoid the costs charged by technology companies or which dislike their products have, from time to time, formulated creative responses to these circumstances. The statistical biases inherent within Web metrics and databases can, it transpires, provide a gateway to public funding if they are fitted correctly to the technocratic logic of public funding schemes. Governments prefer 'hard data' and verifiable goals when allocating resources, and the Internet can help to generate respectable numbers that suit this need.[14] For example, a technologically 'savvy' volunteer for an obscure sport built a basic online management system and website that engaged with members and, most importantly, satisfied the reporting requirements of a government department:

> There's two things that the national and state bodies need: one is to be able to communicate directly with the members and the second thing is demographics. The demographics are to manage the sport. But the most important thing is to suck money out of the Government . . . It might sound funny and suck is not the right word, but you know what I'm getting at—funding to sustain you. Governments need to be able to report when they are going to fund grassroots participation. And so [the sport in question] had in the palm of their hand their national membership. They were able to say, 'We've got "x" number of members as of Monday morning at 10am split by this area in the country and these age groups. Demographics are such that we are targeting this, this, and this [group or objective]'. And the difference in the amount of money given to them was huge.[15] (Interview with author)

This account represents a calculated technology-driven strategy to extract public funding, with the Internet and Web deployed strategically to give government exactly what it wanted—up-to-the-minute, verifiable (or at least plausible) data. The difficulty with success of this type is that other sports and community organizations then learn to generate their statistics in the desired format, creating another rigorously competitive game in lower-level sport for paltry sums of money.

Digital plenitude is not translating into greater financial abundance and wellbeing for the majority of minor sports, and the expansion of online media distribution channels has not created equitable outcomes in the marketplace—or even begun to level them out. There are few viable media, sponsor, and spectator markets for low-profile sports and many would collapse immediately if the support of government or their national organizing body was withdrawn. The people who make money below the elite level are generally running digital technology and software companies that harvest the data and advertising opportunities arising out of mass participation competition. At the elite level, the massive amount of content available for fans online is also consolidating the symbolic and cultural dominance of the major male sports. The attractiveness of professional production and reliable quality content creates a powerful gravitational pull for fans, who are consuming more media than ever about the same established band of professional sports teams and leagues that have long held popular attention. This analytical observation is compatible with the idea that the Internet, despite its incredible diversity and complexity, works to concentrate the minds of like-minded users on similar interests and opinions. The digital plenitude generated by online media has made more material available, but it is misleading to conclude on this basis that sports followers are accessing unfamiliar content in large quantities, or suddenly watching sports that have historically struggled for resources and attention. Ultimately, the inequalities of media access, coverage, and technical and human resources that prevailed in the analogue-broadcast era continue, albeit with different dynamics, in the realm of digital-convergent media. The principal difference so far, then, between broadcast scarcity and digital abundance is not the attenuation of inequality, but the way this stratification is obscured by a seductive mythology of limitless and informed choice.

THE POWER OF THE NETWORK?

A profusion of words has been written about the power of the network as an organizing principle and technological phenomenon that is permanently transforming society, culture, the economy, and politics (see Bollmer 2010). The Internet and Web, it is said, have changed the ways in which power flows and functions, fundamentally altering hierarchical and centralized structures into decentered, self-organizing systems that operate in accordance with a 'centripetal imperative' (Ryan 2010). The emancipatory promise of open, networked information production and exchange is celebrated and reiterated by multiplying terms and neologisms that have entered the vocabulary of technology commentary, media studies scholarship, and general public discourse. Cognitive surplus (Shirky 2010), crowdsourcing

(Howe 2008), the hive mind (Herz 2005), smart mobs (Rheingold 2002), the long tail (Anderson 2004), and produsage (Bruns 2008) all capture different dimensions of irrevocable or purportedly revolutionary change in how people live, feel, and think. The power of the network has, in the process, become a taken-for-granted social fact and a transcendental signifier of democratization and freedom. This is the 'digital sublime' (Mosco 2004), an intoxicating mixture of awe and hype that obscures the purposeful actions and collective decisions that create the Internet and Web out of an evolving constellation of protocols, applications, and everyday uses.

It is timely to shift attention from the potential power that resides within the network and, instead, to consider evidence of the relationship between power and the network (Castells 2009). This approach places evidence of the interests and motivations of individuals, sports, corporations, and institutions squarely in the frame as they act upon and through digital media. Our addition to the rapidly expanding list of neologisms—networked media sport—aims to signify the multi-sided uncertainty, change, and resistance to change that are discovered once sufficient evidence has been collected and weighed. The uses and abuses of the measurement of online audiences and users encapsulate this argument. There is a widely acknowledged need for change in audience measurement systems across the media sector in order accurately to match advertising placement and the behavior of people online, as the emergence and growth of lunchtime workspace audiences attests. But many major media industry players contest this need as they jockey for best position in any proposed new system and, by extension, for first-mover advantage in any new commercial opportunities that might arise. This opportunistic mindset produces a contest over which website metrics count the most and which claims can be made legitimately to attract and protect advertisement and sponsorship revenue. Paradoxically, these actions are generally accompanied by a progressive rhetoric that emphasizes the exciting new opportunities, choices, and openness offered by the Internet and online communities. As was shown above, this rhetoric has distinct limits, with the multiplication of media sport content producing both greater user choice *and* a countervailing urge for control on behalf of content providers and online operators when they construct pay walls. The value of the real estate behind these walls is also dependent on popular clubs and teams cooperating with their league as a whole in order to maintain a modicum of competitive balance on and off the field. Notably, these changes in media conditions have not dismantled the entrenched cultural hierarchies of sports organization, practice, and spectatorship. Digital plenitude has failed so far to produce digital equality. The discovery of an entirely new media sport market was outlined in the section immediately above, but most women's, disabled, and mass participation sports are benefitting from its operation only at the margins. The ability to 'broadcast yourself' online is, at this stage, failing to deliver increased income, government assistance, or substantial public exposure.

This chapter's opening discussion of the Beijing Olympics highlighted that the power to communicate networked media sport exists on a scale and in a manner never before seen. Nevertheless, there is limited evidence of cultural and political democratization or flattened hierarchies. Much of the power exercised by major clubs, leagues, sports organizations, media companies, and digital technology providers is directed towards tracking and controlling the measurement and movement of users, exercising and expanding market influence, entrenching existing interests and structures, containing costs, and improving margins. The critical issue, then, is not the power of the network *per se*. Rather, it is what happens when different users, groups, corporations, and governments seek to exert their power over (i) how the network operates; (ii) the purposes to which it is directed, and; (iii) the ways in which different types of networked digital communication are understood and valued in terms of affordances and limitations. The next part of the book applies this argument, examining the popularity, uses, and regulation of social networking services and blogs. In so doing, we travel even further beyond sport television and websites into the provisionally charted realm of (de)friending and (dis)liking.

4   Blogging, Social Networking Sites, and Information Accidents

Six of the top 10 websites on the Internet include user-generated content and features.[1] The likes of Facebook, YouTube, Baidu Space, Qzone, Tumblr, and Twitter characterize online cultures that see media producers, distributors, and users interact on an unprecedented scale. Users are said to challenge professional media content providers in an environment featuring extensive use of social software systems, reorganizing the industrial production value chain to enable continuous collaboration and modification of digital content (Bruns 2008, pp. 9–36).[2] This is the age of the perpetual-beta (Ryan 2010) where 'produsers' constantly reconfigure information and, as a result, cultural and intellectual life (Bruns 2008, p. 34). Wikipedia is often cited as a prime example of peer-driven, communal knowledge in action, representing a powerful model of knowledge production and exchange where multitudes of users challenge the cultural authority of traditional intellectual gatekeepers and self-appointed guardians of 'legitimate' knowledge.[3] YouTube represents another important site of participatory culture in which emerging norms of media power and control are contested *en masse* (Burgess & Green 2009; Snickars & Vonderau 2009). For those accustomed to the conventional notion that a small number of major media organizations generate and diffuse texts that are consumed by large, heterogeneous and dispersed audiences, the elevation of 'ordinary people' to the status of 'co-creators' has a radical, popular democratic appeal (Carpentier 2011). These are seductive arguments that, depending on subject and context, contain both truths and distortions about so-called 'Web 2.0' media.[4] They are certainly plausible when Axel Bruns (2008) artfully dissects the activities of user communities formed around Flickr, Linux, and Second Life. They are, however, less convincing in the case of sport, when the muddled and ambivalent sets of outcomes produced by blogging, Twitter, and Facebook are examined.

Social software possesses a Janus-faced character. Blogs and social networking sites[5] supply potent tools for the production and dissemination of sport related information *and* challenge the capacity of sports and media organizations to maintain control over information and images in unpredictable online settings. Social software has changed the shape and speed of media sport information circulation, allowing many more people to generate content than ever before. Athletes have been the prime beneficiaries and targets of criticism arising out of these developments. Stars now command their own followers as they post messages and bypass publicists and journalists. As will be shown, however, they can also embarrass themselves if any excesses of their private behavior and opinions are placed on public display. This is a situation of social complexity flowing from the hyper-production and hyper-accumulation of digital information (Gane 2006, p. 29), which makes it difficult to anticipate the potential effects of blog entries, status updates, and tweets. The key challenge for athletes and sports organizations is the prevention and management of *information accidents* (cf. Virilio 2007)—scandalous disclosures, damaging criticism, and embarrassing photographs circulated widely online. In effect, this is a media strategy contest occurring *within* elite sport, as those who play, report on, and officiate seek to deploy social software in order to satisfy their particular needs. The end result for fans and users is that they are drawn into an accelerated, real-time information order that generates round-the-clock attention for the major football codes, basketball, tennis, cricket, baseball, and the Olympics, and which can speedily and efficiently turn any, even tangentially sport related topic, into global news.

TRANSMEDIA SPORT

The alchemy of the so-called 'Sports 2.0 ecosystem' (Coyle Media 2011) is to convert the emotions, experiences, and creativity of sports fans into data that mediate market value. While many media sport industry insiders initially feared that audiences would be lost to them by 'talking amongst themselves', they increasingly view blogs, Facebook, and Twitter as effective vehicles to 'get the brand out there', with customized profiles helping to draw users back to official websites and portals. In replicating the quantitative bias of the broadcast ratings system, the latest manifestation of this market-driven rationale is the tracking of friends and followers, and early attempts at determining the monetary value of a 'like' on Facebook or a re-tweet on Twitter (or, of course, the corresponding cost of inaction by Facebook and Twitter users). Terms like 'trending topic' have entered common currency as measures of popular attention that might be monetized. Corporate consultants and technology commentators, therefore, use the numbers generated by social networking to rate the value of 'sports properties' (see Figure 4.1). Like shares on the stock market, social media 'movers and shakers' rise and announce themselves, while high-value 'blue-chip' brands jostle for top position. For instance, the 10 entities appearing on the Coyle Media ranking in Figure 4.1 are soccer and basketball teams with international fan-bases (7), a globally popular sports league, a sports entertainment federation, and a global media sport company. These ranking exercises have assumed a self-perpetuating logic as leagues, teams, and athletes race each other to collect the greatest number of followers and then publicize their popularity in the news media:

> [Over] two million people follow the NBA on Twitter, a record for any major US sport on the social networking site . . . NBA followers push the league ahead of the National Football League, which has almost 1.7 million followers on Twitter, or Major League Baseball, which needs about 30,000 more. (Pandaram 2010)

Significantly, social networking services are acting to discredit the proposition that the Internet erodes the audience for television sport. While other forms of digital delivery such as IPTV or unauthorized streams nibble away at broadcast television's overall share of the sports audience, platforms such as Facebook and Twitter are working to offset these losses. Fans lavish attention on major sports events through a combination of television viewing, social media use, and website access, creating a *transmedia sport experience* irreducible to its constituent parts. This variation on Henry Jenkins' (2006a, pp. 95–97) concept of transmedia storytelling describes how different media platforms are used selectively to enrich the experience of sports events as a whole by providing access to 'extra-textual elements'

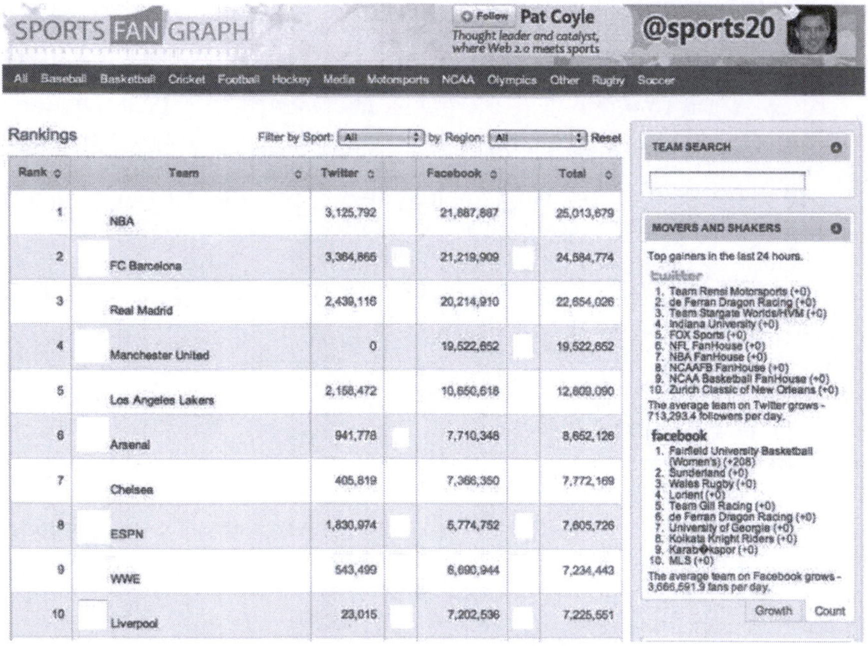

Figure 4.1   Screenshot taken of a 'Sports Fan Graph' on the Coyle Media website. Used with permission of Coyle Media

(Ross 2008, p. 86). These elements include online viewer comments and discussion, fan reactions to coaching and referee decisions, real-time statistics, updates on athlete injuries, behind-the-scenes insights, and replays of contentious and spectacular moments. They also provide many new opportunities for audiences to communicate with each other about sport before, during, and after the event. These transmedia practices surprised network executives who had initially feared that the Internet would continually undercut their chase for viewers. This type of viewer engagement is evident during events such as the NFL's Super Bowl. According to Nielsen (2010), 14 percent of television viewers who watched the 2010 Super Bowl live used the Internet at the same time, an increase of 2 percent on the previous year. For viewers in the US who were multitasking, Facebook was visited during the game by one in 20 Internet-connected home viewers, who spent an average of 19 minutes on the site. This pattern was further evident on Twitter, with a huge number of tweets sent over the course of the game (*Sports Geek* 2010b). At the same time, the television audience for the 2010 Super Bowl was a record, exceeding 100 million people, with television executives recognizing the positive influence of social networking:

> CBS [the Super Bowl Broadcast Network in 2010] Chief Executive Leslie Moonves said social-networking tools such as Twitter have encouraged TV viewing as Americans exchange opinions on what they're watching. (Schechner & Ovide 2010)

In 2011, the Super Bowl TV audience exceeded the previous year's figure, with social media again to the fore (Seidman 2011). Similar transmedia experiences were evident during the most recent summer and winter Olympiads. The IOC, which derives massive revenue from broadcast rights, has embraced social networking in an effort to reach younger audiences. IOC President Jacques Rogge explained the need for the Olympic Movement to utilize 'channels including YouTube, Facebook, and Bebo to reach kids through media that they are immediately comfortable with' (Quoted in Roberts 2009). Our observations of Internet activity during the 2008 Beijing and 2010 Vancouver Olympic Games indicated that thousands of individuals used their profiles to comment on and post Olympic related content. Alan Wurtzel, research president for the Olympic broadcaster, NBC-Universal, is upbeat about these practices, saying that the Internet 'actually fuels interest' after observing viewing and media-use habits over the course of the 2008 Beijing Olympiad (Kiss 2008). Furthermore, the General Manager of Fox Soccer, David Nathanson, has observed that his channel's extensive online media operations complement its television programming: 'The Internet and mobile allow people to delve deeper' (*Sport Business International* 2011d). The interaction between social networking, online coverage, and television commentary has also helped to create an engaging experience during the Tour de France cycling race and various motor racing events. These developments show that social media platforms are catalysts for increased user and viewer attention for sporting moments that already claim mass followings. The dynamic propelling this intense focus is comprehensible when observing trending topics on Twitter, a news feed on Facebook, or the latest results on a StumbleUpon toolbar at the time of a Super Bowl or World Cup final. These tools are digital media awareness systems (Hermida 2010) that actively funnel the attention of followers, 'friends', and 'stumblers' onto events watched by thousands or millions of users.

The key to the future of media sport is the relationship *between* screens. Television, computer, tablet, and mobile phone screens connect different dimensions of live fixtures and events, as well as the secondary and complementary news and social media discussions that occur around them. In Raymond Williams' (1974) classic formulation of the television viewing experience, these transmedia arrangements can be understood as generating a new digitized *media flow*. Williams explained that television viewing results from the mutual interaction between programmers who construct a broadcast schedule and viewers who decide what to watch and when (Williams 1974, p. 93). Interaction between Internet access, social networking, and television is personalizing the flow of viewing sport in a way not previously seen. Event organizers, broadcasters, viewers, and users on social networking platforms are flexibly creating the experience of media spectatorship for the Super Bowl, the World Series, or the FA Cup Final (Johnson 2009, p. 126). The attention awarded to different media is shifting in relation to user choice and collective reactions to sports events. While there will always be those who watch, habitually or selectively, the television screen only, these viewers are now joined by 'multitaskers' who create their own media flow on the run as they watch, post, and follow the contents of two or more screens. The widespread incorporation of fan Twitter feeds into sports broadcasts, which are then discussed by commentators, ensures that no one watching can escape social networking. Live sport is uniquely suited to this flow, as sports events were already a popular social location for the use of mobile instant messaging, ranking behind only 'crowded public transport' and ahead of 'busy meetings', 'campus classrooms', and hospitals (Castells, Fernandez-Ardevol, Qiu, & Sey 2007, p. 177). Solidifying this trend, the NBA, NFL, MLB, UFC, and soccer leagues in different countries all feature frequently in the lead trending topics on Twitter each week (*What the Trend* 2011).

A notable feature of the arrangements that we have outlined is that social networking activities are still reliant on live televised sport, suggesting that services like Facebook, Google+, and Twitter are extensions of the television experience and media activities in their own right. This pattern continues to solidify as resource-rich sports deploy digital media most effectively in the dissemination of entertaining content, and the social networking profiles operated by fans of major leagues only reinforce this online dominance.

Elite sport and its stars are already the recipients of extensive news and media coverage, and user-generated content and comment provide them with more attention in new communicative contexts. Even when fan-produced content and comments are critical in nature, there is rarely a fundamental challenge to those who possess overwhelming symbolic power in defining and anchoring the reality of elite sport—sports organizing bodies, leagues, clubs, media companies, and sponsors (cf. Couldry 2003, 2006). Such gestures of fan defiance struggle to mobilize transformative forces in sport, even if this were the intention of 'dissidents'. Indeed, discussion by fans often concentrates on how officials and executives should improve their performance to achieve greater success for their team on the field, better financial returns off it, and more appealing action for those watching (Scibilia & Hutchins 2012; Wilson, W. 2007). The value of online fans is derived from the accumulated attention that they award to top-level sport, with social networking media proving a successful means of harvesting their time and energy. Discussion now turns to how the globally influential Olympic Movement has responded to the growth and challenges of social software over recent years.

BLOGGING THE OLYMPICS

Blogging is a popular online activity despite the fact that it is no longer fashionable among the technology *commentariat*. The Technocrati search engine continues to track over one-and-a-quarter million active blogs worldwide, with many blogs also linking to Facebook and Twitter profiles.[6] The blogging platform WordPress claimed to be the home of six million new blogs and 23 billion page views during 2010 (Van Grove 2011).[7] Sport has a noteworthy place in the blogosphere despite the neglect of this topic in the literature on blogging (see, for example, Rodzvilla 2002; Gurak, Antonijevic, Johnson, Ratliff & Reyman 2004; Bruns & Jacobs 2006; Barlow 2008; Rettberg 2008). The growth of online activities during the 2006 FIFA World Cup (Dart 2009) was again evident during the 2010 World Cup in South Africa and the Vancouver Winter Olympics, which featured among the most blogged-about topics of 2010. The increasing practice of athletes using the Internet for self-promotion and independent communication now sees many maintain personal, promotional, and officially sponsored blogs. Examples of routinely updated blogs include those of Swedish professional golfer Alex Noren and MLB's Matt Antonelli. These blogs sit alongside that of NBA basketball player, political commentator and poet, Etan Thomas of the Atlanta Hawks, who writes for the *Huffington Post*. Diary-style blogging among sportspeople, however, may not be assiduously practiced. For example, as of July 2011, the last blog post from global soccer celebrity, David Beckham (commencing, 'Hi everyone I'm back in LA now and we're already a couple of matches into the new season'), was sent out on the 23rd of March (*David's Blog* 2011). Further complicating this picture are the blogging activities of professional print and broadcast sports journalists—signaling the rise of the 'j-blogger' (Singer 2005)—who use blogs to interact with readers. *The New York Times*' 'Straight Sets' tennis blog, which posts contributions by tennis writers, is an engaging example of such j-blogging.

The use of digital media devices and the Web to self-produce and distribute media content has been evident for many years in youth-oriented lifestyle sport and movement cultures, including skateboarding, freestyle BMX, surfing, *parkour*, and base-jumping (Beal & Wilson 2004; Puijk 2004; Stauff 2009). These subcultural media practices had reached mainstream professional sport by the time of the Beijing Olympics in August 2008, fuelled by the falling prices of laptop computers and smart phones, and the growing popularity and availability of social software. Costing in the order of US$40 billion to stage, the 2008 Beijing Olympics are an instructive case study because of their stature as the largest sports megaevent in history. This festival represents an achievement of scale and organization projected onto the world stage by a Chinese state that displays acute sensitivity about their representation and mediation (Qing & Richeri 2011). There were 24,562 accredited journalists, presenters, producers, and technical staff from around the world reporting on the sports events, in addition to another 3,654 non-accredited media personnel (IOC 2009b, p. 8). Beijing was the first 'Web 2.0 summer Olympics' (Miah, Garcia & Zhihui 2008), an event in which digital online media were a dominant presence. The IOC sold separate Internet and mobile platform exhibition rights for Beijing, embracing the Internet much like the media preceding it: 'a platform for disseminating coverage of the Olympic Games' and 'an important medium for the communication and promotion of sport and the Olympic Movement' (IOC 2008a). The physical manifestation of a shift towards digital networked communications was the presence of 260 computers installed in six Internet lounges built in the main Olympic village, and the conspicuous presence of an exclusive worldwide Olympic sponsor and computer manufacturer, the Chinese-owned company Lenovo (Humphreys & Finlay 2008, pp. 290–95).

Demonstrating just how fast the digital media landscape changes, blogging was the activity of most concern to Olympics organizers in the lead-up to Beijing. No research interview or search for news articles conducted around the time of the Olympics produced a single mention of Twitter. MySpace and Facebook did receive attention, but were considered to be of lesser significance than blogs. IOC officials grappled with how to respond to the prospect of athlete blogging in the lead-up to the Beijing Olympics, developing valuable knowledge that would then be applied to Twitter and Facebook at the winter Olympics in 2010. IOC officials were (and remain) concerned about the Internet activities of athletes for two principal reasons. The first of these applies to the protection of commercial value: namely, the prevention of ambush marketing and infringement of broadcast media rights by means of uploaded still or moving images. The Olympic Movement had by that time managed to generate over US$10 billion from broadcasting rights since 1980 (Smart 2007, pp. 124–25), and takes seriously any perceived or imminent threat to this extraordinarily profitable arrangement. The second matter involves preventing athletes posting unexpectedly critical, scandalous, or politically charged comments, which is a potential by-product of social communication and exchange in online environments. While we do not focus in detail on the fraught politics of the Beijing Olympics in this chapter (see Close, Askew & Xin 2007; Horne & Whannel 2010; Rowe & McKay 2012), critical issues like journalists' freedom of reporting and movement, political repression in Tibet, and freedom of speech in the host nation play a subsidiary role in our analysis. These issues prompted national and international Olympic officials to be especially vigilant about the possibility of the Web being used to 'hijack' the 'Olympic media platform' (Price 2008) by a dissenting athlete, non-government organization (NGO), or an onlooker armed with a smartphone. For instance, an activist group causing concern was the athlete-led and run Team Darfur, which used a range of media mechanisms to draw attention to the connection between Chinese state investment and the Sudanese government in the midst of a humanitarian crisis.[8]

While short, the history of official responses to the use of blogs and social networking services by athletes is characterized by confusion and backflips. The Secretary General of the Australian Olympic Committee (AOC), Craig Phillips, stated in early 2007 that Australian athletes would be banned from blogging during the Beijing Olympics, citing a curious combination of pious and instrumental reasons. Such activities, it was suggested, would erode the 'sanctuary of the Olympic village' and leave Olympic sponsors open to ambush marketing by athlete sites (Bryant 2007). By May 2008 this position had been overturned, with the IOC and AOC having released detailed guidelines outlining the specific conditions under which athletes could express themselves online. The Chair of the IOC Press Commission, Kevan Gosper, stated the following about these guidelines:

> if athletes had a free run on blogging, they could cut across the protection constraints that exist for broadcasters who pay us a lot of money for broadcasting rights, and journalists themselves. (The Sports Factor 2008)

This sequence of events replicated a controversy at the 2007 Pan-American Games in Rio de Janeiro, where athletes were initially banned from updating their blogs during competition (Sparre 2007a, 2007b).[9] Like the IOC, organizers feared that commercially unauthorized videos or images posted online would compromise the value of the coverage rights purchased by television stations. The response from bloggers to such actions was dismissive:

> It is enough that one spectator buys a ticket and gets into the audience with a cell phone, while another can connect a cable channel line into a video capture board and, at the same time, hundreds of others send all of this to YouTube. Those rights' [sic] owners, broadcasters, recording companies and all the entrepreneurs dealing with information need to rethink their business models. (Sparre 2007a)

The process described in this quotation has since become easier, as the recording and sharing of footage with a mobile smartphone requires minimal technical knowledge when using programs such as Ustream and Qik. The decision of officials to ban blogging at the 2007 event in Rio de Janeiro was discarded within three months of its announcement. Reasons given for the reversal were its unenforceability (the athlete's village had been built with a wireless Internet network and many athletes carried laptop computers) and a policy review undertaken by the IOC in relation to athlete blogging. This high-profile review did not, however, produce uniformity across international multi-sports events. Australian athletes at the 2010 Commonwealth Games in Delhi were banned from using Facebook and other forms of social media over the course of the event, presumably to prevent criticism of Commonwealth Games organizers and fellow athletes (Halloran 2010).

The source of consternation for event organizers is the need to find a quick and effective response to the conditions of 'enhanced autonomy' enjoyed by sportspeople in a networked information economy (Benkler 2006). Athletes now possess the ready-made capacity to communicate digitally outside the control of traditional, centrally controlled media systems. Comparing the present day to Seoul in 1988, when athletes could only speak to a host television channel, radio station, or a limited pool of accredited newspaper journalists based in their home country, reveals the dramatic enhancement of their communicative options in just over two decades. The public profile of many athletes means that they have attentive followers waiting to see and hear their messages, which may be at odds with the official statements, positions, and commercial arrangements of sports organizations and commercial news companies (cf. Poor 2006; Jenkins 2003). A disturbing case of this 'cut through' capacity was presented when, two months prior to the Beijing Opening Ceremony, Ronda Rousey (a judo medal winner for the US), unexpectedly used her personal blog to accuse an official in her sport of molesting young female competitors (Smith 2008). Just a month later, champion Australian road cyclist, Cadel Evans, caused alarm when a 'Free Tibet' announcement and Tibetan flag appeared on his personal website, which contains a blog, and remained there throughout the Olympiad. That Rousey and Evans broke ranks before the commencement of the Olympics was arguably a blessing in disguise for the IOC, placing national team officials on alert for athlete dissent online. Ultimately, events in Beijing demonstrated that careful policy measures and media management techniques can limit the impact of social software to evolutionary, not revolutionary, effect.

The IOC's blogging guidelines (IOC 2008b, 2010, 2011) contain a range of conditions best read in conjunction with the media guidelines issued to accredited members of national teams (AOC 2008). These documents also apply to the use of social networking media. These policies recognize the right of athletes to express themselves, but place tight limits on permitted topics and content. A celebrity gossip blog, *Derober* (2008), accurately summarized the conditions placed upon athletes with a dash of sarcasm:

> The IOC has given athletes the right to blog at the Beijing Games this summer, a first for the Olympics, as long as they follow the many rules it set to protect copyright agreements, confidential information and security. Basically, they are allowed to discuss what they had for breakfast as long as they don't get emotional about it.

No interviews, moving images, or audio coverage were allowed, while advertising or sponsorship should not be 'visible on the screen at the same time as Olympic content' (IOC 2008b, p. 2). A key sentence reads, 'When Accredited Persons at the Games post any Olympic Content, it [is to] be confined *solely* to their own personal Olympic related experience' (p. 1, emphasis added), which effectively excludes photographs of, or comments by, other athletes, and limits discussion to an athlete's own performance. Online entries need to adopt a first-person, diary-like format that cannot be confused with journalism and reporting. The outcome of blogging safely within the guidelines could be seen in the 'Voices of the Summer Games' promotion, which featured over 100 athletes from around 25 countries blogging about their Olympic experiences. The resultant content was often highly descriptive, individualistic, and dull.

While the IOC felt that the blogging rules were fair, one of our interviews elicited a critical response from a media and public relations manager working for a national sport. Tasked with having to understand and explain the guidelines to male and female athletes competing in Beijing, he explained forcefully that his sport's competitors wanted to know what they could say and do in straightforward terms. This need required an applied understanding of the blogging policy and the risk factors associated with social media related activity:

> The news media is just absolutely dying to get an athlete to make a mistake in blogging. If a person performed well over the entire Olympic period and won the gold medal, but in a blog said, 'Asian food sucked and it would be better if Asians just didn't exist at all', then that person would not be remembered for their gold medal or their performance. They will be remembered for a stupid little [racist] blog that they put out when they were in a bad mood. (Interview with author)

After using the guidelines to write a mock blog entry in order to assess their effect, the media manager felt them to be 'completely contradictory' (Interview with author). It was, he said, a 'rather difficult exercise' when attempting to write a blog entry that cannot mention fellow team members or international competitors. Superficially, at least, this sharp response suggests that the IOC is guilty of poor media policy design. However, closer analysis shows that the difficulty described is actually a cunning response to fast-changing digital media conditions. The IOC's blogging policy needed to be general enough to stymie accusations that athletes were being openly censored, particularly when the Fundamental Principles of Olympism (see IOC 2007) emphasize and champion human rights and dignity. However, the policy also sought to circumscribe the range of Olympic experiences that could be referred to in posts, steering discussion away from commercial and political matters. This awkward combination led the media manager quoted above to regard blogging as 'a minefield' (Interview with author). As the IOC no doubt hoped, athletes were then strongly advised by team management to exercise caution when writing posts and uploading photographs and videos. The consequences for those judged to have breached IOC rules were also potentially severe, being at risk of having their Olympics accreditation stripped, which doubled as their visa entitlement to enter and remain in China at that time.

Media minders were also charged with identifying and 'heading-off' risk factors that could produce adverse publicity for athletes over the course of the Olympics. These were flagged during media training and information sessions held in the lead-up to Beijing. It was explained that an athlete accustomed to regular news media exposure at home would be 'at risk' during the Olympics given the number of teams and athletes that attend, meaning that they may receive little or no coverage depending on their performance. The temptation to use a blog or social networking profile to speak out is increased because 'it's when they don't get the attention [that] you have to start worrying', given the routine newsworthiness of elite athletes in their regular media environments:

> Athletes who previously get press at home will largely get ignored. Those athletes will probably want to connect with the outside world, and they'll try and do that through blogging . . . there's going to be athletes in sports who are going to be affected by that lack of attention and they're going to want to connect, and that's where they're going to run into problems with blogging. The biggest danger, or the one we're trying to avoid, is that we have an athlete who is in the middle of something and not concentrating on their sport. (Interview with author)

The identification of risk factors and implementation of preventative measures proved effective in Beijing. No Australian athlete breached the IOC's blogging guidelines or was involved in a media scandal—no doubt to the disappointment of many in what Michael Schudson (2008, p. 57) describes as a necessarily 'unlovable press' peopled largely by journalists that 'relish conflict' and like events that provide 'a recurrent resource for embarrassing the powerful'.[10]

An additional reason for the lack of scandal or breach of Olympic Guidelines was the level of focus and discipline required by elite athletes to compete successfully at an international level. This need produced a natural 'insulating effect' for the IOC when it came to limiting athlete blogging and online communication in general. Most athletes were either unwilling or unable to comment on matters apart from sport because of the physical and psychological demands placed upon them during competition. One elite athlete who maintains a website and social networking profile spoke of the pressures applied by coaches and by the pursuit of personal and team goals over the course of a career. These factors meant that any interest outside sport tended to be sublimated for the duration of the festival:

> I think the biggest thing to bear in mind is that to reach that level of sport . . . you've got to be single-minded, and 100 percent emotionally, physically, mentally committed. And anything short of that, unless it somehow bolsters the commitment to competing, steals away from the long-term goals. (Interview with author)

This comment is consistent with statements made by AOC Communications Manager, Mike Tancred, who expressed a similar sentiment, albeit in cloyingly idealistic terms:

> I lived in the village in Sydney and I lived in the village in Athens . . . The fact [is] that you might be a Communist, a Muslim, a Catholic, a Methodist. You know the fact that you might vote for the Democrats or the Republicans or Labor or whatever. Those sort of issues don't get raised really in the Olympic Village, because the 10,500 athletes who go to the Olympics are elite athletes, and they're there fulfilling a dream. They've worked for four years, eight years, some of them have worked for a lifetime to get to the Olympics, and really their focus is sport and competing, and friendship and harmony. (The Sports Factor 2008)

This literally 'Olympian' take on sport has a familiar Coubertinian ring (Hill 1992), but it should be recognized that the Olympic village and competition are not immune from politics, outside influences, or disruption. The history of the Olympics is one of intermittent political demonstrations, such as the Black Power salute of 1968, and occasionally horrific terrorist acts, as in Munich (1972) and Atlanta (1996) (Guttmann 2002). Neither Tancred nor the athlete quoted above is naïve enough to deny this history. Rather, in different ways, they are pointing to the fact that outside influences, interests, and communication are strategically avoided in the pursuit of peak performance.

There were, then, no major athlete blogging scandals in Beijing, but there were problems that demonstrated the impossibility of *total* information control and data surveillance on the Internet. Unpredictable information flows are inevitable in online environments where the ceaseless production of data and content creates complex communications systems that produce intended and unintended outcomes through the very logic of their operation (cf. Lash 2002); a point emphasized in the remainder of the chapter. Additionally, a tense political atmosphere is susceptible to the generation of media scandals (Rowe 2004a; Thompson 2000). The anxiety of the host nation about internal political agitation and its image on the world stage created an acute sensitivity as international news media reported from China. American track cyclist Mike Friedman unwittingly walked straight into this media force field upon arrival at Beijing International Airport by being photographed wearing an anti-pollution mask. His appearance offended the BOCOG by drawing attention to the city's pollution problem and China's environmental record. US Olympic officials expressed concern at the 'incident' (a symbolic rebuke to China, a country where the wearing of such masks by locals on the street is by no means uncommon) and Friedman offered an apology, which was published on the front page of *China Daily* (Macur 2008; Hutcheon 2008a). The controversy persisted, however, when Friedman defended his actions on his personal blog, which was then accessed by media outlets such as *The New York Times* and Melbourne's *The Age*:

> Well, well, well, this is certainly not how I anticipated starting off my Olympic experience. I can't say much at this point simply because everything is scrutinized severely. It's hard for me to not attach emotion to this, those of you who know me, know what I'm talking about, but what I will say is this. Everyone is entitled to their opinions. I will continue to wear my mask where I deem fit. It's my life and health in the long run, and I would never do something that would purposefully or intently [sic] harm the best interest or the public view of either my Country or other Countries in attendance. (Friedman, M. 2008)

This blog entry generated 94 comments within 18 days, including statements of support, patriotic breast-beating, anti-Chinese sentiment, and condemnation of his actions. Significantly, Friedman's decision to provide his perspective on the story adhered to the requirements of IOC guidelines. He blogged only about his personal Olympic experience and there was no requirement that he delete reader comments from his website. But it nonetheless provoked unease among US and China Olympic authorities.

An unusual use of networked digital media to subvert authority at the Beijing Olympics occurred through an album titled, 'Songs for Tibet—The

Art of Peace', which was available for download through Apple iTunes three days prior to the Opening Ceremony. Featuring well-known Western artists such as Suzanne Vega, Moby, Ben Harper, Sting, and Alanis Morissette, the album was offered as a free download to athletes attending the Olympics. Competitors were asked to listen on their MP3 players to show support for the Dalai Lama and the independence of Tibet (Hutcheon 2008b; *PRLog* 2008). About 40 unidentified athletes showed their solidarity with this cause by taking up the offer. International controversy followed after the album was then linked to the blocking of access to the iTunes store in China, and the appearance of denouncements by 'angry Chinese netizens' in online forums (CRI 2008). These blunt responses provoked another round of officially unwelcome news discussion about the 'Great Firewall of China' (Zhang 2006). This story did not amount to a major blow against the Chinese Communist Party, although it gave offense to its leadership. The album was arguably a technical contravention of Rule 51 of the Olympic Charter, which prevents any 'kind of demonstration or political, religious or racial propaganda' in Olympic sites or venues, but it did not seriously undermine it. Rather, the international attention that the album and its blocking received highlight the constant worry of governments and international sports organizations that networked digital communications and Internet users are undermining their economic power and political influence. On balance, the discussion presented so far suggests roughly the opposite. The compact between the IOC and the states that host Olympic festivals is firmly entrenched, and social software draws additional user and viewer attention to these mega-events. But the paradox of possessing great power is the ever-present worry that it could wane or, worse, be lost altogether.

In the lead-up to the London 2012 and Sochi 2014 Games, the IOC has maintained its record of vigilance and adaptive responses to online media, releasing new 'Social Media, Blogging and Internet Guidelines' for London well in advance of the event (IOC 2011). These guidelines acknowledge that Twitter and Facebook have grown in global popularity and update the conditions imposed on athletes to control their use. Once again, there is an insistence that athletes adopt a 'first-person, diary-style format' when tweeting and updating their profiles (p. 1) and limit their comments to their own performance and experience. This need recognizes the potential of social networking media to disturb orderly and, as the remainder of this chapter demonstrates, hierarchical communication regimes.

TWITTER, FACEBOOK, AND SEXTING

Large numbers of elite athletes communicate with fans, followers, journalists, and friends by sending short, direct messages of 140 characters or less on Twitter. According to the Director of Online Communications for the

2010 Winter Olympics, Graeme Menzies, Twitter recalls Marshall McLuhan's observations about the telegraph (cf. Levinson 1999):

> Twitter has retrieved the telegram. It's a good telegram: Short little sentences and things that are important for the next five minutes, but not so important after that. (Quoted in Silverman 2010)

Menzies' point about disposable short sentences is perhaps accurate in many cases, but requires the addition of three critical dimensions—network speed, scale, and accessibility—to understand the significance of this platform. It also demands recognition that while the message itself may be quickly forgotten, it can act as a catalyst for something much larger and more enduring—after all, those 140 characters may be the gateway to news stories and scandals of substantial consequence. Twitter claims to have 100 million active users who contribute to an estimated 230 million tweets per day (Kiss 2011). The phenomenal growth in attention awarded to this platform occurred from early 2009. While data on usage, audience, and active accounts vary, all show Twitter experiencing a remarkable upsurge in activity from this moment. The site attracted around 44.5 million unique visitors worldwide in June 2009, compared to 'only' 2.9 million in June the previous year (Schonfeld 2009). This explosion in popularity is the result of a number of factors, including the fast-rising use of social networking media, effective website design, canny online promotion, and widespread news coverage garnered through Twitter's adoption by celebrities such as actor Ashton Kutcher, pop star Britney Spears, and basketball player Shaquille O'Neal. These factors coincided with a surge in consumer uptake of personal communications devices ideally suited to tweeting—Internet-enabled 3G smart phones such as the iPhone, Blackberry, and various Android compatible handsets—although it is necessary to note that tweets are easily and commonly sent by sms text messages on 2G phones and via the Web (Goggin 2011, p. 125).

The 2010 Vancouver Winter Olympics provides another snapshot of the media sports cultural complex through the lens of a global mega-event. The nervousness of the IOC and broadcasters about the Internet had dissipated somewhat after reviewing media consumption patterns over the course of the previous Olympiad. Online coverage in its many forms—official, unofficial, news-oriented, and personal—had expanded the collective attention accorded the Beijing Olympics. While still unhappy about unauthorized Internet streams, the IOC noted that viewers who accessed both NBC's television and Internet coverage during the 2008 Olympics 'consumed twice as much content as those who just consumed TV' (Proof Committee Hansard 29 April 2009, p. 15). Seeking to capitalize on heavy consumers of the Olympics, NBC actively promoted Twitter during the 2010 Olympics. The network offered a live feed of American athlete tweets on its website over the course of the Olympics, and produced a 'tracker' that visually traced the amount of Twitter activity. This visual interface displayed images of the specific events and athletes in action at the time that tweets were sent (*YouTube* 2010). It showed between two- and seven-thousand tweets posted every 10 minutes during competition, with Shaun White's virtuoso performance in the half-pipe snowboard a prominent feature. Other standout performers who contributed to peak Twitter traffic included Apolo Ohno in the short track speed skating and gold medalist Lindsey Vonn in the downhill skiing. Vonn was also confused by the IOC rules that governed athlete tweets and Facebook status updates, initially informing her 35,000 plus followers that there was a blackout period in effect for the duration of the Olympics (McClusky 2010a). She was then informed that messages could be posted despite the IOC's blogging guidelines (2010) not specifically mentioning Twitter or Facebook at the time. As with competitors at the summer Olympics, posts were required to be limited to her personal experience and to contain no promotional content. The difference between diary-style blogging and short-form tweeting was best demonstrated by Vonn's teammate and rival in the downhill ski events, Julia Mancuso, who tweeted about her performance *during* the progress of the giant slalom. Having had a poor first run, Mancuso posted and then quickly removed a personal assessment of her progress:

> that yellow flag in the GS [giant slalom] was such . . . I just want to scream. I'm really miffed. Anyway, gotta take that energy and focus it for 2nd run. (McClusky 2010b)

Mancuso also used Twitter to deny a rift with Vonn. Lower profile competitors also enjoyed the spontaneity and freedom offered by Twitter in Vancouver. For instance, aerial skier Jeret Peterson appreciated the capability of announcing himself publicly without having to attract the attention of a journalist, 'It's free, it's instantaneous and it's real . . . It's my message and it's not filtered' (Quoted in Pells 2010).[11]

The word instantaneous is mentioned frequently in discussions of Twitter, which helps to describe what is both intriguing and irritating about this platform. The immediacy and speed of the short messages sent by athletes awards them an appealing unvarnished quality and the occasional 'shock of vitality' (Williams 1974, p. 54) in a media sport setting dominated by hackneyed responses in staged press conferences and media interviews (Boyle, Rowe & Whannel 2010). It is also obvious after following dozens of athletes for a short period that, despite the timeliness and number of micro-messages posted, their content is often banal, disposable, and of negligible insight. Yet, it is precisely these characteristics that make tweets stand out as a form of media sport content. The spectacular representation of athletic feats and contests, and the unremitting adulation and scrutiny of sport celebrities, render otherwise mundane messages from leading footballers and tennis players somehow special. An example in this regard is the Twitter profile of tennis' Serena Williams, which includes observations about video footage she has watched ('Finally my butt is not in the video': 17 January 2011) and her energy levels ('I am so sleepy. It's only 9.15': 18 January 2011). These messages hint at the 'real person' behind the celebrity persona, promising intimate and immediate insight into the backstage dimensions of a sport star's life (Goffman 1990 [1959]; Marwick & boyd 2011, p. 123; Crawford 2009). These types of tweet build a sense of common experience between athletes and their followers, be they fans, observers, or dedicated tweeters. In other words, the cultural distance between the elite athlete and fan appears to be erased momentarily by a repetitive communicative act. The fact that Twitter is so popular at present—Williams has over two million followers at the time of writing—shows that the social performance of tweeting is proving successful in its own terms.

Constant tweets and Facebook status updates by sporting figures and their followers are noteworthy for reasons other than fashion and novelty. The sheer speed and volume of routine digital messaging highlights a longer-term trend of accelerating media communication in modernity. Instantaneous communication has been a precondition for the emergence and disasters of 'fast' or 'turbo-charged' global capitalism (Beck 2005; Elliott & Urry 2010; Hassan 2011). (It has also, we observe in passing, contributed to the advent of a counter-politics based on a philosophy of slow-living and slow food [Parkins and Craig 2006]). Just as hundreds of tweets are sent per second, high-frequency digital trading on world financial markets driven by computerized trading programs and algorithms enable thousands of quotes to be generated each second (Hassan 2011, pp. 379–80).[12] John Tomlinson (2007) employs a term usually associated with information technology research and computing studies to specify what is unique experientially in a world of high-speed interconnectivity, where portable, networked, and wireless communications technologies enable constant contact between individuals and groups. Telepresence—'the possibility, and increasingly for many, the *preference*, of "keeping in touch" without actually, literally, being in touch' (Tomlinson 2007, p. 111, original emphasis)—speaks to a range of techniques in which relations of presence are felt between different social actors in both embodied and disembodied forms. Tele-, meaning 'at a distance', is the pivotal prefix here, opening the possibility of real-time presence at a distance as a readily available method of interaction for people who form and maintain meaningful relationships in and through media systems, including websites, bulletin boards, social networking services, chat rooms, and online games. These types of interaction weave relations between people known to each other through online interaction, offline contact, and more traditional forms of media representation and celebrity. The term highlights a significant difference from that other tele- coupling that has dominated the last half-century—television. As noted earlier in this book, 'seeing at a distance' was the major innovation (Weber 1996) that exposed otherwise inaccessible visual phenomena to new audience formations (Rowe 2011c). Telepresence, by contrast, insinuates more complex, multimodal forms of sociality.

Telepresence sits alongside direct, embodied experience as a pervasive and increasingly normalized feature of contemporary social relations (Tomlinson 2007). Numerous athletes exemplify these communicative-experiential conditions, using social networking to post frequent messages in and out of competition. Importantly, the speed and constancy of these digitally networked connections deepen the interpenetration of sport and media frames, technologies, and corporations (i.e., sport as media). Major finals are, for example, where new records for tweets sent per second are set, with 7,196 tweets sent in a single second during the climactic goal shoot-out in the 2011 women's soccer World Cup final between Japan and the USA (*AP* 2011). This number surpassed the 4,064 tweets sent at 10:07:16 pm during the 2011 Super Bowl, and the 3,283 sent in one second during the FIFA 2010 World Cup (Indvik 2011). Unfolding at the 'speed of light' (Redhead 2007; Virilio 1986), it is becoming harder to divorce the transmission and consumption of sport from media, particularly when growing numbers of athletes, journalists, and fans use social networking sites.

Accidents are integral to the operation of technologies that generate speed, which is an argument that applies as much to communication as motor vehicles. One of Tomlinson's influences, French cultural theorist Paul Virilio (2001, 2007), contends that each new technological breakthrough produces a new kind of accident, which is part and parcel of its very operation. For example, the building of purportedly safe nuclear power stations near residential areas resulted in a new category of horrific experience, 'the major nuclear accident', just as the invention of the airplane gave rise to the violence of 'the air disaster'. Accidents uncover critical flaws in the ceaseless pursuit of scientific progress and the human motives determining the uses of nascent technologies. Indeed, for Virilio, the accident as concept can be said to precede the actual application of new technology. This line of argument reveals that fast, powerful social networking tools such as Twitter and Facebook produce their own negative form, *the information accident*. The desire and ability of telepresent sportspeople to keep in touch ferments accidents that 'scandalize' the individual athlete and/or the organization that they represent, especially when they are used unthinkingly to distribute lewd or embarrassing comments and pictures. These materials are then circulated widely online and reported in the national and international news media, resulting in outrage, calls for punishment, mockery, and so on. The tightly regulated and monitored environment of Olympic festivals and world championship tournaments limits the occurrence of these accidents, which are instead concentrated in regular season competition and out of season downtime for sportspeople. Examples include Australian champion swimmer, Stephanie Rice, who made a tearful public apology after posting a homophobic slur on Twitter in response to the final score of a rugby game that she had just watched late at night (*AAP* 2010). In the previous year, the Australian cricketer Phillip Hughes pre-empted an official team announcement that he had been dropped by 'confiding' the information on Twitter (Miller, A. 2009). Liverpool EPL player, Ryan Babel, was fined for his harsh criticism of a referee and the uploading of an altered photograph suggesting that the official was guilty of biased decision-making (Taylor, D. 2011). These are the types of information accidents resulting from impetuous acts of communication that cause unintentional damage to an athlete's public image. The difficulty for the offender is that unclicking the 'tweet' or 'share' button is impossible once their accident has been exposed and its contents endlessly copied and reposted. The effects of an accident are also hard to predict, relying on responses by many users, as comments, pictures, and videos are delivered to inboxes, websites, and user profiles. They can also be 'repurposed' and reconfigured in a variety of ways, including parody, exaggeration, and misinterpretation.

　　Sports journalists search for information accidents, while athletes, publicists, and sports organizations seek to avoid them. This is a strategic media game played in a round-the-clock digital sport and news environment. Journalists comb through voluminous messages on Twitter, Facebook, and blogs searching for content that may provide the basis—no matter how slim—for a story that would otherwise go unreported. This is a digital search for disagreements and disclosures that elicit responses from the subjects of stories. It is also an example of an almost ineradicable schism that exists between the individual right and ability of sportspeople to express themselves publicly, and the determination of leagues and clubs to exercise tight control over media comment and self-expression in order to keep unwanted stories out of the news, and to detach the athlete from undesirable associations (especially sponsors who are not officially endorsed). Information accident reporting by journalists is producing numerous stories of uneven news value, including claims of personal animosity between teammates and opponents, athlete outrage at official decisions, complaints about playing conditions, and serious matters such as the adequacy of security arrangements at tournaments (Hutchins 2011). An example is EPL player Darren Bent, who shone a light on the inner workings of the player transfer market after an outburst on his Twitter profile was reported. Bent's frustration at delays over a pending transfer deal that would see him move clubs from Tottenham Hotspur to Sunderland saw him post a series of spontaneous tweets appearing to blame Tottenham club chairman, Daniel Levy, for his predicament. Bent's tweets included, 'Why can't anything be simple. Sunderland are not the problem in the slightest', and 'Do I wanna go to Hull? No. Do I wanna go to Stoke? No. Do I wanna go to Sunderland? Yes'. Accessed by journalists and fans, these tweets caused a low-level scandal that initially saw Bent make an apology for his actions, and then later speculate that his outburst may have been beneficial, helping to clear the way for his eventual move to Sunderland (*BBC* 2009a).[13] Given that player transfer speculation is a staple of soccer news reports, often involving fabricated stories by journalists and strategic 'plants' by player agents and clubs to improve their negotiating position, a tweet from the 'horse's mouth' can cut through much of the regular player market noise in the popular media.

Similarly, rugby league and union international, Mat Rogers, expressed spontaneous anger at the suspension of a fellow club player. A news report emerged that Rogers had posted the following message shortly after a player judiciary announced the two-week suspension of a teammate on the repellent charge of biting an opponent:

> No no no no no no no. That is a #%^*+#* joke!!! If he wanted to bite him he wouldve (sic) bitten him. How about 2 weeks for a grapple!! [an illegal form of tackle]

The message was removed but not before journalists had seen and recorded it. While managing to avoid a financial penalty, Rogers' outburst produced a warning from his sport's governing body and an announcement that tweets are considered to 'fall into the category of "public comment" and can have the same consequences as comments in any other form of media' (Quoted in Jackson, Walter & Prichard 2009). This is an approach that has been progressively adopted by many sports governing bodies worldwide. England's Football Association (FA) has warned players who use Facebook, Twitter, and blogs that they should proceed with caution. Comments that are 'offensive, use foul language or contain direct or indirect threats aimed at other participants are likely to be considered improper', and may leave the player open to civil legal proceedings (Cutler 2011b). Again, this determination to control the public utterances of professional sportspeople sets up a revealing tension. As can be seen by a cursory examination of athlete profiles, the routine use of Twitter and Facebook for personal expression clashes with the explicitly public status awarded to *any* comment.

The most damaging scandals arise from messages that move beyond text-based communication to visual content. It is worth recalling that the example of Ryan Babel mentioned earlier involved a photo that left no room for confusion about his thoughts on a referee. Roundly regarded as 'hard evidence', visual images of wrongdoing or mischief are harder to deny or explain away than comments that may be amenable to alternative interpretation. Three different stories—two Australian, one American—demonstrate this point, with each involving sexual indiscretions that once would have remained largely private affairs. A national scandal broke in the Australian news media just prior to Christmas in 2010 about the St Kilda AFL team. Nude photographs of three players, including the team captain, Nick Riewoldt, were circulating on Twitter, Facebook, and online message boards. The photos were posted by a disgruntled 17-year-old girl who alleged poor treatment at the hands of individual players (not including the captain) and the club after claiming to have had a sexual relationship with a member of the team. This disturbing story was fed by accusations of footballers behaving atrociously, an angry minor who continued to use Twitter and Facebook to promulgate her version of events, and, most tellingly, the widening distribution of the photographs on the Internet (which she first claimed to have taken, and then admitted to have stolen) as news stories stimulated curiosity about their contents. In the opinion of one news analyst, social networking had created a new model of media power that was fundamentally different to the analogue-broadcast era:

> Today the material is writ large across the internet in minutes and the story has a momentum that cannot be checked. The take down of Riewoldt and teammate Nick Dal Santo has been stunning in its speed and ferocity. They have learnt the hard way a lesson that all clubs must now face. Social media has an awesome power. But managed badly—and it is hard to manage—it can be seriously anti-social. (Silkstone 2010)

The 'St Kilda schoolgirl' story continued to run for several months, with further revelations, exposures, accusations, and retractions. The most serious of these storylines revolved around unproven allegations that she had taken drugs and engaged in a sexual relationship with leading player agent Ricky Nixon, having circulated a digital picture of him in his underwear in her hotel room. Her active presence in social networking media (with, for example, almost 18,000 Twitter followers in July 2011 and frequent 'lifecasts' on Ustream) fed into and off broadcast television and other 'legacy media' appearances, posing a constant risk of embarrassment to the older, male-dominated institution of Australian rules football (Rowe 2011b).

The difficulty of managing this sort of controversy had been demonstrated a month earlier in the AFL's rival code, rugby league. Australian representative and then Canberra Raider, Joel Monaghan, was embroiled in an incident reported internationally after an embarrassing photograph was posted on Twitter. The photo appeared to show an inebriated Monaghan simulating a sex act with a dog (Walter 2010). The image prompted discussion on- and offline about the possible motivation for such an act and the welfare of the canine in the picture. The consequences of his actions saw Monaghan voluntarily quit his club, tearfully admit his error and embarrassment, and move overseas to take up a playing contract in England where he admitted knowledge of the incident would follow him for the rest of his career. Indeed, a July 2011 Google search for 'Joel Monaghan' found the heading of eight of the first 10 results refer directly to the 'dog issue', which was also covered in his Wikipedia entry. Only a single result in the first 10—a very recent match report—prioritized his performance on the ruby league field.

These cases demonstrate the changed functioning of media power, or 'mediated visibility' via computer-mediated communication (Thompson 2005). Neither incident approaches the seriousness of the Abu Ghraib prison torture photos scandal that John B. Thompson (2005) uses to explain this concept. Nevertheless, each shows how mediated visibility on the Internet can starkly reveal the otherwise unnoticed or unseen, bringing into public view and digitally preserving information accidents that once would have remained hidden due to technical and spatial limitations. The 'gotcha' image—such as the *News of the World's* 2009 front-page picture of leading US swimmer Michael Phelps inhaling cannabis at a University party—has long been a feature of the news media in revealing scandals of a lesser or greater order. But in the 21st century, it is only an uploaded camera phone shot away from global dissemination.

Our third example shifts the focus to another form of digital message, the mobile phone text that does not fall neatly under the heading of social networking media. However, the aforementioned capacity of mobile phones to take and send photos, as well as to post to Facebook and Twitter, highlights a digital messaging ecology. Impromptu, fast, interactive, and multimedia messages have long been a routine feature of online communication via numerous platforms and interfaces (for example, email, listservs, newsgroups, Internet Relay Chat (IRC), instant messaging), satisfying and creating demand among Internet and wireless communications users for established and new forms of interaction. These messages leave behind evidence of a user's habits, which exponentially increases the vulnerability of celebrity athletes to unwanted attention. At about the same time as the St Kilda and Monaghan stories in Australia, champion NFL and 20-year veteran quarterback, Brett Favre, found himself the subject of a scandal in the US (Wilner 2010). It was alleged that Favre sent MySpace messages to female game-day presenter and model, Jenn Sterger, when playing for the New York Jets. These advances were reportedly accompanied by voicemail and text messages to Sterger. The scandal worsened when photographs of a still-unidentified penis taken with a mobile phone began appearing online. The images led many to assume that Favre had been sending Sterger raunchy or sexually explicit messages and photos. 'Sexting' is also evident in other football codes, cricket, and, more broadly, among select teenage users of mobile media (Albury, Funnell & Noonan 2010; *Four Corners* 2009; Goggin 2006, pp. 132–38; Lenhart 2009). The combination of the images and a complaint by Sterger to the NFL tarnished Favre's public standing on the eve of his retirement from the game, led to a comedy skit on *Saturday Night Live*, and eventually saw him fined US$50,000 for failing to cooperate with the NFL investigation into the matter. The next section highlights that sports leagues and organizations are responding to these types of problems by investing in accident prevention strategies and education programs.

ACCIDENT PREVENTION

The repercussions of information accidents are primarily reputational, affecting the image of the individual, their team, and their league. Minor and major scandals are prompting administrators to implement prevention strategies to lessen the likelihood of athletes sending offensive, insensitive, or legally problematic messages. These 'coping' strategies focus on outlining the potential effects of thoughtless or careless social networking use and the potency of visual images attached to profiles. Information and training sessions warn athletes against posting information about injuries, tactics, and team selections. The release of these details can create unnecessary distractions in the lead-up to a fixture, hand opponents a tactical or motivational advantage, and be used in the operation of legal and illegal sports betting markets (Hutchins 2011). According to a communications manager who runs twice-yearly media training sessions for athletes, a prime objective is to minimize the chances of a news media outlet publishing an unflattering or compromising photograph of a sportsperson. This instruction in media routines and capabilities involves explaining the ease with which photos can be 'click, copy, pasted' into an email by a third party, which comes as a surprise to some sportsmen and women:

> We can keep tabs on most [athletes] and sort of suggest gently when it [an image] is inappropriate and take it down. If it's said in the right terminology, i.e., 'this is damaging to your brand when you're an Olympic medalist. Do you want that to come out in the paper?' People go 'oh no' and quickly remove them. (Interview with author)

It is also stressed that materials posted on profiles set to private can still end up being publicly circulated. Another manager promoted the same wariness of visual media. He advises players to set their Facebook profiles to private and remove any images of them consuming alcohol in social situations. The advent of tawdry websites such as Drunk Athlete (Sanderson 2009a), which publishes images of sporting identities partying and drinking, heightens the need for this instruction. The likelihood of a sportsperson posting a photograph taken at a private social event is explained by a common misconception that Facebook and Twitter profiles are a 'personal space' despite the public or semi-public availability of their contents (Interview with author). The aforementioned Australian swimmer Stephanie Rice, for example, created a minor stir (much exaggerated by a tabloid sensibility and an implicit assumption that captured Facebook images are *ipso facto* evidence of undesirable behavior) when a newspaper published images from her Facebook profile of her in party mode, including dancing in a police uniform. The newspaper then gleefully reported the reaction of Swimming Australia:

> HAPPY snaps of Stephanie Rice partying have been deemed too raunchy for Swimming Australia, with all of the swimmers ordered to block public access to their Facebook profile pages . . .
>   Instead of finding sexy images of Rice in a police officer's uniform, curious web users instead found more wholesome images of her

modeling Speedo swimsuits and posing with a winning medal when they searched the social networking website yesterday. (Saurine 2008)

The Daily Telegraph linked the story to its 'Gallery: See the pics too raunchy for Swimming Australia here', while quoting the Swimming Australia media director that 'It's something we had counselled them [the swim team] on in the past two years to be careful of' (in Saurine 2008). Thus, as is commonly the case, the story drew its force not from the innocuous images of a young female athlete at play, but the method of their capture and the reaction of sports administrators to them.

This contest to control the use and content of social networking media extends to combating mischievous and fraudulent users. An impostor sending tweets for several months motivated the (recently retired) NBA's Shaquille O'Neal to start using Twitter, who has now collected over four-and-a-half million followers (Beck 2008). Canadian ice-hockey great, Wayne Gretzky, has been the victim of identity fraud (Arceneaux & Weiss 2010, p. 1273), and World Darts Champion, Phil 'The Power' Taylor, joined both Facebook and Twitter because of several profiles pretending to be him (Church-Sanders 2010). Fake profiles, which are easy to find and can be amusing when they cleverly parody a sportsperson,[14] undercut the control of athletes and sports over their public image, take considerable time to remove, and impact upon clubs and organizations in broader terms. With fraud perpetrators being difficult to locate, deceptive messages are a serious concern when the hoaxer attempts to achieve a degree of authenticity in posts, making it hard to distinguish the actual athlete from their fake portrayal. English cricketer Ian Bell, for example, was forced to declare that he was not tweeting after a hoax profile appeared featuring credible messages about his preparation for a forthcoming Test match (*BBC* 2009b). Such deception confuses fans because of the speed and volume of information circulation online, meaning that deliberately mischievous or inaccurate speculation about an injury, teammate, opponent, or personal opinion can be distributed swiftly among large numbers of fans and journalists, taking on the status of assumed but erroneous fact. As in the case of newspaper and other media retractions, the splashed headlines and heated online conversations first produced are rarely matched by equally visible corrections and apologies. Both Twitter and Facebook have introduced verification and complaints procedures designed to reduce identity confusion. Such measures are, however, of minimal use when a profile is deliberately hacked. Nefarious online behavior can then involve time-consuming and costly legal processes, much to the frustration of those officials charged with handling them:

> The worst part is that it may not be your athlete that screws you up. We had a guy who had his Facebook profile hacked. Someone put up a link, 'How to get good marijuana', and 'Where to get this great

marijuana—click on this link'. And this was on a 20-year-old athlete's site who's in the mix for the national team. That involved us having to send letters to Facebook, having to inform our lawyers, having to go through all due diligence, so that if it came up again we have to say, 'Well, this did occur on this day at which time we took this action and reported it to these people'. We're now having to protect our athlete from the site . . . It's a completely personal site, yet we as an organization are now dealing with lawyers. (Interview with author)

This example and many others show that 'getting the brand out there' and 'engaging with fans' on Facebook and Twitter has a flip side when it involves the loss of control over information and photos, and that for leading sportspeople there can be no such thing as a 'a completely personal site'.

There is a belief in many sports organizations that social networking sites platforms can be harnessed and managed successfully, a conviction informed by the IOC's experience and, most pertinently, an array of consultants and corporate services that sell this promise. An increasing number of 'social media intelligence firms'[15]—an Orwellian term of uncertain provenance—offer risk management strategies, including advice on user policies and guidance in the provision of media training. The spread of digital media 'minders' is incrementally reducing the unpredictability of social networking communication and the chances of information accidents. For instance, workshops on the 'safe' use of social media began as early as March 2011 for likely Australian representatives at the 2012 London Olympics, and involved the AOC using the examples of Stephanie Rice and Joel Monaghan to warn other athletes about the pitfalls of thoughtless or impetuous posts (Halloran 2011). Yet, imposing this strict discipline undercuts the spontaneity, freedom, and open-ended interaction that makes social networking attractive to users, detracting from the sense of immediacy characterizing tweets and status updates by telepresent sporting identities. The relatively slight possibility of athlete dissent, political comment, and provocative expression are also effectively foreclosed. Deliberate commercial sanitization is already in evidence. James Griffin, a partner with the social media firm SR7, appears to regret that it has not happened earlier in Australia:

Unfortunately, many Australian athletes are still dealing with social media scandals and problems as opposed to reaping the commercial rewards of social media like many in the US have begun to do. (Quoted in Pierik 2010)

Clubs, sports, and player agents are also starting to avail themselves of companies providing 'online reputation management' services. Techniques applied by these operators include the attempted manipulation of search rankings by the creation of (or linking to) positive online mentions and listings, which then reduce the prominence of troublesome content in search results. Removal of negative content about an individual or team is also pursued where possible. The strategic avoidance and attempted erasure of information accidents is set to concentrate the minds of media sport executives and managers in the next few years because of legal issues, scandals, and journalists hunting for easily gathered, high-impact stories. This focus is also likely to tame much genuine self-expression on Twitter and Facebook, subjecting sports fans to carefully managed brand maintenance operating under the deceptive label of social media 'conversations'. Yet, as the history of media and technology, from copyright infringement to invasion of privacy reminds us, each attempt at control is under constant challenge from those seeking to circumvent or destroy it.

IMAGE RIGHTS AND RESPONSIBILITIES

The enhanced autonomy offered to sportspeople by social software systems is leading to vigorous claims for increased control over their public image. This advocacy is another step along from clubs demanding the right to manage online content and identities separate from their competition authority (see Chapter 2). Conditions of digital plenitude enable sportspeople to assert their own 'image rights'—'the commercial appropriation of someone's personality, including indexes of their image, voice, name and signature' (Haynes 2004, p. 101)—above and beyond that of their team, league, and/or sport. Known as publicity rights in the US (Cianfrone & Baker 2010; Evans 2007–2008), image rights involve a recognized contractual agreement above and beyond the 'standard form agreement' in English soccer (Boyle & Haynes 2004, p. 74). The value of these rights can be considerable and involves measuring the relative enhancement of a player's image and a club brand when they are associated with each other (Smart 2005, pp. 160–61). Disagreement over this equation led to long-winded negotiations between (then) Manchester United and star-player-turned-celebrity-icon, David Beckham, in 2002 (Cashmore 2004, pp. 63–65). Notorious EPL midfielder Joey Barton (who has two convictions for violence, one leading to a jail sentence) was paid approximately £13,000 a week for his image rights when playing for Newcastle United (White 2009).[16] The notion that such rights should feature in the negotiation of player contracts reflects the burgeoning value of individuals as cultural signs and commodities, as demonstrated by the growth of celebrity culture in both sport and the wider entertainment industries (Andrews & Jackson 2001; Smart 2005; Whannel 2002). Blogs, social networking profiles, and websites that promote an athlete's image, communicate their preferred messages, and sell merchandise are a logical extension of this commercial and cultural order. Seven-time Tour de France winner, Lance Armstrong, is a conspicuous example of this practice, using Twitter and a blog on his personal website to exert tight control over his public image and statements. Such online activities help to explain the strong efforts made to quash fake blogs and profiles that are deemed to infringe athlete image rights and to harm their brand.

The wider cultural question of whether 'property in personality' is a 'commodification too far' (Boyle & Haynes 2004, p. 76) is forgotten in the rush to capitalize on the growth of image rights.[17] Image rights have only just been introduced into rugby union player contracts in Australia, with player unions and management agencies advocating their introduction into other sports (see, for example, Australian Athletes' Alliance 2009). Negotiations over a new collective bargaining agreement between the AFL and its Players' Association produced disagreement over whether individual players should control their own digital media rights (Pierik 2011; see also Mulholland 2007). Following negotiations with their players' union, Cricket Australia (CA) also introduced a diluted form of image rights into contracts. This condition offered a return calculated on the basis of a player's individual market value and the extent of their voluntary promotional activities. The players' union, the Australian Cricketers' Association (ACA), has actively encouraged its members to be more active and proprietorial in the management of their public images and life stories over recent years (Haigh 2006, pp. 145–51). According to a union official for another sport, these actions represent a welcome development and reflect the form of labor relations practiced in North American sport:

> You have the right that you develop your own personality. It's who you are. You have the right not to have somebody else exploit it and you have the right to control it. If you decide to exploit it yourself, fine. But, if you don't, the idea that somebody [a club or league] could take who you are for their own economic gain . . . it's just considered against your human rights, against your dignity, whereas in Australia, you don't care. It should just be your right to control who you are and how you're used. (Interview with author)

This is a fair argument when assessed against the limited career span of most professional athletes, their economic vulnerability in an often over-supplied sport labor market, and the fact that leagues and media companies make considerable profits from their physical exertion and inevitable injury (Miller, Rowe, McKay & Lawrence 2003). However, it also clashes with the popular notion that sport is a public good, an enriching collective cultural and national experience that should be widely accessible and shared by fans in the public domain (cf. Rowe 2004c; Evens & Lefever 2011; Scherer & Whitson 2009). Image rights work against this collectivist understanding by escalating the enclosure and annexation of media content and intellectual property on the Internet and other media, including statistics, photographs, and images.[18] Boyle and Haynes (2004) show that these disputes began several years ago, including a Premier League footballer who attempted to limit the use of his image by a television news outlet because it allegedly encroached on his image rights, and a German player who sued a video game publisher for using his likeness in a football game without permission. Social networking and blogs are but the latest demonstration that the command of images—moving, still, or otherwise culturally represented—is a crucial source of power in the media sport content economy.

With rights, though, come responsibilities. The rewarding of image rights for athletes is offset by the onerous responsibility of accepting the uncertain consequences of independent content distribution through social software. It is difficult for sportspeople, having demanded individual image control, to blame a league or club authorities for failing to shield them from adverse publicity, particularly when they are guilty of misjudgment or misbehavior that is exposed online by self-instigated messages.[19] The developments described in this chapter show that information accidents are the product of an unpredictable relationship between intention and outcome, which is explicable by the newness, speed, and quantity of messages, and the desire of sportspeople to use—indeed, exploit—blogs and social networking services. Under prevailing and foreseeable circumstances, this combination of factors makes it difficult for athletes always to anticipate and manage the outcome of their various online activities. An accelerated media information order presents many opportunities for sportspeople to connect with fans and capitalize on their image, but travelling alongside these affordances is the damage wrought when they post before clearly thinking through the implications of their messages. In the digital media sport environment, information accidents are not so much waiting to happen. Rather, the contending parties within the media sports complex are working strenuously to, by turns, exploit, eradicate, and contain them. Our gaze now turns to the online activities of sports fans and followers whose opinions about the triumphs and travails of leagues, teams and athletes are also increasingly announced online.

5   Online Crowds and Fandom

The media sector deals with the anxieties and challenges associated with online media by seeking to corral, appropriate, and tap into the energies of users. A proposed antidote to the fickleness and unpredictability of netizens is 'crowdsourcing'—people on the Internet 'coming together to perform tasks, usually for little or no money, that were once the sole province of employees' (Howe 2008, p. 8). Presented in Jeff Howe's popular book, *Crowdsourcing: Why the Power of the Crowd is Driving the Future of Business,*[1] this approach appropriates the lessons learnt from the open source programming movement for the generation of new business ideas, market research, design tasks, and corporate content creation. The anti-establishment collectivism of the 1960s counterculture movement is recast as the 'gateway to economic cornucopia', which is a trait shared by other 'Web 2.0 business manifestos' (Van Dijck & Nieborg 2009, p. 857). Howe promises the reader that the psychology of the 'human network' can be harnessed so that large numbers of people actually enjoy expending their mental energy and private time to make profits for others.

Tapping into the 'wisdom of crowds' (Surowiecki 2005) is a seductive sales pitch when the successful case studies of online consumer engagement are presented. However, these stories conveniently underplay the fact that peer production and communication do not dissolve power imbalances or work well across all domains of economic, social, and cultural activity (Kreiss *et al.* 2011). When stripped of its pretensions to innovation, a sense of foreboding shadows proactive instructions on how business should deal with geographically dispersed and dynamic online communities. Crowds are volatile. An unhappy crowd has the potential, with little warning, to behave like an angry mob and desert once-profitable commercial portals and online businesses. Such unpredictable behavior poses an ever-present threat to the orderly accumulation of capital and profits (Sundaram 2010, p. 137). MySpace offers a portent of this danger. A thriving social networking platform in 2006, it was sold by News Corporation for a small fraction of its purchase price after much conjecture over its pending sale and rumors about workforce layoffs.[2] The reasons for this poor performance are complicated—although the rapid rise of Facebook as the predominant social networking service is a powerful one—but it is clear that a failure to engage and channel the energy of a crowd risks potentially terminal irrelevance.

This chapter critically adapts the idea of online crowds and examines their actions in different areas of media sport activity. Sporting codes are used to housing, rationalizing, and profiting from the 'affective power' of crowds (Marshall 1997), given that they are historically the home of large and zealous fan communities. Well before the advent of black-and-white television, sports teams were the focus of intense collective passion by mostly male fans connected by geography, community, common experience, and the embrace of shared sporting symbols and myths. In their seminal figurational sociological analysis of the institutional development of sport and leisure, *Quest for Excitement* (1986), Norbert Elias and Eric Dunning demonstrate that men's sport became an important site for the permissible expression of intense emotion and excitement in modernizing industrial societies of the nineteenth century. Organized, rationalized sport, in largely supplanting relatively unstructured, intermittent folk past times and games, was a distinct social form at a time when the self-regulation of behavior and exercise of personal restraint were read as indicators of 'civilized' conduct under modernity (Rowe 2011b).[3] The collective effervescence evident in the behavior of crowds also helps to explain the religious and ritual meanings attributed to sport in celebratory accounts of its development and experience (Novak 1976). The means by which fans express their feelings and opinions about players, teams, and leagues are our main concerns here. Fans watch and know sport through media, having done so for many decades through magazines, fanzines, newspapers, talkback radio, phone-in television programs, and broadcasts (Rowe 1995; Crawford 2004; Cleland 2011). The ubiquity of computing, portable digital devices, and online platforms means that the expression of individual and collective fan approval and outrage occurs in and through media more than ever. Indeed, these expressions are not only *relayed* but also *multiplied and magnified*.

The geometry of fan expression and action has changed as a result of the Internet and Web. Digital media formats and technologies are now the communicative 'bridge' that links crowds and the sports that they follow (cf. Urry 2007, pp. 31–32), as well as structuring relationships and interactions between them. These circumstances produce unpredictable group dynamics as fans meet online to comment, argue, advocate, and watch sport. The public face-to-face banter between large numbers of supporters[4] that once mainly occurred in physical locations like bars, pubs, clubs, playing fields, and stadiums is augmented by extensive distantiated online screen-based activities. These activities are administered by official sports organizations, commercially run media portals, and independent websites, each possessing their own internal cultures and user regulations. The following sections highlight that the development of networked media sport has engendered new ways for fans to comment on online message and bulletin boards, and opportunities to experiment with the control and administration of team sport. Online crowds are shown to possess characteristics that are subject to considerable variation. Groups of fans and users can represent, by turns or in combination, a source of harsh criticism, an exploitable and profitable source of free labor, and an economic force that claims ownership of sport. A consistent feature of our analysis is the unease experienced by sports clubs and administrators as they are compelled to deal with crowds that are rarely easy to control. The challenge of exercising control is made especially difficult by a media sport content economy where norms of practice, access, and exchange are in flux, and open to disputation by online fans who may demonstrate minimal regard for the interests or feelings of sport's formal powerbrokers. We conclude this chapter by discussing how, crucially, the relationship between fandom, sport, and the nation is affected by these developments in a potentially radical reconfiguration of national identities, loyalties, and mobilizations.

ONLINE MESSAGE BOARDS AND DISCUSSION FORUMS

Online message boards are popular sites for the expression of support, complaint, disagreement, gossip, and connectedness among sports fans (Malec 1995; Berg & Harthcock 2008; Otto, Metz & Ensmenger 2011; Rowe, Ruddock & Hutchins 2010; Sanderson 2010; Scibilia & Hutchins 2012; Watts 2008; Wilson, W. 2007). The most popular boards feature thousands of threads, each devoted to a user-nominated topic, and posts (or messages) numbering in the thousands or millions. Depending on how they are run, message boards require users to register and to consent to their comments being moderated by paid workers and/or volunteers. A distinct hierarchy is evident in terms of users, with heavy 'posters' often possessing informally acknowledged authority in the user community, both by means of agenda-setting and sheer visibility. The most active members build a reputation for their dedication, ability to convey 'insider knowledge' about players and teams, and their capacity to locate and share hard-to-find snippets of news and information. Depending on the type of message board in question, threads may contain an array of messages that feature intelligent analysis and in-depth discussion, basic information and items that are met by questions or comments, and debate between fans about team lineups, athletes, and current issues impacting upon a team or sport. Heated arguments, abuse, and chauvinism, as well as antagonistic baiting ('trolling') and puerile declamation, are also common. These often heavily populated forums are spaces where active supporters perpetuate fierce historically rooted rivalries between teams (cf. Theodoropoulou 2007). Regarded as evidence of a new 'grassroots of fandom' (Watts 2008, p. 243), they constitute spaces where individual and collective identities are expressed and negotiated through round-the-clock interaction and activity by aficionados and, in some cases, obsessive participants. As will be made clear, message boards produce guarded and ambivalent responses from sports officials because of the antagonism evident in some online exchanges, and the legally suspect status of the rumors and innuendo that can appear in posts, not to mention their sometimes questionable relationship to copyright ownership.

Message boards present a problem for sports clubs and administrators when fans react with hostility to official decisions and poor team performances, particularly when the news media report the revolt. This behavior represents a sporting inflection on the 'snarkiness' found on popular television and film message boards.[5] Snarking refers to the generalized skepticism and critical savvy found on fan message boards that, despite all the archness and intermittent venom on display, betrays deep emotional investment in the object of fan attention (Andrejevic 2008). The lifelong devotion of many fans to their club and team makes sport peculiarly susceptible to outspoken complaints by fans and supporters. Premier and Football League soccer in England, for example, has witnessed many incidents of heavy-handed responses to outbursts by users, leading to overreactions by club directors who have called in lawyers, and as a result provoked loud accusations by fans of bullying and censorship. For example, an unofficial Sheffield Wednesday fan forum, Owlstalk, was the subject of national press attention following legal threats made against it by the club's chairman and directors (*WSC* 2007; Monbiot 2008). The offending posts coincided with a poor start to the playing season and saw users such as 'Auckland Owl' and 'Halfpint' named as key offenders. The club's action surprised the site operators and forum members because they had received no complaint prior to the legal threat and had enjoyed a generally harmonious relationship with the Sheffield Wednesday club. In Australia, the Melbourne Storm rugby league club has been openly accused of censoring 'hundreds' of messages posted by fans on their website after the club was punished severely for breaking competition salary cap rules (Hawthorne 2010). This development saw many Storm fans move to an independent forum, Mad Fan, although this did not prevent the club chairman threatening to sue a fan for comments made about him (Hawthorne 2011).

Club directors and sports officials have learnt that establishing a constructive relationship with message board operators is preferable to arguing with supporters in the public domain and news media. There has also been a realization that giving the appearance of ignoring 'the boards' can often be an effective response to fan discontent. Complaint and disappointment are habitual dimensions of sports fandom, as the great majority of teams fail to win championships with any regularity. Indeed, as interviews with ardent sports fans clearly demonstrate, following a losing team or club can be a frustrating and even depressing experience that elicits a variety of coping mechanisms (Bryant & Cummins 2010; Cash & Damousi 2009, pp. 30–47; Sandvoss 2003, pp. 29–30; Wann, Melnick, Russell & Pease 2001). Alternatively, a 'culture of complaint' in sport may constitute one of its perverse pleasures (Hornby 1992; Rowe *et al.* 2010).

The difference between current fan expression and that of two decades ago is that frustration and anger about a team's underachievement are no longer limited to verbal complaints made to fellow supporters, or evident in a limited sample of letters-to-the-editor, phone calls to radio stations, or small-circulation paper fanzines (Haynes 1995). Instead, complaints are written and posted online where they can be accessed and read for a lengthy period of time. Messages in fan forums are difficult to ignore when they contain legally sensitive information and potentially defamatory or libelous accusations. The online naming of soccer players alleged to have raped a 17-year-old girl in 2003, for example, emphasized the potentially serious ramifications of unmoderated fan discussion, especially when the case was still under police investigation in the UK. Sections of an online forum were closed in an effort to avoid legal problems on this occasion (Boyle & Haynes 2004, pp. 154–55; Kelso 2003). The challenge of regulating free-flowing and plentiful user posts explains why many sports and clubs no longer host message boards, which are instead operated by independent websites and Internet fan groups.[6] In Australia, the legal risk associated with online bulletin boards is cited as the reason for the closure of many official club-hosted forums, despite the fact that many fans enjoy reading discussion threads on the website of the sport or team that they follow.[7] Concerns are also raised by club directors about the wisdom of sponsoring fan forums that openly criticize their performance and undermine their public standing. A communications manager conceded that shutting down a fan forum leads to a fall in traffic for a club website, but countered that the cost of paying moderators and the risk of legal difficulties are too great:

> The concern is the moderation of it and how you can avoid various legal issues and the minefields that arise. We have considered it, but at the end of the day the decision has been that short of having 24-hour-a-day moderation and all posts being vetted, which is nearly impossible without a huge staff, then effectively that is not an option . . . The legal concerns are legitimate. I think a lot of forums have felt that over the years, and a number have been closed down for that reason. (Interview with author)

Cases for libel or defamation on a message board are not commonly pursued in the court system, but no sports organization wants to incur the expense of being a legal test case in which they are sued for 'publishing' a user comment. This wariness explains a preference for hosted live-chat sessions with coaches and players, where 'crowd control' is much easier during time-limited discussions. Comments and exchanges in such cases can be closely monitored and users 'terminated' immediately when they make inappropriate, embarrassing, or actionable comments.

While not openly acknowledging it, many sports monitor online communities in order to assess the feelings of their fan-base. Online discussion provides information that complements other satisfaction indicators such as game-day experience, fan emails, and conventional market research methods. The monitoring of board content is rarely publicly acknowledged but, when approached constructively, sensitizes decision makers to the range of opinions and depth of feeling that exist among sports fans. For instance, insights derived from observation of 'the boards' can help to pre-empt fan protests when administrators are forced to make difficult commercial and strategic decisions. Website operators and board moderators are sometimes offered limited behind-the-scenes access to a club media manager or official so that the 'full story' behind a contentious decision or incident can be distributed among the user community.[8] According to a communications manager, 'taking the temperature' of fans online has become part of his media management duties and, on occasion, may extend to club staff intervening in fan forums under the cover of oblique usernames:

> I do go on the fan boards from time to time and I know some other staff do as well, some more than others. But it's more like a litmus test. You get to judge the feeling in the supporter base as opposed to being a contributor. However, there have been times when club staff have contributed to the forum. (Interview with the author)

The extent to which sports administrators, team support staff, and players surreptitiously participate in online discussions is the subject of speculation because of the anonymity offered by usernames. A national media manager stated that he was aware of a club chief executive officer and a coach who posted on message boards semi-regularly in order to 'quash rumors' (Interview with author). At its most extreme, this type of online intervention can be used to generate support for particular individuals in the lead-up to the election of a club board or major decisions about financial matters (Lane 2010), and so has a specific political purpose at an organizational level.

Message board moderators and heavy users are attuned to messages that signal a strategic intervention in a forum debate or discussion, and note the usernames associated with them. For moderators, part of 'the game' unfolding in fan message forums is working out the characters, personalities, and agendas among different sections of their user community. Users who spend considerable amounts of time online and follow the flow of media information about their sport or team closely also notice when clubs or leagues react to what fans have said. A moderator explained this awareness by reference to the sudden appearance of a press release after voluble complaints by supporters began to appear on his site:

> It's really a fantastic case study in how the club's communication strategy is being driven by responses on fan sites. The press release they put out about [a player] saying that they were disappointed and explaining why he was leaving [the club] was absolutely the result of fans going

ballistic on the forum. It's absolutely a reaction to what's happened on the bulletin board—they've actually listened. (Interview with author)

Fans possess power, although caution is necessary to ensure that it is not over-stated. This informant is arguably exaggerating the level of influence exercised by message board activity in an effort to emphasize the influence of supporters and, by extension, his own role in the club-fan feedback process. Nonetheless, the evidence of our research suggests that major sports organizations do pay attention to what supporters are saying on the Internet and intervene in different ways depending on prevailing circumstances.

Club responses to fan dissent and agitation demonstrate that message boards 'shadow' the news media (Interview with author).[9] Discussion forums provide an additional level of information about a club or sport that sits behind the coverage provided by officially accredited news media outlets. One reason that message boards are read by fans is the level of detail and discussion that is unavailable elsewhere. Thus, a regular visitor to a fan forum explained that he visited daily during the season because he wanted to know 'stuff like who trained, how they went, who's got an injury, and which players are coming through' (Interview with author). Only the most passionate fans are interested in this depth of information and trivia, which is why online forums and message boards are significant as a category of fan-produced media. Users shadow every movement, performance, decision, action, and story associated with a team in forums where posts constantly appear, meaning that there are always new messages to read about an object of shared attention and, commonly, devotion. This need for information is the motivation for a website operator and board moderator to 'invest a hell of a lot of time'[10] in a site devoted to his favorite club:

> If you're a fan you will read everything to do with your club, and it doesn't matter if you're a fan of a celebrity, or a fan of a football club, or a fan of a certain make of cars. You cannot get too much information. The traditional news media does not generate enough content to satisfy your thirst for information on that particular subject matter. (Interview with author)

As the legal issues already mentioned highlight, the dilemma posed by an insatiable thirst is that fans are susceptible to 'imbibing' almost anything provided by the boards, including distortions of fact, scurrilous rumors, and scuttlebutt. For instance, the cloak of anonymity lends itself to bold talk, over-excitement, and the erroneous piecing together of disconnected evidence when it comes to fathoming the reasons for confidential club decisions.

The excitability of fan communities online causes occasional difficulties for sports officials when journalists, some of whom admit to reading message boards (Interview with author), ring or email with questions about issues under discussion online. This situation is made trickier when

journalists deliberately attempt to incite fans by posting inflammatory messages. A flurry of responses then provides an automatic basis for a story about conflict within a sport, which forces an official response. A communications manager for a national sport expressed dismay at this questionable behavior:

> We'll have media issues where we have a couple of journos who love to get into forums and 'have a go' [criticize] under their real name, which is absolutely unbelievable. There's one Sydney journalist who jumps into one of the forums and inflames things. (Interview with author)

The unusual feature here is that the journalists freely identify themselves when posting, leaving open the possibility that other members of the fourth estate are less forthcoming and prefer the cloak of anonymity. This is a particular problem for the sport discussed in the above quotation, which possesses a history of infighting between the federations and officials who sit on its national governing body. Message board comments are, in effect, used by journalists to sow discontent among fans and inflame administrative rivalries, producing both compelling news and poor organizational outcomes. This example also demonstrates how message forums sit within an ecology of media sport practices—fan-produced media, journalism and news media reporting, and official comment by media officers working for sports organizations.

The shadow cast by self-organizing fan communities is considerable for lower-tier competitions with limited budgets, resources, and news media coverage. Message boards are a valuable resource for maintaining a consistent, mediated connection with dedicated groups of supporters, in spite of the problems that may result from interacting with them. Whereas major sports organizations are reticent about acknowledging the influence of discussion forums, less popular codes and leagues (with sufficient available staff) are able to treat them as 'action-contexts' where it can be *openly* demonstrated that fan feedback is listened to, considered seriously, and acted upon (cf. Couldry, Livingstone & Markham 2007, pp. 124–25; Freeman 2011). This process involves a media officer 'doing the rounds' of the most populated message boards to observe and respond to user comments about significant issues affecting the sport:

> There is one particular message board that is well visited and we are happy to go on there and some others. What I do is post under my own name in various forums to show that we are trying to stay in touch with the fans. (Interview with author)

This activity provides an opportunity to post clarifications when 'factually incorrect' statements begin circulating among users. The benefits of generating a sense of responsiveness to supporters tend to outweigh any difficulties

experienced when an individual user unfairly criticizes or taunts a media official. To the contrary, a diplomatic response or dignified refusal to engage in an adversarial fashion with a provocateur is an opportunity for a sport to earn respect within the user community. User groups may also exercise their own discipline by vigorously challenging unwarranted criticism and/or insisting that a moderator suspend an offending user for a period of time.

The affective energy of online communities is considerable. This energy, and the free labor that it delivers, can also be susceptible to appropriation by commercial interests, particularly when volunteer-run websites and chat forums begin to generate a large membership base. These sites are attractive to advertisers precisely because of the time that dedicated fans spend reading and contributing to their content. Furthermore, the informal nature of user community management and administration presents few formal legal barriers to takeover, particularly when website operators are tempted by money that promises to turn their favorite hobby into a remunerated occupation. The prospect of being paid to do what one loves is a powerful incentive, but it poses particular difficulties when the property auctioned to the highest bidder has been created by the unpaid labor of an online user community.

Sanjay Joshi (2007) offers a nostalgic yet incisive account of what happens when amateur website operators replace the language of grassroots community with that of capital investment, stock offerings, equity holdings, and profit margins. Presently owned and operated by ESPN, Cricinfo is the world's most popular cricket website, and claims to reach over 20 million users worldwide each month.[11] A Cricinfo enthusiast in its early days, Joshi recalls that the site began life in 1993 as a 'bot' on IRC, designed to retrieve and organize cricket scorecards. It was written by Simon King, a British researcher working at the University of Minnesota, and catered for expatriate cricket fans from the Indian subcontinent living in the US. King was assisted by a volunteer collective and a sizable user community that enjoyed detailed online discussions, exchanging messages about the latest cricket news, and relaying live match scores and ball-by-ball commentaries for those unable to access broadcast coverage. The popularity of the Cricinfo community saw the addition of a Web interface that claimed 3.5 million visitors by 1995.

The popularity of Cricinfo was built on an extensive database. Much like baseball (Schell 1999), statistics are the *lingua franca* of cricket commentary and debates about players and teams from the past and present. The Internet has provided the potential to make an incredible range of cricket statistics available at a few keyboard strokes, which could then be mulled over and parsed by users. Significantly, the massive task of initial data entry was completed by hundreds of volunteers who submitted typed and scanned scorecards, match reports, and statistics from games throughout the sport's history (Joshi 2007, p. 1232). Alongside live match updates,

the scale and quality of this database formed the basis for user interaction and fostered a spirit of shared ownership of Cricinfo.

A sign that Cricinfo's community spirit was under threat occurred in 1995 when free registration was required to access the most up-to-date version of the website. Although the site's managers continued to employ the rhetoric of volunteerism and community, Simon King registered Cricinfo as a privately held company in the UK in the following year. A combination of venture capital, stock holdings, and buyouts during the dot.com boom of the late 1990s saw King and the other members of the Cricinfo board end up owning a half-share in a US$150 million firm (Joshi 2007, pp. 1234–37). They had, in the words of Joshi, become 'millionaires effectively on the back of the labour of others' (p. 1237). Dispiritingly, a board member and later chairman of Cricinfo, Alex Balfour, brazenly promoted the dark side of the crowdsourcing ethos—user exploitation—in the print media:

> A web entrepreneur starts with a solid idea . . . and publishes a basic site. Internet users come to the site . . . The entrepreneur listens to the users . . . or, better still, encourages the user to help make those changes. Delighted to see the site incorporate their ideas the users return, and continue to help . . . In time the entrepreneur has a large pool of volunteer labour and advisers to draw on . . . As long as the entrepreneur is sufficiently charming and well organized to keep the volunteers happy . . . the site will continue to develop rapidly. If volunteers believe that their work is helping to build something which they will find useful, if they can see that their work and ideas making an immediate difference . . . they will work hard. (Quoted in Joshi 2007, p. 1236)

As a source of premium media content, sport is a powerful generator of sustained user attention for large online communities. These qualities increase the likelihood that corporate media and advertising interests will attempt to commodify the labor and time of online fans. Intentionally or otherwise, this commodification then risks dissolving the user community and volunteer ethic that gives birth to fan-generated websites and forums in the first place. After its transformation into a corporate site, Cricinfo experienced financial difficulties that saw it merge with the Wisden group in 2003 before being taken over by ESPN in 2007. Cricinfo's managing director responded to this move in language far removed from that of the casual fan chat that characterized the site's operation in the 1990s. 'Brand recognition' and ESPN's 'expertise in sports marketing and digital media' now defined the mission of the site (Cricinfo staff 2007); commercial corporatist concepts that sports fans frequently ridicule and resist within their everyday communitarian conversations. The next section of this chapter investigates what happens when fans attempt to take back control of a sport and test the idea that they know how it should be run.

AN EXPERIMENT IN FAN DEMOCRACY

Democracy is the worst form of government except for all those other forms that have been tried from time to time. This abridged version of a statement by Winston Churchill in the British House of Commons in 1947 has entered popular usage as shorthand for the struggle faced by elected representatives and voters as they strive to build governance mechanisms that balance popular will, the need for just social conditions, and the facilitation of peaceful disagreement in complex modern societies (Keane 1991, 2009). The demotic retort to this conundrum in sport is the cry that soccer is 'the people's game', despite its status as a media spectacle substantially owned and controlled by transnational corporate and geopolitical interests (Sugden & Tomlinson 1998; Giulianotti & Robertson 2009). The voice of 'the people' can be heard throughout sport worldwide whenever officials and players claim that their exertions are 'all about the fans'. Despite such heart-warming sentiment, few organizations have ever contemplated indulging fan sovereignty to the degree that they hand over financial and material control of their club or code to them.

'Crowdsourcing Soccer in the UK' (Kuhn 2007), 'Football Gathers Crowd Through Web' (*Economic Times* 2007), and 'User-Generated Soccer' (Malone 2007) are three of the headlines that appeared internationally after the founding of MyFootballClub (MFC) in the UK in 2007. MFC was the brainchild of English journalist Will Brooks, who had become frustrated with the lack of fan input into a sport whose governance is increasingly the province of entrepreneurial club owners and media/leisure corporate interests. While there was nothing at all original about his unease, Brooks proffered an inventive solution. Levying a membership charge of £35, MFC aimed to purchase a controlling stake in an English soccer team, which would then be managed by members through a website. Team tactics, transfers, admission prices, sponsorship proposals, and so on would be determined by popular vote, with no member or 'co-owner' being allowed more than one vote. In February 2008, MFC paid £635,000 (just over US$1,000,000) for a controlling share in Ebbsfleet United, a semi-professional club located in Gravesend, Kent, which presently plays some four divisions below the EPL. A combination of an appealing concept and canny marketing attracted over 30,000 paid-up members from over 80 countries around the globe, including continental Europe, North America, and Australasia. The website (see Figure 5.1) announced that this was 'the world's first internet community to buy and takeover a real-world football club'. MFC's example also spawned similar attempts at online ownership and control of lower-level clubs in Italy, Germany, Poland, Spain, and England. An effort has also been made to start a professional cycling team run along the same lines.

MFC stands out as an example of Web-based fan democracy in action for a number of reasons. It is a sign of the formidable challenge posed

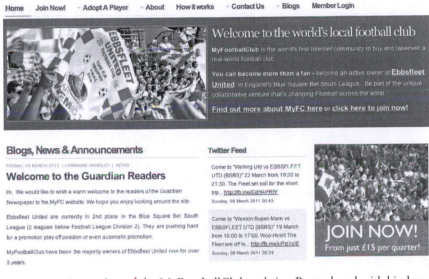

Figure 5.1 Screenshot of the MyFootballClub website. Reproduced with kind permission of www.myfootballclub.co.uk.

by governance models that enable 'participatory democracy' via the Internet and online voting mechanisms. With majestic detail and insight, John Keane (2009) explains in *The Life and Death of Democracy* that disagreements between advocates of participatory democracy and representative democracy have endured for well over two centuries. One school of thought demands the right of citizens to participate *directly* in the decisions that impact upon their lives. The other prefers a system of representatives elected by citizens at regular intervals. These leaders are then charged with *representing* the interests of electors. The latter's ascendency coincided with the emergence of print culture and has been widely regarded as an effective method of building workable government in large-scale modern polities. However, the 'communicative abundance' (Keane 2009, pp. 736–47) fuelled by the Internet and digital media has challenged this orthodoxy because of the growing capacity and willingness of users and citizens to speak, vote, and respond online. The networked communications tools required to realize participatory democracy on a widespread basis have, according to the optimists, finally arrived. The introduction of sophisticated e-government and 'government 2.0' initiatives in the US, UK, Australia, and Italy highlight that citizens can contribute directly to public policy formulation and respond directly to decisions made by elected officials (Freeman 2011). MFC is a manifestation of this phenomenon in the realm of sport and popular culture. No longer does the election of club directors by a show of hands at a public gathering of members necessarily hold sway. Internet driven fan democracy presents a theoretically attractive means of toppling 'autocratic' and 'out-of-touch' moneyed club owners. MFC went beyond bold talk and established a living, breathing, participatory mode of governance. It is, therefore, a significant experiment in the uses and possibilities of networked media sport (Hutchins, Rowe & Ruddock 2009).

This online soccer club tapped into the zeitgeist by following closely on the heels of *Time* magazine's intoxicated announcement that the 2006 'Person of the Year' was 'You':

> But look at 2006 through a different lens . . . It's a story about community and collaboration on a scale never seen before. It's about the cosmic compendium of knowledge Wikipedia and the million-channel people's network YouTube and the online metropolis MySpace. It's about the many wresting power from the few and helping one another for nothing and how that will not only change the world, but also change the way the world changes. (Grossman 2006)

Reflecting a hunger for stories about networked collaboration, MFC was reported by the BBC, CNN, ABC (in the US and Australia), ESPN, Al Jazeera, Wired, Fox Sports Australia, The Malaysian Star, The Guardian, and The Times. Jeff Howe (2008) went as far as nominating Ebbsfleet United as an example of why the adaptability of his crowdsourcing concept makes it so 'pervasive and powerful' (p. 18). This was an astounding degree of attention for an obscure non-league club (that is, below the level of the main 92 football teams in the four strongest divisions) that had experienced limited success since 1946, struggled consistently to achieve attendances of more than 1,000 spectators, and received little regular coverage outside the local *Gravesend Reporter* newspaper.

The initial hype surrounding MFC was such that it even managed to generate its own anti-MFC online community, freemyfc.com, in 2009, populated by a group of ex-members who were disillusioned that the MFC experience failed to deliver on its democratic promise, especially majority voting on team lineups and tactics (Rowe *et al.* 2010). This point was later conceded by Will Brooks, who, after having relinquished his stake in the club in late 2009, commented in *The Guardian*, 'Maybe the idea of [fans] making decisions was more exciting than the reality' (Taylor, L. 2011). MFC subsequently struggled to stay afloat because of dwindling interest and financial difficulties, claiming around 1,400 members at the time of writing.[12] Nonetheless, contrary to the initial predictions of many critics, the team has experienced some on-field success and has survived for over four years under perilous economic conditions for soccer clubs at all levels, particularly after the 2009 collapse of the non-League broadcaster, Setanta.[13] Ebbsfleet's survival has, for example, seen it mentioned in *The Guardian* newspaper as an example of a membership-based club governance model, listed alongside global powerhouse clubs like Barcelona and Real Madrid (Callow 2010).

MFC represents an imaginative, enterprising, and opportunistic response to the disenfranchisement of fans caused by the spiraling commodification of sport and the unrelenting commercial valuation of supporter loyalty. The ambivalence associated with sports fandom springs from the knowledge that fan devotion alone cannot sustain a successful professional team, while still resenting the fact that marketers and sponsors insist on articulating emotional fealty with the calculation of consumer spending habits. The encroachment of corporate capital into the lifeworld of supporters over the past 40 years has produced consistently spectacular athletic competition, full-time professional players, and appealing media coverage. It has also increased the distance between fans, celebrity athletes, and club directors and owners whose profit-seeking motives transcend sport and encompass other sectors of the global economy, including media, marketing, property, transport, oil, and banking. Speaking on the MFC podcast in 2008, newspaper journalist Brian Reade argued that Ebbsfleet United tapped into a collective disaffection generated by these large-scale developments:

> I don't particularly like that [Premier League] players who don't have a left foot and are just going through the motions are actually earning £40,000 a week, and I'm being charged £35 for a ticket. You know, I don't actually like that. I don't actually like the fact that it's so polarized around a few big clubs that keep getting this massive investment from Europe every year by qualifying in the top four. I actually want to start again. I think there's something there [in MFC], something liberating there that a lot of fans can identify with because it gets you back to why you fell in love with the game in the first place.

MFC applied a technological salve to the 'wound' of fan disillusionment that had been, to a significant degree, itself inflicted by another, earlier form of media technology—commercial broadcast television (Rowe 2011b). The Internet and Web were deployed as tools that made it possible for fans and supporters to extend their involvement in soccer beyond the realm of the cultural and the textual—the purchase, display, and appropriation of club symbols, and the reception of mediated sport texts—to the political and economic sphere. As owners, they were granted a formal 'property interest' in the club and made decisions about how it should be run (Margalit 2008). The operators of MFC also promised members a level of management efficiency rarely achieved under conventional club management structures:

> The way we put it is that it can be very hard to get eight men sitting around a board room table to agree on anything; it can be very easy to get 50,000 people to vote on a website and the computer makes the decision for you instantly. That's the way we like to put it. I think

it's possibly less cumbersome than the way things are traditionally run. (Tim Glynne-Jones, MFC Spokesman, quoted on The Sports Factor 2007)

This model also presented a welcome initiative in an online media environment where myriad website polls, feedback forums, and comment sections relentlessly seek user opinions (Hermes 2006). Yet these opinions tend to produce little or no change, instead being directed towards the accrual of user data and online advertising. MFC was brave enough to attempt to put user opinion into practice and to act upon the decisions—and often the egoistic fantasies—of 'armchair' soccer experts. Perhaps unsurprisingly, the results were uneven and involved many arguments, in the process laying bare the tensions evident where rationalized calculation co-exists with affective commitment and casual involvement.

THE JOYS AND SORROWS OF A FAN-RUN CLUB

Sport experienced and controlled by a crowd through a Web interface proved to be an intriguing experience at the outset. Many of MFC's new members had never heard of Ebbsfleet United or contemplated watching non-league soccer regularly, particularly if they were based overseas. In the early stages of the website's development, this required the transformation of an unremarkable club and home ground, Stonebridge Road, into an attractive destination in the imagination of members. The generation of a romanticized 'place image' (Adams 2009) involved a combination of representation, discourse, and technical connectivity. MFC members were shown the club on the website, told how to get there, and given a sense of what the embodied Ebbsfleet experience might be like. Features included vision of training sessions and club clerical staff working in the offices, discussion of the atmosphere on game day, and forums for members wanting to discuss ticket prices, the club bar, and training facilities. Accounts were provided of the stereotypically earthy characters that work and volunteer at the club, including the secretary and 'Jo—the lady who runs the bar' who 'always seems to be smiling, calm and good company'. Seeking to engender intimacy at a distance, audiovisual content included (and still includes) match highlights and features from the training ground and main pitch. Clips welcomed viewers to Stonebridge Road and showed interviews with players, with coach, Liam Daish, and with club cult figure and groundsman, Peter Norton.[14] One member believed that this video content penetrated the barriers imposed by the formulaic conventions of broadcast television and top-flight sports coverage formats:

This is broadcasting without boundaries. It allows us to see beyond the realms of conventional television as MyFC's coverage endeavours to reach inside the heart and soul of Ebbsfleet United. We have the unique opportunity to ask the questions and find the answers to affairs of the day while other lowly football fans are subjected to the same stock answers to the same clichéd questions. (Ware 2008)

It is precisely the comparative accessibility and informality of grassroots, semi-professional football that marked MFC as attractive. Ebbsfleet United's lowly status as a non-league team that received minimal attention also meant that, unlike major EPL and European clubs, packaging content for the MFC website did not contravene existing sponsorship and coverage contracts.

The other dimension of selling MFC involved an inversion of the soccer competition pyramid. Members had to be convinced that MFC could revive the organic community bonds that had sustained soccer in the past, and had the capacity to restore the voice of 'the people', which had been effectively silenced by multinational business and media interests (Robertson 2004, p. 301). An idealistic investment in redressing this situation would enable supporters to look past the modest standard of non-league matches and facilities, especially compared to the branded wizardry on display in well-appointed EPL stadiums. Members were instead urged to invest in 'the real sort of football that's going on' alongside 'proper football fans', and to connect with 'community in the truest sense' (MFC Podcast 2007–2009). Caroline Barker, host of the *Non-League Football Show* on BBC London Radio, expressed skepticism towards the MFC takeover of Ebbsfleet United, but this was out of concern for 'grassroots football' and the belief that many people in the media think that non-league competition 'doesn't matter, it doesn't care, when, in fact, non-league football more so cares about the way the game is treated' (MFC Podcast 2007–2009). MFC spokespeople ignored Barker's doubts but embraced and promoted her sentiment. This framing of non-league soccer inverts the hierarchy of media coverage and spectatorship. The 'hard core' fan-base who populate non-league teams and grounds are elevated to the ascendant position of *truly* caring for and defending the game's traditions, thereby consigning top-tier competitions, their global television audiences, and multi-millionaire entrepreneur owners to the status of the 'unworthy'. Its recruitment of tens of thousands of members indicates that MFC successfully executed this impressive sleight-of-hand, at least for short period. This popularity was a stunning achievement given that the club marketed a glaring contradiction: it was using media in order to revive 'the people's game' while simultaneously blaming media for the demise of community involvement in the sport (Ruddock, Hutchins & Rowe 2010, p. 325).

The MFC experiment has produced moments of genuine excitement. Ebbsfleet's 1–0 victory over Torquay United in the 2008 FA Trophy Final— the first in the club's history—was an outstanding performance before more than 40,000 fans at the remodeled 'home of football', Wembley Stadium in London (Denton 2008). The final was a media stage that announced the MFC project to the wider soccer community and offered validation of the notion that a club managed through a website could experience success. (The fact that the MFC takeover of Ebbsfleet United was completed in the lead-up to the final and could not claim direct credit for the performance was conveniently downplayed in the afterglow of victory.) The club produced an appropriately titled book, *the fleet@wembley: Ebbsfleet United—FA Trophy Winners 2008* (Denton 2008), to commemorate the event, which announced on its cover that 'the Fleet' had been embraced far beyond the borders of Kent county: 'Hundreds of pictures and thousands of words by those watching at Wembley and from around the world'. Featuring excellent photography, the 15 short essays by lifelong Ebbsfleet fans and new MFC members are joyful, proud, clichéd, and evince an air of slight disbelief. A photo of a small boy holding a sign in the Wembley crowd, 'I'm from Ebbsfleet and I'm finally proud of it!!!', captures the sense that the club had unexpectedly moved out of obscurity and into a privileged 'media space' (Couldry & McCarthy 2004) that it could only dream about prior to 2008. Chapter four, 'Ebbswhat?', is written by an American member who made the transatlantic flight in order to attend the Trophy Final. The reward for the lengthy journey was a sense of belonging, as he discovered a 'second home in Kent' where he was 'treated like family' (Friedman, J. 2008).[15] The trope of community is reiterated throughout the book in different ways, embedded within heartfelt tales of togetherness and fans reclaiming ownership of their favorite sport:

> Some people say that technology is destroying humanity and our connection with our fellow man but we are living proof that, when used properly, technology helps to bring people together and breaks down barriers between people of all nations. Our future is boundless and our joys will, hopefully, grow as we work together, moving forward and helping to place our football club as a model for the rest of the world to follow. (Groshell 2008, p. 90)

> I knew why I'd joined [MFC] in the first place. In a time where the Premier League is more concerned with money and celebrity than the game itself, Ebbsfleet United and MyFC have just started out on a new path where the fans truly come first because they are nurturing their own club, not being treated as a cash-cow by some billionaire foreign owner. (Sanna 2008, p. 59)

Once the euphoria of the Trophy Final had subsided, Ebbsfleet finished the 2007–08 season in mid-table (11th) of the Blue Square Premier League. The following season, the first full year of MFC control, produced a similar mid-table finish (14th). MFC also managed to attract media attention again during this season after a major player transfer was completed by an online member vote. Following extensive message-board debate, over 7,000 members voted on whether the promising 19-year-old striker, John Akinde, should be transferred to Football League Championship side, Bristol City, for £140,000. Over 80 percent of votes were in favor of Akinde's transfer, a decision that was endorsed by the team manager (*BBC* 2008). This transfer saw the National Football Museum in England request a signed Akinde playing strip for possible display to mark the completion of the first-ever player transfer decided by an Internet community. After first gaining entry to media space, the once-unnoticed Ebbsfleet United gained access to a commemorative space that constructs and maps sporting tradition and history.

The initial success and publicity attracted by MFC masked fundamental flaws in crowdsourcing the management of a soccer club. Foremost among these was the exponential conflict generated by mixing the following: (1) the unavoidable politics involved in the administration and funding of a team or club; (2) the fractious politics of online debate about complicated management issues conducted on message boards, which then culminate in simplistic 'point and click' voting decisions, and; (3) the different types and levels of emotional investment in Ebbsfleet United held by long-term 'local' fans and new online 'global' members.[16] Cumulatively, these intersecting issues have seen MFC buckle under the weight of a technological conceit: namely, that it's 'less cumbersome' to run a club through a website because 'the computer makes the decision for you instantly' (Glynne-Jones on The Sports Factor 2007).

The dream of a functioning fan democracy was undermined on a number of fronts. The savage tone of much online discussion and the intensity of message board arguments between members indicated that the threat of ochlocracy (or mobocracy) was ever-present, especially once success on the playing field and the budget spreadsheet ebbed. A relatively small number of agitated and highly vocal members felt that their opinions and demands were insufficiently acknowledged and posted frequently harsh criticism of the club and its principals. These members exhibited open contempt for the MFC operators, disrespect for fellow members, and disregard for Ebbsfleet stalwarts. Their often uncivil, and sometimes offensive behavior disenchanted many less-engaged members who supported the MFC project, but preferred to 'lurk' silently reading the message boards or limited their involvement to a vote after reading a relevant article. Club secretary of 15-years standing, Roly Edwards, expressed dismay at the fierce arguments that occurred day and night in the MFC discussion forums. Writing as a 'lifelong Ebbsfleet supporter', he posted an article that lamented the attacks on MFC board members, the unfair expectations placed on the shoulders of the website operators, and the unrelenting criticism of volunteers who donated their time to making MFC a viable proposition:

> If this is the future of MyFC I don't give it a hope in hell. What do people want for their £35—does it really give licence to criticise and accuse those volunteers that have chosen to work on our behalf . . . Our representatives clearly need to communicate but cannot/must not live in fear feeling the need to justify their positions at every turn. (Edwards 2008)

Edwards pinpointed the likelihood that widespread disharmony lessened the chances of people renewing their membership, thereby causing the club financial trouble. He later resigned from the club, telling the BBC that he believed Ebbsfleet United could 'never progress so long as MyFootballClub was involved' (Lee, D. 2010).

A prime source of discontent on the message boards and among members was the right and ability of members to pick the team that would play each week. MFC had heavily promoted this feature of membership through the motto, 'Own the Club, Pick the Team', since its inception. Brooks promised that MFC would be a vehicle to 'pool fans' opinions, passion and wealth and turn fantasy football into reality' (Sinnott 2007). The reference to fantasy football deliberately capitalized on the immense popularity of fantasy soccer competitions and soccer management computer games (e.g., *Championship Manager* and *Football Manager*) for PC and console platforms, particularly among men (Davis & Duncan 2006; Crawford 2006).[17] Fans and journalists took the cue offered by Brooks:

> It's [MFC] an opportunity for an average person with no experience to have a go at management. It's like playing *Championship Manager*, except it's real life. (Chelsea fan, Tom Dear, quoted in Dart 2007)

Having members pick the Ebbsfleet United side each week proved unworkable in practice. Choosing the members of a fantasy EPL team is made possible by the popularity of elite level players and the amount of information made available about their performance by extensive media coverage and collation of detailed performance statistics (although, of course, this highly filtered and processed information can never entirely substitute for intimate, intra-organizational knowledge). In contrast, selecting a non-league team from a group of unknown semi-professional players is akin to a guessing game. This remained the case even after the limited information available about the Ebbsfleet United squad was posted for the benefit of members. Incomplete knowledge about team members was compounded by the fact that only coach Liam Daish was fully aware of niggling injuries, performances at training, the psychology of team members, and the likely success of positional variations week to week. Many MFC members had never seen the team play a full game or visited Stonebridge Road, let alone watched pre-season games and intra-club matches. The closest that MFC came to fulfilling its original promise to members was a weekly vote on a team that was then 'recommended' to the coach who, at least from our observations, promptly dismissed it. Daish, not unreasonably, had no intention of ceding his right to select the team or determine team tactics and formation to an online crowd that displayed limited wisdom, intermittent hostility, and questionable regard for the tenuous career status of players earning subsistence level non-league wages. Daish's stance saw a section of the MFC community call for his sacking, while other members argued that he deserved their full support. Effectively, MFC could not re-draft the traditional team coach's job description of making key decisions, as opposed to implementing the will of shifting member voting configurations on a weekly basis.

Another divisive feature of MFC's operation was that the 'world's local football club' (see Figure 5.1) showed itself to be rather more local than worldly in terms of member control. Despite the notable number of overseas members, the seven people of the inaugural elected Society Trust Board were all based in the UK. Six were from the local area in which Ebbsfleet United is located and many had been involved directly in the Gravesend and North-fleet club that was rebadged as Ebbsfleet United in 2007. The results of this member election, which featured pitches by individual candidates, prompted complaints from those living outside Kent and overseas. A proposal was put forward to introduce quotas on the Board for overseas members. This election result highlighted the persistence of older spatially-oriented fan histories even within a dispersed and apparently democratic online setting. It also exacerbated tensions on the message boards between those caricatured as 'original and old-timer' fans of Ebbsfleet United and the 'MFC newbies and interlopers'. These divisions remain evident in the continued existence of two separate websites for the club, with the Ebbsfleet United Football Club Official Website overlapping with the MFC site as a source of club news, information, and results. Notably, the former has its own separate and active online fan message board, thereby revealing the resilience of place, history, and direct social group relations in football fandom, as well as the perplexities and complexities of 'executive fandom' (Rowe 2011b).

Online complaints, arguments, and insults revealed a debilitating condition for the MFC experiment. Running a club is not always fun and 'playing fantasy football with a real team' is an onerous, serious undertaking with real consequences for flesh-and-blood human subjects. The situation worsened during the 2009–10 season when a weakened financial state caused by expenditure demands and falling membership (and, some complained, excessive compensation for principals such as Brooks), combined with poor on-field performances, saw Ebbsfleet suffer the indignity of relegation to a lower division. Membership numbers dropped consistently over this period. The survival of a commercial venture that had limited revenue and mounting debts began to demand a great deal more work than play for members (Rowe *et al.* 2010, p. 309), involving votes on the mundane operational matters that enable Ebbsfleet United to compete each season and survive to the next. The number of active voting members fell away as difficult, technical decisions were made about expenditure on advertising, cash advances, preparation of accounts, budget allocations, loan arrangements, unsold ground hoardings, and responses to government tax rate changes. A lack of on-field success made these matters seem tiresome for all but the most dedicated members which, unsurprisingly, were often Kent-based, long-term Ebbsfleet United fans, thus shifting the balance of power back in favor of the original club at the expense of MFC. A source of hope for MFC is that the team managed to secure instant promotion back to the Blue Square Premier League after a strong 2010–11 season in the less competitive Blue Square Bet South League. This success has not, however, translated into many more paying members.

Ultimately, MFC exhibited too many of the features of present day democratic systems. It was shown to be conflicted, frustrating, undermined by voter disengagement, prone to financial deficit, and based on the exhausting pursuit of a worthwhile ideal—a truly fan-owned and controlled club. For all the optimistic claims-making attached to its meteoric rise and the potential potency of its online operation, MFC is an enticing idea consigned to a list of governance models that 'have been tried from time to time' without great success. Despite this outcome, it is likely that MFC will doggedly persist in its struggle for survival, and experiments similar to it will be attempted elsewhere in the future.[18] The appeal of participatory democracy continues, the Internet offers the ready opportunity for users to speak and to act, and many fans possess an unshakable faith in their beliefs about how sport should be managed. Without venturing anywhere near the politics of football fandom, Geoffrey Pleyers (2010, p. 226) makes an important point in *Alter-Globalization: Becoming Actors in the Global Age* when proposing new, locally-globally flexible activist citizens' negotiations with globalization:

> At the core of alter-globalization alternatives and organizational principles, participation is inscribed within a will to give the central place to citizens, displacing purely systemic logics, whether embodied by a model of inflexible planning, the invisible hand of the market or the internal contradictions of capitalism.

MFC's small-scale experiment in football fan democracy may not have been an unquestionable success, but nor has it been an unmitigated failure. It has been highly instructive about the limits and possibilities of popular mobilization in sport, providing a combination of promising development and cautionary tale that can help guide other online innovations in the persistent battle for the souls and wallets of sports fans.

SPORT AND THE NATION

The Internet and Web have altered the geometry of sports fandom. The examples of online message boards and MFC's international members show that the operation of transnationally networked communications technologies allows users, viewers, and expatriate communities to establish and/or maintain mediated connections with national sports leagues and teams from a great distance. According to Richard Giulianotti and Roland Robertson (2009, pp. 134–37), this digital connectivity represents 'the social electrification of globalization processes', promising the availability of almost any league or event via a broadband Internet connection. The transnational projection of media sport content links with the determination of leagues around the world to enter new markets through a combination of broadcast platforms and online media exposure and coverage. Examples in soccer include the growth of club and representative Champions League competitions, and a formal partnership between EPL club Chelsea and the Asian Football Federation to develop the game throughout the Asian region (Cutler 2011c).[19] In a single week in July 2011, EPL clubs Arsenal, Chelsea, and Liverpool all played matches in Malaysia. The NFL travels to London to stage matches and the NBA plays regular season fixtures in Europe. The ICC persists with associate and affiliate membership status for countries that continue to display limited interest in the game, including Canada, the Netherlands, and Kenya. Rugby league has ambitions of expanding into the US, and the AFL has staged exhibition matches in China before quizzical onlookers in an attempt to gain a commercial foothold.

Developments in globalized media sport create anxiety for those who worry about whether crowds of impassioned patriots will continue to gather excitedly and cheer national teams as they have done throughout the 19th and 20th centuries. This was certainly a concern for a sports journalist who interviewed an author of this book for a magazine feature about digital television and the question of what media sport would be like 'in 2020' (Scott 2007). He sought repeated confirmation that 'we are losing something as a nation of sport lovers' because of the range of choices available on the Internet and the distracted attention that it creates. While he was politely disagreed with, the journalist had touched upon the unexamined relationship between networked media sport and nationalism. His anxiety recalls the theory of Daniel Dayan and Elihu Katz (1992; Dayan 2008) about the social and cultural function of 'media events'. Television broadcasts of sporting contests, commemorations, and feats of human achievement watched by mass audiences have for many decades acted to integrate nations as political and social communities (see also Whannel 1992). The power of these media events is, at least in prospect, threatened as users gravitate towards fragmented online special-interest communities and bathe in 'a culture of real virtuality' (Castells 2000a). The individualization of online reception forestalls the 'upsurge of fellow feeling' and 'epidemic of communitas' that is said to occur when national communities congregate to watch their countrymen and women compete at the Olympics (Dayan & Katz 1992, p. 196).[20] Compared to broadcast television in the analogue era, the Internet offers fewer of these 'high holidays of mass communication' (p. 1), or perhaps too many competing ones.

The specters of audience atomization and user isolation lead to an imagined future where media sport spectacle is drained of its affective power to mobilize nationalism. This projection overplays the power of technology to determine human behavior and underplays the role of culture, which are best understood as intricately intertwined. Perpetuating the myth that the Internet and Web are 'placeless' technologies, such arguments underestimate the role played by space, place, language, and national and regional cultures in shaping online interaction (Adams 2009; Miller and Slater 2000). Evidence of these factors is available, including the institutional specificity, linguistic complexity, and class dynamics of the Internet in China (Qiu 2009). Studies of online play highlight that 'location still matters' even in the fantastical worlds of massively multiplayer online games (MMOGs) like *World of Warcraft* (Taylor 2006a, p. 319). The national identity and language of players influences the actions of millions of avatars that populate the virtual land of Azeroth. These experiences and the use of digital media technologies in general are sustained by chains of production that produce geographically uneven impacts and reflect management decisions coordinated across multiple national sites (Johns 2006). Moreover, the material infrastructure of networked digital communications—the Internet's 'backbone'—are spread across physical sites and regulated by the policy parameters of national governments. The vectors of networked digital media may be more complicated and territorially diffuse than broadcast systems designed to address designated national publics, but national cultures and contexts still play a major role in digital communication practices (Turner 2009). This is especially the case with sport. The websites and online media coverage of national sports, leagues, and teams display symbols that perpetuate nationalist discourses informed by popular histories involving stories of famous victories, heroic defeats, and great individual performances. These stories and symbols are generated by unique cultural forms and practices—Australian rules football, baseball, Gaelic football, cricket, American football, ice hockey—that are the source of nation-building myths and rituals in many countries. International contests, furthermore, derive their principal meaning frames from the nation, irrespective of the technologically mediated form of delivery.

The interplay between technological diversity and cultural unity characterizes media sport. The expansion of individualized consumption options has proceeded through the operation of growing numbers of content providers, online platforms, digital devices, and mobile media. But these changes in communications technology do not automatically produce cultural fragmentation or disunity. Those moments where national flags fly and anthems are sung—grand finals, cup finals, the Olympics, world championships, world series, and tournament finales—are arguably more important than ever because of their ability to focus intensive national attention within a fractured world of online choice and narrowcast audiences. Watching their nation's participants in international competitions ranks among the top reasons why audience members are willing to pay to watch sport (Hammervold & Solberg 2006). Sport is a source of cherished shared moments where partisan fans identifying with nations stop to watch and cheer it—and in Durkheimian terms—themselves. For instance, the final of the men's ice hockey between Canada and the US at the 2010 Olympics was the most watched broadcast in Canadian history (Paul 2010), and the 2011 Super Bowl was the most viewed broadcast in the history of the US (Nielsen 2011). As the previous chapter discussed, the collective attention focused on these moments is now a transmedia phenomenon that involves more than broadcast television. Enormously popular media events are also the subject of real-time Internet streams, on-the-run highlights, bulletin board chat, online and sms updates, and extensive Facebook and Twitter use. This interplay between variegated technology use and cultural nationalism parallels a clear lesson of globalization—heterogenization and homogenization are two sides of the same coin. Economic globalization and the dismantling of regulatory and technological barriers to trade and finance have travelled hand-in-hand with the acclamation and resurgence of claims to cultural identity and nationhood (Bauman 2000; Castells 2004a; Pleyers 2010). Media systems have increased the awareness of these claims of difference, with place-based national cultures, identities, and rivalries projected in global media flows that travel through digital communications networks. As a popular cultural form, sport is both a motor of this process and a mirror through which it can be glimpsed and understood (Giulianotti & Robertson 2009, p. xii).

Understanding the power of the nation and nationalism in the media sports cultural complex also requires acknowledgement of the difference between weak and strong emotional ties or attachments. Websites and Internet streams make it possible for sports enthusiasts to follow domestic leagues and tournaments located in other countries, but the strength of the attachments formed with these distant events is highly variable. Sitting at home in Melbourne or Sydney and opportunistically sampling from a range of mediated sports available around the world—cycling in Italy, Argentinean soccer, golf in Dubai—may be a sign of sophisticated consumption and cosmopolitan taste, but it often lacks the 'thick solidarity' and 'grounded identities' that characterize dedicated fandom (Giulianotti 2002). In such instances, sport is simply sampled from the menu of diverting television options, and can be easily substituted by other types of content, such as cooking shows and travel programs. By contrast, the major national leagues and domestic teams that fans grow up with, follow in local print, broadcast, and digital media each day, and build dense social networks through, possess enduring resonance and meaning. These competitions and clubs still provide the materials for fashioning emotional ties that anchor deeply felt and resilient identities that inscribe the autobiographies of those who identify with sport. This point remains true for many who follow a team from afar after having once lived close to a home ground or in the same city. It is notable that many of the members most dedicated to the survival of MFC, as well as those fans who spend considerable time posting in online message forums, live in the vicinity of their club and/or refresh their bond with them through media on a daily basis. The interpenetration of sport and media continues at astonishing speed, but place, space, and the relative autonomy of culture (Alexander 1990) ensure that the significance of fandom is about rather more than the capacity of digital technologies to harness the human network for commercial gain. There is no doubt that developments in media and in the wider communications sphere create extensive opportunities for diverse permutations of sports fandom, but 'sticky' social relations and topophiliac identifications still operate as fetters for the global sports fan. Chapter 6 deals with the professionals who interpret, report, and experience this complicated mix of continuity and discontinuity in media sport—journalists.

6 Sports Journalism
Convergence and a Leaking Craft

Sports journalism is a craft or, if preferred, a profession that lends itself to caricature. Long derided by peers on other, more 'serious' reporting rounds such as politics and business as the 'toy department of the news media' (Rowe 2007), sports journalists have struggled to enhance their occupational prestige despite high levels of consumption of their textual products (Boyle, Rowe & Whannel 2010). The disparagement of the skills required by sports journalists might in many cases be unfair. The pressure of deadlines and the need to file copy quickly demands specialist skills, while those sports journalists who have successfully broken with straight reporting and become sports feature writers are in high demand and are commensurately rewarded (Boyle 2006).

The stereotypical image of a print sports journalist, though, has proven resilient. Crudely exaggerated for the purposes of argument, it is that of a star-struck, sports-loving newspaperman who 'got lucky' by being paid to do what other people who aren't celebrities or dignitaries have to pay for—watch sports events from the best seat in the house. In return for this privilege he (and it is still usually a male) was required to describe, interpret, and judge sports events on behalf of those who had not seen them, to elicit comments from professional sports personnel (athletes, managers, coaches, and so on) to whom they did not have access, and to provide 'privileged' information by drawing on contacts and knowledge derived from their proximity to the sports industry. In this sense, the sports journalist 'stood in' for the sports fan—indeed, the ambiguous nature of their journalistic and fan related roles has been a key source of their professional disparagement, with their fourth estate responsibilities regarded as incompatible with the passionate subjectivity of the fan (Rowe 2005).

With the arrival of broadcasting—first radio, then television—there was less of a requirement to have sports contests described by print journalists after the event. Live radio commentators could paint word pictures with ambient stadium sound as a backdrop, while those working in television offered descriptive words alongside the evidence placed before viewers' own eyes. Although multimedia technologies meant that many of those who heard and/or saw mediated events still consulted print sports journalism and reportage, the practices of sports journalists were necessarily changed by the assumption that their audiences had encountered the action on screen. Reporters and commentators sought to 'add value' to the experience of spectatorship through evaluative analysis, provision of 'insider' information, and the provocation of controversy. The co-existence of print and broadcasting gradually eroded working distinctions between commentary and journalism, while single-medium journalism also receded. Broadcast journalists often appeared in print, and print journalists on radio and television. However, while the everyday tasks of sports journalists may have changed and their uses of communications technologies expanded, until quite recently there was reasonable certainty about their place (interposed between the institution of sport and its audiences), role (professional, remunerated producer of aural, literary and visual media sport texts), and product (professionally 'manufactured' media material over which they had control, and which is readily identifiable as sports journalism).

The relative clarity of these arrangements has increasingly given way to ambiguity and confusion. We argue in this chapter that sports journalists and journalism in the digital age are subject to many of the changes that we have described and analyzed elsewhere in this book. The impact of digitization and networked content distribution throws considerable light on the contemporary sports media labor process, and disputes over the distinctions between sports news and closely controlled intellectual property in online environments. Unlike elite sport at the level of event staging, content provision, and athletic labor (see Chapter 2), the distinction between professional journalism and 'amateur' or unpaid media sport commentary and analysis has been complicated and, on occasion, confused (cf. Bruns 2005). Watching amateur sport on a regular basis may not appeal to many sports fans, but the same cannot always be said for reading and listening to the opinions of keen, unpaid sports bloggers, amateur podcast presenters, and self-styled citizen journalists.

During the interviews conducted for this book, newspaper, radio, and television journalists all spoke about the changes in their routine professional practices as a result of the Internet and the digital delivery of news. A distinctive feature of this chapter is a particular emphasis on the voices of media professionals who produce and control sports news, and whose practices testify to the lived experience of technological change. Their comments and opinions are connected to the broad-scale commercial and policy schisms triggered by the transition from analogue-broadcast to digital-convergent communications media. This approach provides analytical insight into how journalists are rearticulating their occupational roles and routines, and announces the emergence of *convergent sports journalism*. This mode of media practice places demands upon journalists to file and produce stories for multiple platforms simultaneously, to report stories and provide additional news related content via blogs and podcasts for little or no additional remuneration, and to position their professional practice in relation to specialist online journalists and editors. These developments are impacting upon the very idea of sports news, changing the amount and immediacy of discussion between journalists and their audiences, and placing demands upon journalists both to observe and, occasionally, to compete with independent bloggers and commentators.

DETERMINING THE NEWS

Like weather and stock market reports, developments in sport have been an historical staple of radio and television news bulletins, while all major newspapers have had their own, distinct sports section produced by a large, dedicated 'news desk' of sports journalism personnel with its own editor. With the coming of the Internet, text, still, and moving images could all be placed in the sport sections of online newspapers and on dedicated sports news websites, with the addition of easily updated breaking news and live scores. However, as we show, the 'good news' that there could be a great deal more sports coverage in a range of forms was not received with universal approval in the media sport industry.

Sports news has been a source of controversy well before the World Wide Web because of the major role played by exclusive television broadcast rights in the media sport market. Rival networks and non-rights-holders, for obvious reasons, sought to get as much live sports action for broadcast as often as possible from rights-holders. In response, rights-owners rigorously policed access to sport stadiums and monitored the amount of sports footage used by third parties in order to protect their costly investments in exclusively controlled intellectual property. Although it was not always easy to achieve widespread agreement between the various television networks without resort to the courts, broadcast conventions were developed that provided reasonable satisfaction for all parties. One well-known unwritten industry convention in Australia is the so-called '3 x 3 x 3' rule, by which television broadcasters agree to show no more than three minutes of each others' footage, three times a day, three hours apart (see deZwart 2009). While there have been variations and also infractions of such rules, they have tended to hold in the name of reciprocity and mutual protection. However, as discussed in earlier chapters, broadcasting's monopoly on carrying audiovisual sports texts has come under challenge from online sports highlights shown on websites, and the growing capacity of sports organizations to independently produce and retransmit content. The outcome here has been worsening confusion and conflict over who has the right to show what content, when, and how often.

Online operators, website hosts, and other digital media organizations can now all lay claim to being sports news producers, gatherers, and/or aggregators, with uncertainties over what constitutes legitimate news coverage and *de facto* competing sports content. This change threatens established revenue streams based on expensively sold and acquired coverage rights that, in turn, are traded for advertising exposure, branded sponsorship and audience subscriptions. Thus, orderly relations and arrangements between recognized news media companies; between news media companies and digital content transmitters such as telecommunication companies; and between sports leagues/clubs and media organizations, have begun to break down alongside currently operative market regulations and policies (Hutchins & Rowe 2009b, 2010). The resultant uncertainties have seen actual and projected changes in audience behavior emerge alongside new digital media sport services, such as on-demand viewing and high-rotation content provision across different platforms. As is conventional under these circumstances in the media and sport industries, the court system has constituted a site of potential recourse when the various parties have felt their rights to be infringed (Hutchins & Rowe 2009a; Battersby 2011).

The Australian media sport environment is characterized by a clear hierarchy of well-funded sports organizations in a crowded field of competing sports; a still developing subscription and pay-per-view broadcast sector; a significant public service broadcasting tradition of news provision; and a history of tight, state-enforced regulation of broadcast sport. According to Anthony Edgar, head of media operations for the IOC, Australia also possesses a fiercely competitive sports news market:

> . . . it is an aggressive media environment, it is a very strong media environment and it pushes the boundaries. If you want to take the Olympic Games, generally we have more trouble with the Australian media than we do with all other media in the world put together . . . In saying that, that does not mean it is a problem for us; it is that they push the boundaries. (Proof Committee Hansard, 29 April, 2009, p. 6)

Fierce competition and the challenges of media convergence have combined to produce widespread discord and dissent, leading to a pioneering parliamentary inquiry into 'The Reporting of Sports News and the Emergence of Digital Media'. The terms of reference for this 2009 investigation of the Senate Standing Committee on Environment, Communications and the Arts were wide-ranging:

(a) The balance of commercial and public interests in the reporting and broadcasting of sports news;
(b) The nature of sports news reporting in the digital age, and the effect of new technologies (including video streaming on the Internet, archived photo galleries and mobile devices) on the nature of sports news reporting;
(c) Whether and why sporting organisations want digital reporting of sports regulated, and what should be protected by such regulation;

(d) The appropriate balance between sporting and media organisations' respective commercial interests in the issue;

(e) The appropriate balance between regulation and commercial negotiation in ensuring that competing organisations get fair access to sporting events for reporting purposes;

(f) The appropriate balance between the public's right to access alternative sources of information using new types of digital media, and the rights of sporting organisations to control or limit access to ensure a fair commercial return or for other reasons;

(g) Should sporting organisations be able to apply frequency limitations to news reports in the digital media;

(h) The current accreditation processes for journalists and media representatives at sporting events, and the use of accreditation for controlling reporting on events; and

(i) Options other than regulation or commercial negotiation (such as industry guidelines for sports and news agencies in sports reporting, dispute resolution mechanisms and codes of practice) to manage sports news to balance commercial interests and public interests (Parliament of Australia Senate Standing Committee 2009, p. 1).

These terms of reference are a useful way of summarizing key issues of contention arising from the fact that the most unequivocally public dimension of sport, news, is in conflict with its highly prized commercial function as a media property to be exploited through commodity exchange. Although the inquiry was established in Australia, such concerns apply to all mature and emergent media sport markets. It is for this reason that the inquiry became a 'test site' watched closely by major sport and media organizations from across the world, many of which made submissions to and appeared before the Committee.

As Table 6.1 below reveals, those who made submissions included some of the most prominent international organizations with interests in media sport, including the News Limited company (owned by News Corporation) and press agencies Agence France-Presse (AFP) and Associated Press (AP); the International Cricket Council (ICC) and IOC among peak sports organizations; the Belgium-based News Media Coalition (NMC) and the World Association of Newspapers (WAN) among media representative bodies; leading telecommunications and digital media companies Hutchison Telecoms and Yahoo!7; as well as Australian sports bodies and government agencies. The wide scope and high level of interest in a formal inquiry into sports news (which was empowered but declined to make binding recommendations) and its relationship with networked digital communications is testament to the importance of its competitive stakes, and links directly to the ownership and control of globally mediated sport (Rowe 2011b).

The range of stakeholders contributing to the inquiry constitutes a rough map of the media sports cultural complex with one missing element—sports

Table 6.1   Submissions to the Senate Standing Committee Inquiry into 'The Reporting
of Sports News and the Emergence of Digital Media' (Total: 44)

News Media Companies, Agencies, and Corporations (12)	Agence France-Presse (AFP), Associated Press (AP), Australian Associated Press (AAP), Australian Broadcasting Corporation (ABC), Getty Images, Fairfax Media, News Limited, Premier Media Group (PMG), Reuters News, Special Broadcasting Service (SBS), Sports Media Publishing (SMP), West Australian Newspapers
Sports Organizations (11)	Australian Football League (AFL), Australian Racing Board, Cricket Australia, International Cricket Council (ICC), International Olympic Committee (IOC), National Rugby League (NRL), Softball Australia, Newcastle Knights Rugby League club, Racing Victoria, Tennis Australia, Victoria Racing Club (VRC)
News Media Associations and Representative Bodies (7)	Australian Press Council, Australian Sub-scription Television and Radio Association (ASTRA), Free TV Australia, News Media Coalition (NMC), Pacific Area Newspaper Publishers' Association (PANPA), South African National Editors' Forum (SANEF), World Association of Newspapers (WAN)
Telecommunications and Digital Media Companies (4)	Hutchison Telecoms, Optus, Yahoo!7, ninemsn
Sports Industry Bodies and Associations (4)	Coalition of Major Professional Sports (COMPS), Australian Athletes' Alliance (AAA), Australian and New Zealand Sports Law Association (ANZLA), Australian Womensport and Recreation Association
Government Departments/Agencies (2)	Australian Sports Commission (ASC), Department of Health and Ageing
Individuals (2)	Dr. Kayt Davies (Edith Cowan University), Mr. David Smith (Edith Cowan University)
Other (2)	Confidential submission, Lander & Rogers Lawyers

Source: Hutchins and Rowe 2010

fans. Unlike another Australian government inquiry conducted around the same time, *Sport on Television: A Review of the Anti-Siphoning Scheme in the Contemporary Digital Environment*[1] (Department of Broadband, Communications and the Digital Economy 2010a), which attracted over 330 submissions, there were no impassioned statements from sports fans such as the following:

I signed up for Pay TV to watch sport, unfortunately I pay $40 per month and NO sport month (sic) and no sport is included. They force people to pay the premium amount to get any sport. This is massively unfair and ordinary families cannot afford this. The Government wants people to engage their families in sport and the opportunity to watch ones chosen sport is being taken away by pay TV (sic). (Elaine Crowther, Submission 100)

Sport supporters in Australia cover a broad spectrum of the Australian community but by and large, the majority are average wage earners who are doing their best to ensure that their standard of living and those of their dependents, is moderate, comfortable and within their means. The introduction of new digital channels gives Government and the free-to-air networks the opportunity to ensure that the millions of sports fans in this country can access the sports they want to view free of charge thus allowing supporters to enjoy the sports they love without any additional costs. (Sport Supporters Australia, Submission 283).

Such voices were largely absent from the inquiry into sports reporting and digital media, despite its direct relevance to the amount, type, and frequency of media sport images and information made available to sports fans. This absence reveals starkly that this is territory dominated and (pre) occupied by professionals and organizations with vested interests in the control and exploitation of media sport content.

That such appealing content can now be provided by many professional organizations with a website means that the boundaries between professional news media and sports organizations, in particular, are being eroded. Hence, the Group Editorial Director for News Limited, Campbell Reid, argued before the Committee:

. . . actually, what appears to be going on here is that sporting bodies want to act as news providers themselves, so they want to restrict competition by limiting the existing news providers. There is nothing to stop sports bodies becoming media organisations that produce and distribute their own content—in fact, in the digital age the barriers to entry are low, and they are doing it already. (Proof Committee Hansard, 16 April, 2009, p. 48)

If the sports organisations wish to compete as media organisations and suppliers, they are not coming from a backward position in this. In the past they would have had to buy a printing press, but now they simply have to have a Web site. (Proof Committee Hansard, 16 April, 2009, p. 51)

The principal objection of media companies to this move of sports organizations onto their 'patch' is that the familiar division of responsibility between news source and news provider, and between rights seller and purchaser, has the potential to be monopolized by the source/seller. Sports organizations were coy about their ambitions in this regard when appearing before the Committee, as the following exchange with the Confederation of Major Professional Sports[2] (COMPS), a coalition of all the major sports in Australia, reveals:

> CHAIR—Other witnesses have said, to paraphrase it, that it is not so much the media organisations taking over the sports organisations' business, which is to promote and run sporting events, but the sports organisations are taking over the media's role of reporting those events. What do you say to those allegations? You all have your own websites. Clearly they are in competition with the other websites that provide sports news . . .
>
> Mr McLachlan [Chief Operating Officer, Australian Football League]—We are frustrated with it as well at times. Ultimately I guess there is the fact there are no barriers to entry to running your own website, and there are no barriers to entry and it is very cheap and easy. There is a proliferation of news websites, which in fact is the core of what the media companies are talking about. It is actually the core of our problem today. I do not think we have aspirations to become media companies, but the fact that news is able to be so easily disseminated and so easily reported, and the fact that these fair dealing provisions enable anyone really to grab copyrighted material and use it for the reporting of news means that we have this proliferation, and that is at the heart of this. Because it is a cheap and easy tool for which we do not need a licence, unlike a television station or the huge amount of capital that is required to run a newspaper, all sports will continue to run websites as a communication tool. I do not think they were aspiring ultimately to be media companies, although if you look overseas they potentially do as well . . .
>
> CHAIR—Is it not a little disingenuous to say that you are not setting yourselves up in competition against media organisations by having your own Web sites that we all have programmed into our PDAs or whatever?
>
> Mr McLachlan—I did not say we were not competing with them in the online space. There is no doubt about that. Your comment was that we were aspiring to be a media company. In this space we do compete. There is no doubt about that. (Proof Committee Hansard, 15 April, 2009, p. 25)

The distinction between competing in an online media environment and aspiring to be a media company may be abstract and questionable, but it takes on a bluntly material character when one party physically obstructs or prevents another from reporting on the sport that it controls.

This occurred, notoriously, in Brisbane in late 2007 during an Australia v Sri Lanka Test cricket series, with CA demanding that news agencies cede all rights to photographic images taken at its matches and pay fees for access, or be locked out of the cricket ground. In response the leading news agencies AFP, AP, and Reuters temporarily suspended all coverage of the series until agreement could be reached. The Media, Entertainment and Arts Alliance (MEAA), the trade union and professional organization representing workers in the media, entertainment, sports, and arts industries across Australia, made this complaint:

> News coverage should not be up for sale. That is the basic issue at stake here . . . a Test match involving the national team is a public event and news about it should be freely available to the public. At present CA is simply being greedy. (Chris Warren, Federal Secretary MEAA, quoted in Al Jazeera 2007)

Unsurprisingly, CA argued that developments in digital media were eroding their media property rights, as a range of enterprises began to access and circulate match highlights and images. This development was also apparent in relation to so-called unauthorized reproduction of match highlights by news services available through different mobile handset carriers, which contributed to the following statement from CA:

> The emergence of the digital media has not altered the remit of CA . . . CA derives the funding for its investment into community through the sale of its media rights which represents up to 80 per cent of its income in certain years. The value of the media rights is based on the exclusivity provided to media organisations to transmit the event from a venue.
>
> At the same time, CA has and continues to provide non rights media free access to venues, players and private events to be able to report news of the events we stage in a full, frank and fearless manner, without restriction. We believe we go out of our way to assist media to perform its role and pride ourselves on the level of service we provide. (Cricket Australia 2009, p. 7)

So, while CA encouraged news reporting of its events—and it would be extraordinary if it did not avail itself of the free publicity that it affords—its main concern was not with the quality of the sports news. Instead, it emphasized its exploitation by others under circumstances where 'the lines of what has traditionally been regarded as news reporting have been clouded and blurred by new media developments', meaning that 'the definition of what is news—where it starts and where it stops—has been completely turned on its head' (p. 7). Whereas the digital media environment is constantly described as an opportunity for innovative media genres and forms, and for vastly extended user reach and convenience, CA identifies a problem of disorder: the 'increasing creep and stretch of news reporting boundaries offers no regulatory framework, no limits on what can be done and no guidance to resolve disputes' (p. 7). Here, then, the organization that describes itself as the 'custodian' of Australia's dominant summer sport views the practitioners of convergent sports journalism as capable of undermining the economic substructure of the sport, rather than as the bearers of the news that help insinuate cricket deeply into the national consciousness.

In the Senate Committee's final report, cricket coverage received particular attention, alongside a dispute between the Australian Football League (AFL) and Australian Associated Press (AAP), a news agency servicing many subscribing media outlets. For many years, AAP journalists and news photographers (commonly referred to as photojournalists) had attended sports events and sent out text reports and photographic images 'on the wire'. However, in 2007, AAP and the AFL could not agree on the terms and conditions of journalists' access to Australian football games, and events such as award ceremonies and press conferences. A key point of disagreement had arisen over the growth in online reproduction, circulation, and archiving of digital photographs of AFL matches on news websites, which the AFL sought to limit by imposing strict photojournalist accreditation conditions. Despite the intervention of the Australian Press Council, AAP, Reuters, and AP were still refused accreditation to enter AFL venues in order to cover fixtures. The dispute continued in the following football season, with the Australian Press Council (2009) submission invoking the principle of press freedom to support its case:

> This issue is a serious threat to press freedom—the freedom of the press to inform the public on matters of interest and to report properly on news events without the intermediation of those seeking to 'manage' the news. (p. 3)

At the inquiry, the following exchange on the subject occurred between a member of the Senate Committee and the AFL Chief Operating Officer:

> Senator LUNDY—Why were they [the photojournalists] excluded?
> Mr McLachlan—They are not a publisher, they are a syndicator of content. In their submission they talk about the fact that they are selling those images to other entities. We accredit their journalists. All their journalists are allowed to come in and cover the game, but in terms of actually selling those photographs, we were very happy for them to continue to provide the photographs—
> Senator LUNDY—Some of those photographs would have been used for news purposes?
> Mr McLachlan—Yes. They were sold to newspaper companies.
> Senator LUNDY—That is for news.

Mr McLachlan—Yes, but the images are equally available from any number of sources for sale. Essentially, we were restricting someone who was syndicating and selling our photographs.

Mr Lethlean [AFL Broadcasting, Legal and Business Affairs Manager]—Just to clarify that, we did not exclude them from entering the grounds. They would not agree to our accreditation terms by which they were not able to syndicate to non-news reporting agencies. (Proof Committee Hansard, 15 April, 2009, p. 35)

With continuing disputes over accreditation terms and conditions for journalists, the inquiry recorded, 'This case can be summarized as a contractual disagreement over accreditation' (p. 18). Contractual disagreements, negotiations over terms and conditions, and organizational maneuvering are no doubt familiar to those with executive and managerial duties in the media and sport industries. But journalists and news photographers are predominantly concerned with the familiar routines of meeting deadlines, devising 'angles', accessing sources, arranging interviews, chasing 'scoops' and exclusives, and taking the best shots. It is instructive, therefore, to explore journalists' responses to the factors that enable and constrain their professional practices under conditions where their sources (sports) challenge prevailing definitions of news, and their employers (news media organizations) are increasingly demanding on matters of speed and flexibility, while their clients (audiences and users) respond to them directly and may also aspire to emulate them as sports communicators.

JOURNALISTS AT WORK: ACCESS SEEKING AND DIGITAL MULTITASKING

Sports journalism has been commonly regarded as 'nice work if you can get it'. Journalists are charged with the enviable task of being paid for gaining privileged entry to sports events and access to sportspeople, in return for the tasks of describing, commenting, and interviewing in ways that contribute to audience appreciation of sport. Of course, this is a benign picture of an activity that requires, in various measures, accuracy, speed, imagination, and interpretive-analytical acumen. But what established sports journalists have not typically experienced are the compromises to their everyday work practices caused by the conflict described earlier between news media and sports organizations. One senior sport journalist, with a lengthy career in print and broadcasting, discussed the confusion and frustration experienced by journalists caught up in the 2007 Brisbane Test cricket match lockout discussed above. While wishing to concentrate on their primary occupational tasks, he and other journalists felt bewildered as the 'foot soldiers' subject to the specialist organizational negotiations taking place among the so-called 'heavies' (Interview with author):

You hear talk about the negotiations going on . . . at the level the foot
soldiers [you] have actually got no idea. So we ran into this situation
where, well the first we knew of it—the foot soldiers—was we couldn't
get accreditation. And we had some idea of what was going on and what
the reason was, but the actual nitty-gritty, none of the foot soldiers
knew what was going on. I mean it is an incredibly complex area, which
you really need to be 'degreed' [university educated] to understand. It's
incredibly complex. It comes down often to numbers of images or the
number of images that can be transmitted per session or per hour. Or
they may reach a specific agreement with one organization and allow 60
images a minute, an hour, a day, or a session, and it could be 120 images
for another organization . . . from the outside, to someone who doesn't
understand the intricacies of it, there doesn't seem to be any rhyme or
reason to the way it goes on. (Interview with author)

The denial of journalist accreditation in Brisbane produced farcical scenes
that were, ironically, transmitted in the news media and became as much a
part of the news as the cricket match itself:

There was a very amusing photograph that you might have seen of two
or three [other journalists] and myself and a couple of others standing
outside a wire gate. It looked like from one side of prison to another,
and James Sutherland, a Chief Executive [of CA], a very affable man,
on the other side. And we were told we couldn't go in. The 'populars'
didn't file, from what I recall, but I was instructed to file as a freelancer.
My colleagues, staffers, didn't. I don't think I sought a directive from
the MEAA. They're awkward situations . . . we wandered around the
corner . . . and found a coffee shop, and we just propped there and you
could hear the crowd . . .

We took it lightly, that situation, but we were angry. We're professional people who care about the game. Often people are quite oblivi-
ous to that fact because at times we can be critical. The people who
write cricket for a living, who write a sport for a living, do generally
care about the welfare of its people and the game . . . So yes, there was
disappointment, there was some anger . . . I don't understand what's
going on with the agencies and how different their requirements are
and what they want to deliver. But there is nothing more fundamental
to the coverage of sport or the coverage of anything in society as the
agencies. (Senior sport journalist, Interview with author)

Here the affective investment of the journalist in sport itself is clearly
articulated, and extends beyond their specific role to the primacy of sports
news dissemination—'in a press box—there is no one more important role,
in that, it doesn't matter how many celebrated byline writers you've got,
one thing or another, the news has got to get out' (Interview with author).[3]

While recognizing that 'it is an incredibly complex area', there is considerable resentment expressed here towards obstruction to the news gathering process caused by denial of accreditation: 'I just find the attitude of the sports, that they could marginalize the agencies, I just find it unbelievable' (Senior sport journalist, Interview with author). A technology journalist, although questioning how much live sports should be watched as of right, similarly insisted that, in news terms, sports fans should not be 'deprived of the information' (Interview with author).

The restrictions imposed by sports on journalistic access apply to more than the enclosed sports event, extending to everyday contact with sportspeople. As a sports broadcaster for a public service media organization noted:

> Everything now is very tightly controlled. Clubs basically have a policy where you're prohibited from ringing coaches and players directly. So the only way you can actually do that is if you have a personal relationship *with* them, so they're a source rather than a point of inquiry. Requests for interviews basically all go through clubs . . . They'll either be approved or knocked back by the club on their willingness to have it done or the level of controversy attached to the story, so they get to micro manage everything. If they want a player at the center of a . . . news story to give an interview, they'll handpick where they want that interview to go. It's much more tightly controlled from that point of view, and I think, particularly for journos [common Australian vernacular for journalists] coming into it now. It's extremely hard to establish any relationships, to establish your off-the-record contacts because if you ring a player and you don't know the player, the player will report it to the club, and you'll be struck-off [the club journalist accreditation list] fairly theatrically. (Interview with author)

Because of the limited range of well-placed legitimate sports sources, all but the most eminent, established sports journalists fear ostracism by key contacts and organizations on their rounds (Rowe 2005). Refusal to communicate with sports journalists is traditionally caused by unfair criticism or the breaching of confidences. But in an age of tight media management of sportspeople, merely seeking direct, unfiltered access to an athlete can lead to a journalist being 'struck-off fairly theatrically'.

The adversarial nature of the struggle over the reporting and presentation of sports news is evident in CA's (Cricket Australia 2009, pp. 11–12) submission to the inquiry into sports news and digital media, with fans uneasily positioned between sports rights-holders and news providers:

> Cricket can reach new fans in new ways and part of that is through embracing the delivery of content, including the provision of news to fans in the many new and old [media] forms the fan chooses to consume . . .

It is not up to cricket or media organisations to dictate how information is to be received or consumed. This is the fans' choice . . .

. . . Broadcasting content (audio visual) is now seen as the key driver of the news model by media publishers and news agencies in attracting customers in an increasingly fragmented market where consumers have more choice.

Traditional newspapers and traditional radio groups have diversified their business and acquired audio visual assets and other commercial businesses and become production houses and syndicators of content.

This bodes well for ensuring fans have access to 'news' and more choice, but does not bode well for CA as the value of our exclusive offering is becoming diminished as the principles of fair dealing do not stand up in the digital era, simply because the characteristics of the digital age have no bounds or limitations.

These issues—often polarized—repeatedly came to the fore in the authors' interviews with a wide range of actors in the media and sport field. As the editor of a metropolitan newspaper argued:

Well it's something that they've [sports organizations] realized the commercial value of [visual content]. And they're having an argument: who owns that? Who's got the right to have that, to make money out of it really? Thirty years ago you think about an iconic photograph of a tied Test [a very rare case in cricket where both teams have scored the same number of runs], the last ball, the fifth day of a tied Test between Australia and the West Indies; a fantastic photograph. No one made much money out of it other than it was in the newspaper. You bought the newspaper, you got the photograph. Now people have realized that [it's] commercial. You can continue to slice and dice it and get all sorts of value from it. They're fighting over it. That's a kind of business fight that's going on. I just think it's worth sounding an alarm about: what are the potential risks if it's purely a business fight between various competing business interests and what it does mean for us as a culture and as a society? (Interview with author)

Journalists felt especially compromised by the conflict between their occupational values and practices and the increasing range of constraints imposed on their profession in, ironically, circumstances of unprecedented digital plenitude. For those older sports journalists who are still grasping the possibilities of digital media, both the present and future of their work environment are uncertain: 'So, I suppose in short, mate, I've got no idea what's going to happen. I don't think anybody in the industry has at any level. That both frightens and challenges' (Senior sport journalist, Interview with author). These are not matters that apply only to the sports round, but pertain also to journalism in general. As Jane B. Singer (2011, p.

103) argues, 'Perhaps the most obvious change to journalism has involved the introduction and rapid incorporation of new tasks and the tools needed to accomplish them'. For example, another senior print journalist who writes substantially about sport while also discharging a wider editorial role described how

> . . . my base has always been in print and, I must confess, it's the medium I most enjoy still. But, I do stuff on radio—not regularly—but I mean one or two times a month maybe. And I do television occasionally as well. (Former sports editor, Interview with author)

This journalist discussed the pressures of having to file from major sports tournaments on both print and online platforms, especially given the necessary responsiveness of the text and its rhythm of production relative to the time available:

> In more recent years, the stuff I write and I produce goes onto the Internet, and increasingly that has become part of the job. I would say my primary responsibility is to the newspaper, to the print form, but we're expected to file for the Internet . . . A few years ago in Germany [at the 2006 soccer World Cup] in games that Australia would play, the deadlines were such that I was filing almost every quarter of an hour, sometimes doing running, stream of consciousness stuff to our Internet site, and certainly filing stuff immediately for the net, and, if we had more time, doing more considered stuff for the newspaper. It depends very much on the time factor and obviously there's a lot of pressure, wrongly in my view, to go for immediacy and instantaneity on the Internet. So we are under a lot of pressure to produce something immediately when something happens [and] I suspect at times . . . without sufficient reflection or checking for accuracy. But obviously if I have a whole half-a-day to produce stuff for print media, I don't see any problem producing it for the Internet first. (Former sports editor, Interview with author)

The imperative of getting online material 'out' and correcting it later as required is conspicuous here. Interspersed on occasion with radio and television appearances, the necessity is to produce online material that is part prepared, part spontaneous, with more considered, reflective, and technically honed text reserved for print:

> For example, there was the same sort of pressure to file for the Internet for the Beijing Olympics, although the time difference was only two hours. Most events you'd be filing for the Internet soon, very quick, I wouldn't say off the top of your head, but certainly within seconds of an event finishing. You can pre-write certain parts of it in a sense:

who's lining up, who the game's about, the moment the bell goes for the race or the event is over, you whack something down for the Internet, and you still have the option of doing stuff for the paper later . . . And then coming back to the office or wherever you are, you'd go back and then talk to some of the participants in the event and search out some historical parallels, or unpack the context, or probably do a more reflective piece more with background color and movement and different voices. By the time they [the reader] pick up the newspaper it might be several hours later, possibly even 12, 24 hours. And they [the reader] would expect far more than what was just dished up and could easily be read on the Internet, or what they would have seen on television or heard on the radio. So I think there the pressure is really on us to provide added value, and that's in the form of this color and movement and voices, people commenting, the fall out, what does it mean? Is it the greatest day ever? What's it mean for the next events or what are the implications for sport or us or the team, or where do we go from here? (Former sports editor, Interview with author)

Such 'hyperactive', multitasked journalistic routines contrast with the slower, single-medium practices of the past, where the absolute necessity of filing on time was no less pressing, but the accelerated speed and voluminous quantity of copy was neither possible nor required.[4] A clear, generationally inflected preference for the print medium and for the 'luxury' of only writing for it is evident. As a freelance sports journalist recalled:

During the [2006–07] Ashes series, it was the first time that daily journalists—especially the British journalists—had been forced to blog to any great degree. So they were often maintaining blogs independent of their daily newspaper writing. And it seemed that no one had a particularly clear idea of the relationship between blogs and what they would print in their column, and what they would print in their match report, so there was a fair degree of overlap between them. And I know that the British journalists were pretty contemptuous of what they were doing for the blogosphere. Michael Jones from the *Trumpet* [identity disguised] used to walk around saying he was the only one that wasn't keeping a blog, and he really rather enjoyed the status of being the only print journalist who wasn't expected to write for online (laughs). And he was saying that he was glad he lived his entire newspaper journalism career without having dirtied his hands with blogging. (Interview with author)

Yet this journalist, as a freelancer, had been involved in a specialist sports news website for about a decade and was comfortable with the experience of writing for an online readership. He saw the advantages of being in contact with online 'enthusiasts or experts on the game, rather than being read by a general readership that happens to be reading through the omnibus sports pages of the newspaper' (Interview with author). At the same time, he weighed the advantages and disadvantages of having 'actively solicited [online] comments from readers [who] you tend to be insulated from when writing for a newspaper. And that's kind of interesting and potentially annoying at the same time'. Thus, instead of seeing the increased incidence of journalistic blogging as an imposition, he actually welcomed the rise of blogs *in sport*, adding, 'I perhaps don't welcome them quite so much in other areas of discourse, like politics' (Interview with author). From this perspective, something resembling a 'community of practice' (Wenger 1998) can be glimpsed involving shared concerns and competencies among dispersed networks in the area of sport, although in the domain of politics this journalist feels that 'there's a lot of inexpert writing' by 'sectional interests'.

The emergence of convergent sports journalism has led to exhausting reporting routines. The same freelance journalist, although in a different position in the labor market than a 'staffer', has found himself engaged in four different types of journalism each day: filing for a newspaper website; writing a blog for a sports website; speaking for a podcast; and completing a regular story for another newspaper (which would also usually place it on its website). This multitasking has meant producing up to 2,500 words per day (plus spoken material), which he described as 'taxing' not just in terms of quantity but also in trying 'to do that without repeating yourself incessantly' (Interview with author). The unrelenting job of producing content also creates an unenviable situation when play is 'boring': 'You find yourself, not *making* things up, but you find yourself saying things for the sake of saying things. Saying things in order to create content'. The need to operate across media platforms also led to occasions where this journalist has covered matches with three screens open simultaneously for his specialist website article, blog, and daily newspaper column, seeking to work out what 'might work' for one or all of them with suitable adjustments and strategic repetitions. The 'creative cannibalization' (Curran 2011, following Phillips 2010)—of both journalists' own and others' writing—encouraged by such convergent journalism practices is discussed in the next section.

ONLINE PLATFORMS AND 'CREATIVE CANNIBALIZATION'

Unrelenting news content 'over-production' and journalistic multitasking are not only the lot of unsalaried freelance journalists who need to patch together a range of paying tasks to make a living. These demands are a structural feature of the contemporary news media in general. As James Curran (2011, p. 116) notes of British journalism:

British journalists are under strong pressure to produce more, in less time, as a consequence of newsroom redundancies, and the work generated by websites established by traditional news media, requiring stories to be updated in a 24-hour news cycle. This is fostering 'creative cannibalisation', the mutual lifting of stories from rivals' websites, as a way of increasing output.

Alongside analogous 'creative cannibalization' among the sport journalists and editors interviewed, it was also observed that digital technologies make possible what we might call high-levels of 'content cooking and consumption' (to extend the gastronomic metaphor). However, although sport journalists may be busily cannibalizing each others' content, the rate of consumption and disposal of their *own* textual product is accelerating across platforms, with print still retaining its prime place in the news media hierarchy. As one professional sports journalist of over two decades standing put it:

> What's changed? I mean the most obvious part is the journalist's workload has been increased by 24 hour access but it's *still* an area in flux. Because we still haven't got total integration between online and print media . . . we're still in an *ad hoc* basis of filing for online. We have separate staff online but we're on call occasionally to file—I wish I could remember the name they give for it—I think it's 'disposable exclusives'. They're stories that we know will be an exclusive at 3pm on the Internet . . . If you've got a story that you know we can have first on the Web, but the opposition have got a sniff of it, or TV have got a sniff of it, there's an impetus to get it on the Web and have us brand the story as our own as an exclusive at 3 o'clock. (Broadsheet sport journalist, Interview with author)

Another journalist views online media as a place to post questionable material of 'a lesser standard in my opinion', but that can be used to stimulate interest and discussion: 'As an industry the media is grappling with what is an acceptable form of material to generate people looking [at the website] and blogs'. Again, online media are characterized as engaging in the activity of attention grabbing rather than simply providing sports news:

> I think what websites do . . . and even newspaper websites is they'll fly stuff online that they would never print in the newspaper because it hadn't met various standards of proof. And they'll do it to generate blogs and to generate discussion and then the following day's paper will have the real story . . . (Public service sports broadcaster, Interview with author)

But within professional sports journalism—and even inside the same organization—there are now occupational distinctions whereby some newspaper editors and journalists are primarily committed to online journalism rather than paper-based reportage. Thus, an online sports editor for the same newspaper has been 'working with media companies' in 'a fairly slow evolution to accept online as a legitimate and a major aspect of coverage' (Interview with author). In striving for this acceptance, the primacy of communicative speed is acknowledged:

> Immediacy is vital because as we all know the Web has opened up the world to news and information so . . . the rules have changed and the goalposts have moved. Where if you wanted information years ago about American baseball, you might have been in a situation where you had shortwave radio or had to wait for a weekly publication that came to your newsagent three days later . . . you can now get it in a matter of minutes. (Online sports editor, Interview with author)

The emphasis here on rapid-fire online textual production does not make accuracy incidental:

> The onus on being right and accurate is still there, and it's probably tested more than it was previously [when] newspaper journalists could rely on a deadline that might be five or six hours away. Now that deadline could be much sooner, and there's an acknowledgment that . . . you don't necessary file a story once, you might file a story and update it three or four times during a day. (Interview with author)

Although the chances of instant correction are now much enhanced, the likelihood of making a mistake is correspondingly increased.

The notion that material for the Web version of the newspaper is designated as high rotation and so easily discarded, in contrast with the more considered and weighty print stories meriting a longer lifespan, is echoed by the association between Web-based journalism and unpaid blogging or citizen journalism. For example, a senior sport journalist was quite open about his belief that newspaper journalism is superior to blogging:

> I hate the term 'blog' for a newspaper. For me a blogger is someone who is not a journalist having a say. I hate that print news is on our websites and we say . . . we're going to blog on it . . . I'm eternally frustrated that . . . so-called citizen journalists make grand assumptions, puts themselves on a par with the [trained professional] journalist in presenting opinions. Everything I write is based on the fact that I've spoken to people, I've been at the event, that I know stuff off-the-record. Just yesterday I went to a media briefing for instance. We wrote about half of it, and half of it stays in the back of your mind for when you write. It's an informed opinion. (Interview with author)

The idea that people outside the professional network and organiza-tional setting of the newsroom could be confused with journalists is, for this reporter, 'eternally frustrating'. He believes that it helps to foster the notion that journalists are 'redundant' and must suffer the perceived indignity of being rendered outsiders: 'For us to reduce ourselves to that level as outside the ring spectators—bloggers—even in branding, I find quite annoying'. Bloggers, in his mind, lack the professional journalis-tic status and authority deriving from directly sourced knowledge and professional experience. The problem for the 'institutionalized' sports journalist under these circumstances is that the surfeit of opinion avail-able on the Internet undermines the hierarchy of credibility on which the masthead relies.

The creative cannibalization to which Curran refers also involves the use of the material generated by other journalists in their everyday profes-sional rounds as the source material for their opinion—that is, informed opinion at second hand. Or it might be, as the professional above argues, 'uninformed opinion', or perhaps, *differently* informed opinion. This is a defensive response to the kind of citizen journalism that is celebrated by some as the sign of a *'renaissance'* in media and democracy (Curran 2011, p. 117). Michael Schudson (2008, p. 25) notes that citizen journalism is reconfiguring the balance between the various functions of journalism:

> With the arrival of the Web and the blogosphere, the public forum and mobilizing functions of journalism have grown relative to the inform-ing and investigative and social empathy functions. The Web also helps create an incipient new function of journalism for democracy, one in which the divide between the journalist and the audience for journal-ism disappears. Some people talk about this as 'citizen journalism'. It has always existed to a degree. Every time a citizen calls up a news organization and says, 'I have a hot tip for you,' this is citizen journal-ism. Every letter to the editor is citizen journalism. But now citizens can simply go online and publish the tip or letter on their own. This is a new self-organizing journalism, already making waves, already enact-ing something new and exciting.

Among the users of 'self-organizing journalism', intriguingly, are some professional media workers, such as this radio producer who describes his personal media consumption as follows:

> I'm listening to a mix of 'pro-am' or 'pro' [professional] and 'am' [ama-teur], which is possibly what we're seeing in the media space as well . . . Professional journalists filtering, publishing, and also a combination of—I don't necessarily like using the term—but dare I say citizen jour-nalism . . . that mix of the two. (Interview with author)

The 'pro-am' model of media use outlined in this manner reveals that the boundaries between professional and amateur/citizen journalism and media production are no longer clearly drawn (Bruns 2005, 2008).

The 'excitement' that might attend the publication of information or opinion in sport by unpaid bloggers and writers is not universally shared, as we have seen, by those who make their principal living from it. But the availability of the Web to the audience-turned-producer, while infuriating for some, is less of a threat than sports organizations bypassing news organizations altogether and effectively operating their own media platforms. The broadsheet journalist quoted above is far more concerned by official sports websites that are able to access their principal sources 'exclusively' and so prevent them from being subjected to journalistic scrutiny:

> Clubs now attempt to run the agenda, siphon away contact with athletes [through their official websites]. That's becoming a greater issue. I've noticed even over the last six months or so the number of times where announcements are made [on the club website], which is fine. But access is given, and it's totally unquestioned of course . . . it's basically press releases put on the Internet, rather than given to the journalists and then digested, who then ask questions and run a more journalistic version. They [club media managers] cottoned on to that as a very good way of staying 'on message' . . . and the Internet's a very powerful tool for doing that, because they can say, 'We're releasing it on the Internet, look we've provided all this information for our fans . . . ' (Interview with author)

A sports broadcaster found this use of websites as potential competition for established news organizations 'shocking' given the potential to marginalize journalists and to substitute critical journalism with 'propaganda':

> I think that's a shocking development. There was another case recently where [a player] was charged by police. The club did a press conference during the day where the chief executive spelt out everything to everyone and then [the player] did an interview for the club website. That's appalling on a whole number of levels, not least of which is that it's just propaganda . . . Why would the official website ask [the player] any of the relevant questions? He was able to mount his defense, his club endorsed defense without any scrutiny. Journalistically that's a shocking development . . . That's not the role of a club website anyway. They shouldn't be dealing with serious controversies. (Interview with author).

An ironic aspect of such complaints is that it is precisely the frequent wholesale reproduction of press releases, the uncritical reporting of leading athletes and clubs, absorption in matters of 'trivial controversy', and so on that has caused sports journalism to be criticized for failing to discharge its inquisitive, investigative, skeptical fourth-estate function (Boyle *et al.* 2010; Rowe 2005, 2007). Thus, in criticizing bloggers or official sports organization websites, there is a frequently unacknowledged gap between the idealized claims that professional sports journalism makes about itself, and the actual quality and nature of the work that it produces.[5]

In a networked digital media environment it is also increasingly difficult to separate and determine content authorship, origin, platform, cost, and benefit according to an agreed set of rules. The online sports editor discussed the use of his newspaper's material by fan-run websites:

> I have no problem with that because we then benefit from it. I think, again, the same rule should be applied that we use in stories. You need to attribute your material if you sourced it from someone, you need to actually acknowledge that, so it's the same thing for a fan site. And therefore the responsibility falls to the administrator of that site to ensure that the rules are followed . . . we're not hard and fast [about preventing use of our content] because we benefit from people linking to us. (Interview with author)

One of the aforementioned benefits of a light-touch approach to intellectual property rights is that, if the story is properly acknowledged, users of the fan site may link back to the newspaper website (depending, of course, on attribution). This constant shifting across and between sites and platforms presents the oft-mentioned problem of 'stickiness'—staying with a site for long enough to register and absorb textual content and, crucially, to be receptive to the advertising messages that underwrite it. There is, therefore, a continuing concern with enhancement, the 'value adding' that attracts users from other sites, and enables material that has been devised in one medium to be effectively repurposed for another:[6]

> The main thing is that you've just got to be conscious of providing depth to your coverage . . . and if you've sourced that story from a newspaper version, looking and saying, 'Well what else do we need to have with this story that is valuable to people who are seeing it in an online environment?' (Online sports editor, Interview with author)

There was also considerable awareness among our interviewees that, to some degree, large, formal media organizations (dubbed 'big media') had been 'dethroned' in a congested digital media environment. As a Web editor for a public broadcaster acknowledged, this trend has caused changes to his professional practice as a media worker and in his informal capacity as a sports fan:

> It really does demand of me that I know really quickly and well how to navigate the sites that I find most useful, most rewarding, most

interesting, because there's a lot of dross. That's the other thing . . . it seems to me once the journalist's job was actually finding information for people who simply didn't have information . . . That's the way the media worked in what seems to be its infancy or its middle period. People relied on organized media because it was impossible to do otherwise and now we are in a media space where organized media simply has to compete. It's a bigger competitor because of its technical and financial resources, but there's all sorts of extraordinary media exchanges and productions and collaborations that are occurring with no reference what so [ever] to the big media. (Interview with author)

Thus 'big media' constantly search for audiences and anxiously deploy multiple means of reaching them. The desperate, haphazard nature of this quest to match audiences and content is strikingly captured by the freelance sport journalist quoted above when describing media coverage mobilization around one major sports event:

I don't think anyone realized or really knew what sort of content was going to be consumed. So we were creating *all* these different contents hoping that we'd be serving the reader—or the consumer—in some way. But not really being sure how they liked their news, how they liked their coverage. And I think some newspapers actually invested so heavily in their online coverage that they stinted on their print coverage. (Interview with author)

The difficulty of navigating a digitally networked media terrain, where desirable content and the loyalty of users can be transitory, is a substantial problem for major media organizations. As a radio producer whose job also involves program website maintenance commented about the widespread use of social media:

The interesting thing the 'big media company' [organization name disguised] has found is that people are discussing you [online] whether you know about it or not. The same with [a major sports organization] . . . I'm sure these discussions are happening now. It's the case of whether you tap into that, how you engage with that in a way that doesn't just dominate the conversation, or censor comment . . . because you can't. (Interview with author)

Once again, the issue of control and release—both of media and their audiences—is emphasized. Sport journalists have found themselves reluctantly embroiled in struggles between large, formal news media companies and sports organizations on one side, and small, informal Web-based competitors on the other. In the digital environment, sports journalism is losing its double-edged reputation as the toy department *of* the news media. Instead, it appears to be one that is toyed *with* by competing corporate entities,

while its textual products become, in various ways and with both positive
and negative outcomes, the playthings of proliferating media platforms and
online users.

NEW TECHNOLOGIES, ONGOING DISPUTES

This chapter, after a brief overview of the development of sports journalism, focused first on legally contentious issues involved in the reporting
of sports news at a moment when the very definition of news and of the
accreditation of the journalists who report it are disputed. It addressed,
with specific reference to a landmark Australian parliamentary inquiry, the
vexed subject of fair and reasonable reportage in the context of actually
and potentially commodifiable media sport content. The Senate Standing
Committee report on 'The Reporting of Sports News and the Emergence of
Digital Media' (2009) was mostly inconclusive, and its recommendations
little more than tentative suggestions and reflections:

Recommendation 1
5.21 The committee urges the government to take into account
the opportunities and challenges presented by digital media to sports
organisations current and future revenue prospects and options, and
recommends that the current Crawford review of sports pay particular
attention to the capacity of sports to invest in digital innovation.[7]

Recommendation 2
5.23 The committee recommends that the parliament should not
amend copyright law to clarify the application of the news fair dealing exception, unless future specific case law outcomes appear to
warrant it.

Recommendation 3
5.25 The committee recommends that the government consider
and respond to the Copyright Law Review Committee report and its
recommendations.

Recommendation 4
5.38 The committee recommends that stakeholders negotiate media
access to sporting events based on the principle that all bona fide journalists, including photojournalists and news agencies, should be able to
access sporting events regardless of their technological platform.

Recommendation 5
5.39 In the event that these negotiations are unsuccessful, the committee recommends that the Minister consider initiating the process for

consideration of a code under Section 51AE of the Trade Practices Act.[8] (see Parliament of Australia Senate Standing Committee 2009, p. vii)

The inquiry had, however, brought together the contending parties in a manner that enabled the federal Minister for Broadband, Communications and the Digital Economy, Stephen Conroy, to convene a series of post-inquiry meetings presided over by the Chair of the ACCC. The clear implication of this arrangement was that, if no agreement on a code of practice could be reached, the mooted action under the Trade Practices Act (Recommendation 5) would force one. The outcome of these meetings was a 'Code of Practice for Sports News Reporting—Text, Photography and Data' (Department of Broadband, Communications and the Digital Economy 2010b). The code dealt only with digitized text, photographs, and factual information such as scores and team lists, and the accreditation of journalists, ignoring the most contentious matters surrounding the online retransmission of audiovisual footage from sports events, which were a key focus of debate during the inquiry's hearings. Instead, complicated disagreements over text-based and still image sports content could now be referred to an appointed mediator, whose powers are limited to acting in an 'advisory capacity' (p. 9). In the event that mediation does not resolve a dispute between a sport and news outlet over such matters as journalist accreditation, 'parties may pursue other commercial or legal options' (p.6)—just as they could prior to the inquiry. In other words, little changed, with the important exception that a new mechanism was created to *hear* disputes between aggrieved parties, but not to enforce rulings. In the key and most vexed area of online audiovisual footage, there was no advance.

Even in the restricted area where progress seemed to have been made, journalist accreditation, the capacity for rancorous disputation remained, especially at international sports events. Less than 18 months after the 'Code of Practice for Sports News Reporting—Text, Photography and Data' came into effect, and on the eve of the 2011 Rugby World Cup (RWC) in New Zealand, a dispute occurred between elements of the news media and tournament organizers. The cause of the conflict was the familiar issue of accreditation terms imposed by tournament organizers:

> Fairfax Media [publisher of *The Age* and *Sydney Morning Herald* national newspapers] . . . announced today that it refuses to sign accreditation for the Rugby World Cup to protect its editorial freedom.
>
> The publisher . . . will send journalists to cover the event but will be denied access to official World Cup venues by tournament organisers.
>
> Fairfax Media has been joined in its stance by News Ltd. (*Sydney Morning Herald* 2011)

The International Rugby Board (IRB) took the position that the amount of news reporting video material displayed on the websites of newspaper publishers should be restricted, and that, with particular concern for the 'ambushing' of event sponsors, video-based advertisements should not accompany match highlights. Echoing earlier complaints, newspaper publishers saw this requirement as an attempt 'to dictate what material may legitimately be used to report news', as well as part of a more general attempt to control how journalism is delivered, the number of photographs produced and circulated, and the types of platform on which they appear. Therefore, attention falls on the second principal focus of this chapter—the conflicted practices of sports journalists working in a chaotic, complex and contentious institutional and commercial environment.

According to Marcel Broersma (2010, pp. 30–31), drawing on Bourdieu's (2005) well-known concepts of *field* and *habitus*, 'Journalism can be conceptualized as a dynamic field of relations with specific conventions and routines—its *habitus*'. Journalism—like sport itself—has 'its own "rules of the game" that sustain belief in the structures and principles of the field, and are at stake in a continuous battle for symbolic power at the same time'. This chapter's analysis of the field of sports journalism has revealed how its 'structures and principles' are in flux, the 'rules of the game' have become loose and contentious, and the once relatively robust *habitus* of (especially male, print-based) sports journalists has turned fragile and permeable. These 'foot soldiers', as one of their number described them earlier, are not without symbolic power or cultural potency, but have been forced to retreat in some respects, and in others to advance with many more weapons in their productive armory. However, on the evidence available, the corporate and managerial 'generals' who direct sports journalists in the rapidly shifting field of networked media sport possess uneven conceptual and operational command of its current positions and emergent trajectories. In our punning chapter title description of sports journalism as a 'leaking craft', we have highlighted the difficulties of an occupational group that is increasingly permeable in the new environment of networked digital media sport. The next, penultimate chapter continues to investigate the changing experiences and future directions of media sport, albeit in a very different context—that of the sports computer game.

7   Computer Games and the Refashioning of Media Sport

The first sponsor to appear on the website of MFC (see Chapter 5) was Electronic Arts (EA) Sports, the globally dominant computer games developer and publisher. The conjunction of MFC and EA Sports encapsulates the intricate interaction between sport and computer gaming in the media sports cultural complex. Best-selling soccer games such as EA's *FIFA 11*—part of a series that has sold an estimated 100 million units over the past 18 years (Justin 2010)—are integrated into the routine experience of sport for many younger players and fans (Crawford 2006; Crawford & Gosling 2009; Conway 2010). EA Sports' decision to sponsor MFC was a clever marketing decision given the international news coverage Ebbsfleet United was receiving at the time of its takeover by MFC, but it also highlighted a significant feature of contemporary media sport: computer games play an ever-increasing but underappreciated role in the experience, form, and economics of sport.

The analysis in this book has sought to untangle many of the continuous and discontinuous dimensions of media sport as the shift from analogue-broadcast to digital-convergent systems proceeds. The following sections pursue this established line of investigation, analyzing EA Sports and the computer games industry, the interaction between games and broadcast television, the popularity of fantasy sports leagues, and the issue of gender and sports games. Familiar patterns of commodification are revealed, as well as examples of why it is appropriate to speak of sport *as* media, or sporting experiences that are ontologically and materially indivisible from media platforms and technologies. This chapter also reinforces the notion that an understanding of media sport requires appreciation of the interaction between different screens. Games are a pivotal link in transmedia sport experience, played on and moving between the television, desktop computer, tablet, and smartphone screen.

The intermeshing of digital interactive games, networked communications, and sport is producing outcomes that are unexpected and, to a degree, transformative. As the second-most popular genre behind action releases (Kuhn 2009, p. 267), sports games no longer just simulate competition and play, but interact directly with the social and physical world. An example of this phenomenon is the real-time weather feature of EA Sports' annually updated and hugely popular *Madden NFL* and *Tiger Woods PGA* [Professional Golfers' Association] *Tour* titles. For those playing with an Internet connection, in-game playing conditions are updated according to the prevailing local weather conditions at an actual course or stadium (for example, at Augusta, or Lambeau Field in Wisconsin). The gamer observes that snow or rain must be falling at this physical location as the game screen changes. Changeable weather introduces an element of unpredictability into game play conditions that parallels the challenges faced by professional athletes, as this comment posted in an online forum about the *Tiger Woods PGA Tour* game suggests:

> Then halfway through round 4, after all the CPU [central processing unit] players had finished, it started raining! This threw off my game, since I had already locked in my putting tempo, and now suddenly the greens were twice as slow . . . I had some trouble making birdies for a few holes. I hung in there and finished in the top 15, but it was touch and go there for a while. I have to admit, I felt really screwed, since all the other golfers had finished before the rain came (and I assume that the rainy conditions would affect their scores). So check the weather before you start playing. You never know. (brianlevine 2009)

The notable issue here is not the need for meteorological awareness by gamers, but the invisibility of the commercial relationship that makes this weather feature possible. The highly profitable Weather Channel, which is present in over 90 percent of cabled American households, provides a live data feed to EA Sports that affects in-game play. This arrangement reflects a development outlined in Toby Miller's (2007, pp. 144–76) critique of neo-liberal media marketization and the Weather Channel. This television channel has managed successfully to commercialize and mediatize the natural elements, distancing the viewer from the 'direct experience of life' by diverting attention from the heavens outside and towards the screen inside. Networked sports gaming is producing a similar dynamic, traversing the boundaries of the real and simulated, technology and nature, and outdoor and indoor sport.

Sports games produce a remediating effect that is manifest in representational, economic, and material terms. Presented in their widely read 1999 book, *Remediation: Understanding New Media*, Jay Bolter and Richard Grusin argue that no medium or screen works in isolation from others. New technologies refashion older media, which then adjust to and answer the challenge of new media (p. 15). Remediation has been occurring for several centuries in painting, printing, and photography, each medium responding to the others by absorbing and critiquing their aesthetics and social effects. This multi-directional repurposing of media influences ways of seeing and perceiving reality and informs cultural assumptions about the logic of immediacy. A spin-off technology from the invention and mass production of the microprocessor in the mid-1970s (Winston 1998, pp. 232–37), computer games played a minor role in the remediation processes in media sport for several decades. However, the advent of networked gaming, high-speed computing, and the popularity of powerful consoles sold by multinational firms such as Microsoft, Sony, and Nintendo altered this situation, enabling photo-realistic rendering and greater sensory immersion in games (Kline, Dyer-Witheford & de Peuter 2003; King & Krzywinska 2006). Applying the argument of Bolter and Grusin, games now perform potent cultural 'work' as a lucrative and popular form of media that circulates through transnational communications networks. Games are also present intertextually in film, television, art, and tactical media (Dyer-Witheford & de Peuter 2009; Jenkins 2005; Rehak 2003; Silberman 2009).[1]

In the case of sport, games are a force for remediation as they appropriate 'the techniques, forms, and social significance' of popular media sport texts and 'rival or refashion them in the name of the real' (see Bolter & Grusin 1999, p. 63; Plymire 2009). EA Sports' long-standing motto, 'If it's in the game, it's in the game',[2] captures this notion perfectly, seeking to elevate the measure of realistic media sport representation to the level of hypermediacy through computer games. Titles such as *NHL 12* assimilate the aesthetic conventions of television coverage and the information-processing capacities of computing and the Internet. Seeing 'through' the types of camera angles and commentary used in the broadcast of matches, the gamer is invited into a digital media space featuring avatars that resemble the appearance and abilities of professional athletes from the past and the present. This is an interactive social experience where gamers control much of the action. As discussed later in the chapter, the seductiveness and appeal of this experience has meant that game technologies and aesthetics have begun to infiltrate live sports television broadcasts and influence the on-field performance of athletes.

Released in 2006, the final and sixth installment of the famed *Rocky* boxing movies, *Rocky Balboa*, is a good example of remediation in action. The familiar narrative of this film about the frequently battered and retired champion fighter played by Sylvester Stallone (Cummins 2006) uses a computer game as a trigger for the drama that follows. The all-male members of a weekly television sport panel show are seen debating the identity of the greatest fighter of all time. Rather than limit discussion to the usual clichéd to-and-fro between panel members that is characteristic of such programs, the host declares, 'Let's see what the computer has to say'. Attention turns to a computer game that resembles EA Sports' *Fight Night* (cf. Baerg 2007) and a simulation of a fight between the reigning world champion, Mason 'The Line' Dixon, and the champion of yesteryear, Rocky 'The Italian Stallion' Balboa. During the course of the in-game fight, cut-away scenes show television viewers at home and in bars cheering on the digital combatants, culminating in a 'murderous right hook' by Balboa's avatar that knocks out Dixon. This result produces 'real-world' effects, upsetting Dixon and members of his entourage and setting in train a series of events that sees Balboa emerge from retirement for one last fight against Dixon, during which Rocky heroically sustains another beating. Film, television sport, and computer game move in and through each other in this example, each performing different roles in the structure of the text and the creation of meaning. The intersections between these different media forms are made apparent by the fact that the *Rocky* films had previously been made into several tie-in computer game releases between 1983 and 2006 (Crawford 2008, p. 141). The use of a computer game in *Rocky Balboa* signals a normalization of this medium in the presentation of media sport, and reflects the high level of realism that sports games are able to sustain. We now turn to the business practices that have led to this situation.

'WASH, RINSE, AND REPEAT'

As discussed at the outset of this book, the stereotypical distinction between 'jocks' and 'geeks' has become increasingly meaningless—or at least compromised in both experiential and symbolic terms—over recent years. Interactive entertainment technologies and gaming cultures are now an important feature of global media sport, with EA and its specialist sport division, EA Sports, central to this change. EA is not the only major developer of sports titles—others include 2K Sports and Konami—but it has performed a pioneering role in their development, publication, and marketing since the 1980s. The company's founder, Trip Hawkins, is credited with the invention and refinement of a technique that has produced consistently and, at times, spectacularly profitable sports titles. He began by paying US$25,000 to Philadelphia 76ers legend Julius 'Dr J.' Irving for the right to use his name and image in a basketball game. Hawkins later acknowledged that this deal was a bargain: 'Of course, you'd be lucky to do anything today for even ten times that amount' (Kent 2001, p. 265). Irving's consent led to an approach by Hawkins to the manager of Boston Celtic star Larry Bird[3] and the subsequent 1984 release of *Dr J. and Larry Bird Go One-on-One* for the Commodore 64 and Apple II personal computers (Kent 2001, pp. 265–66). The success of Hawkins' strategy led to another sports title produced along the same lines, *Madden NFL* (first released in 1986), which has since become one of the biggest game franchises of all time (Oates 2009; Dittmer 2009). Highlighting a long-term relationship between television aesthetics and game play, the icon of this series is NFL television commentator of almost 30 years standing, John Madden.[4]

Impressive sales figures for EA Sports titles entrenched a widely applied formula where sports games are developed, released, and then re-released on an annual basis with new cover art, updated team lists, the latest rules, and 'tweaked' game mechanics. In this regard, the practice resembles the rapid turnover of playing strip designs and colors in several team sports that seek to stimulate a continuous upgrading of paraphernalia. Presently producing many games from its Canadian headquarters, EA Sports has mastered the production of 'wash, rinse, and repeat' sports games (Florian 2004; Dyer-Witheford & de Peuter 2009). These games are licensed by professional sports federations across a range of codes and competitions, including golf, ice hockey, baseball, motor racing (NASCAR[5]), soccer, rugby union, and cricket. Once staffed by a handful of programmers and support staff working under the guidance of Hawkins, the entire EA operation has expanded to employ almost 9,000 people in multiple international locations, regularly reports annual net revenue in the range of US\$4 billion, and publishes around 70 titles a year across all genres (Dyer-Witheford & de Peuter 2009, p. 39; *Electronic Arts* 2010).

The influence of EA Sports in the global media sport industries has, then, been considerable. It has helped to build an entirely new layer of mediatization and commodification of sport, both simulating sports competitions and altering the ways in which they are played and watched by millions of people (Dyer-Witheford & de Peuter 2009, p. 47). EA Sports' groundbreaking commercial success has seen the emergence of competing developers and publishers that specialize in the sport genre and release titles for console, desktop, and handheld computer game devices. An experienced director of media and communications for a national sport, who admitted to having no personal interest in gaming, outlined how his mindset changed over time as he observed a marked expansion in the number of sports games available for purchase. His sport ultimately negotiated a deal to produce a game in partnership with a competitor of EA Sports, but which replicated the proven wash, rinse, and repeat sequence. An initial multiplatform game release was followed shortly after by another edition that contained updated player and team lineups:

> We didn't have one for many years and then several years ago got one out and then got another one out and they're huge! They both sold extremely well, the game and the redo . . . There's no doubt gaming is part of the [sports] world and people love it. (Interview with author)

Opinions such as this indicate that digital games are an integral part of an overall media strategy that interlocks with broadcast, print, online, and mobile media, with each medium used to promote and direct attention towards the other. Gaming is, therefore, increasingly seen as 'part of the [sports] world' rather than as a contrived simulation of it. For example, advertisements and user forums dedicated to a game are displayed on the website of a sport, the website is mentioned or shown during television broadcasts, text messages are sent to the mobile phones of fans announcing competitions to win the latest computer game, and official game-day

programs feature advertisements and stories about athlete appearances at
the official launch of an updated game title. In turn, the computer game
release reproduces the logos and sponsors of the sport, the teams, players,
and the voices of television network commentators. The release of a title
that sells well and makes a solid return on investment also introduces the
option of additional licensing contracts, with more remuneration potentially available if a sport is willing to sign a deal for a platform-exclusive
game (i.e., available only on Xbox, Playstation, or Wii). The media manager
of an internationally staged sports competition outlined during a research
interview that his sport completed a deal with a game studio connected to
Microsoft Xbox. The popularity of the Xbox console among 'hardcore'
gamers and the proven ability of the studio to produce quality follow-up
releases informed this decision:

> It [the game] was unbelievably successful in this part of the world and
> even in others. It was the highest selling game for several years in a
> platform sense and continues to do so with the Xbox 360. We haven't
> updated it in the last 18 months but there is a view from Xbox that they
> will do a new version in the next year. I think that makes a difference
> to the gamer because we change deliveries every year, we change venues
> every year, and we grow every year. Things change a lot and that cur-
> rency is really important in our sort of game. (Interview with author)

Sports games are a relatively new cultural and technological commodity
designed to service an age-old profit maximization strategy. Their commercial appeal lies in their capture and stimulation of concentrated fan and
gamer attention and the additional exposure that they offer to sponsors,
advertisers, teams, and athletes.

Writing in *Games of Empire: Global Capitalism and Video Games*
(2009, pp. 35–68), Nick Dyer-Witheford and Greig de Peuter offer an incisive assessment of EA Sports as an exemplar of 'cognitive capitalism'—a
mode of production in which knowledge and knowledge workers are the
productive forces that generate valuable media content:

> EA's game development studios, rinse-and-repeat game franchises,
> high-intensity marketing, fanatical corporate culture, and U.S.-based
> but transnationally distributed production webs provide a state-of-the-
> art example of how to make billions from digital play. (pp. xxx–xxxi)

Elite level sport is prized intellectual property in the console game market,
which is why smaller developers and publishers attempt to compete with EA
Sports for licensing rights. High-profile leagues and competitions such as the
NFL, NBA, and EPL are established brands connected to massive fan-bases
that invest considerable time, emotion, and capital following the fortunes of
competitors and teams. A title that allows gamers to enter and interact with

the environments that they see on television and in stadiums is, from the perspective of those positioned to capitalize on these sporting commitments, a 'low-risk cash cow' (p. 46). While reliable figures are difficult to locate, the cost of updating a title such as *Madden NFL* is thought to be in the vicinity of US$10 million or more. The President of EA Sports, Peter Moore, has stated publicly that the 2009 iteration of *Madden NFL* generated US$133 million in its first month of release (Dumitrescu 2008). EA Sports' investment also produces spin-off products such as *Madden* for mobile, a game that appears regularly in 'most downloaded title' lists. The interpenetration of game and television screens that underpins this popularity is both socially and textually evident. In 2008, Nielsen research reported that television ratings for NFL fixtures were 44 percent higher in video-gaming households than non-gaming households (Foran 2008). The capital generated by game sales also led to the production of a tie-in reality television series, *Madden Nation*. Screened on ESPN and running for four seasons from 2005, this show featured skilled *Madden NFL* players competing for a US$100,000 prize in an elimination format competition that travelled from city to city and culminated in a final, staged in Times Square, New York.

An observation made in the field of computer games studies is that the large-scale business and commercial interests described here have broken the 'magic circle' of free play—a bounded space set apart from normal life that has historically existed as a cherished part of cultural life and human interaction (Huizinga 1955; Harambam, Aupers & Houtman 2011). This contentious critique (Consalvo 2009) connects with the experience of many workers who have pursued superficially 'exciting' careers in the production and development of sports computer games, only to find that life at the lower end of the production chain involves deadening workplace routines and no time for free play (Miller 2006, 2010b; Johns 2006). The opportunities for creation and enjoyment of 'gamespace' (Wark 2007) belie the labor conditions and commercial strategies that create them. EA Sports became synonymous with game production and delivery systems that removed the fun from games in the mid-2000s. The coding, design, artistic, writing, audio, and testing requirements of major titles are resource intensive, involving teams of 100 or more people working long hours. A blog post titled, 'EA: The Human Story', written by ea_spouse (2004), uncovered a high level of discontent among employees working for many games studios. Having been the subject of widespread attention and detailed analysis (see Dyer-Witheford & de Peuter 2009; Miller 2010b; Briton 2010), this online post is a savage condemnation of worker exploitation in the creative industries, characterized by short-term employment contracts, uneven wage structures, and demanding production schedules (see McRobbie 2005; Deuze 2007; Ross 2009; Sennett 1998). The commentary authored by ea_spouse pinpointed the instrumentalist logic of EA Sports' mass consumption games and the high level of stress endured in their production:

EA's bright and shiny new corporate trademark is 'Challenge Everything'. Where this applies is not exactly clear. Churning out one licensed football game after another doesn't sound like challenging much of anything to me; it sounds like a money farm . . . The current mandatory hours are 9am to 10pm—seven days a week—with the occasional Saturday evening off for good behavior (at 6:30pm). This averages out to an eighty-five hour work week . . . The stress is taking its toll. After a certain number of hours spent working the eyes start to lose focus; after a certain number of weeks with only one day off fatigue starts to accrue and accumulate exponentially. There is a reason why there are two days in a weekend—bad things happen to one's physical, emotional, and mental health if these days are cut short . . . And the kicker: for the honor of this treatment EA salaried employees receive a) no overtime; b) no compensation time! ('comp' time is the equalization of time off for overtime—any hours spent during a crunch accrue into days off after the product has shipped); c) no additional sick or vacation leave. The time just goes away. (ea_spouse 2004)

Significantly, this critique has been followed by another online complaint by 'Rockstar Spouse' (2010; Huntemann 2010), relaying a complaint about unpaid overtime and workplace stress at the Rockstar Games studio in San Diego. Another report has emerged about allegedly 'appalling working conditions' at Team Bondi Studios in Sydney (McMillen 2011).[6]

The consistent focus of discontent for game development staff is 'crunch time': an 'ostensibly unusual period of crisis in the production schedule' when the race to debug, test, and complete a game by its scheduled launch date places severe demands on employees (Dyer-Witheford & de Peuter 2009, p. 59). The accusation made by disgruntled staff against major developers is that crunch time is no longer unusual, but a deliberately planned feature of production. This 'crisis' period places unreasonable demands on employees often working in non-unionized workplaces, and demoralizes those unable to keep up the exhausting pace, especially those with family responsibilities and domestic commitments. Indeed, the male dominance of sport depicted in many of the games churned out annually tends to mirror gender divisions in the workplace. Industry surveys suggest that between 4 and 11 percent of staff are female, with women concentrated in support roles such as public relations, human resources, and operations (IGDA 2005, p. 13; Crossley 2010). The response of some game development companies to these widespread complaints and imbalances has been to revise policies applying to overtime compensation and working conditions, while for others it is to transfer production activities to overseas sites where labor laws are less rigorously developed, applied or enforced. Following a fall in market valuation during 2008, EA Sports announced that it would be moving up to 20 percent of its production activities to 'low-cost regions' in India and eastern Europe, highlighting the transience and precariousness that characterize working life for many so-called knowledge workers (Dyer-Witheford & de Peuter 2009, p. 68). The next section outlines additional significant connections between games, commercial strategies, and social spaces, such as television presentation and athlete performance.

CHANGING TELEVISION, CHANGING SPORT

Computer games have become an identifiable presence in the broadcast and coverage of professional sport. Jacob Dittmer (2009) describes the gradual appearance of a 'Madden aesthetic' in the television coverage of NFL matches with the use of above-the-field camera angles that resemble the perspective of the gamer in *Madden NFL*. Similar practices are evident in soccer and motor racing, where the camera angles used during broadcasts and the perspectives offered in games develop symbiotically; a phenomenon that is understandable given the international best-selling status of *FIFA Soccer* and numerous racing titles. The most notable examples of remediation are when made-for-television sport attempts to simulate computer games. Played between 2002 and 2008 in a professional league format, Slamball was promoted as 'non-stop, hard-hitting, human video game action' (Waters 2003, p. 5). Screened in the US, Portugal, Spain, Italy, and Australia, Slamball is a form of basketball with four trampolines placed in front of each net and played on a court surrounded by plexiglass walls. The high-flying acrobatics of the professional players and the body contact on display were designed to portray 'video-gaming gone human' (Waters 2003, p. 5). Deliberately manipulating the line between a sport and computer game saw Slamball attract Microsoft Xbox as a principal advertiser. Television commercials were screened during breaks in play for new release Nintendo, Sega, and Xbox games. Slamball's significance lies not in its long-term appeal (our observation is that boredom tends to set in for the viewer once the novelty of the Slamball format subsides). Rather, Slamball matters because enough ESPN and CBS network executives were convinced that a sport–computer game hybrid was worth investing in and screening. Slamball held out the promise of bridging the sport–game divide and delivering new advertisers, sponsors, and audiences.

The remediation of television sport extends beyond aesthetics and the mutation of sporting codes to the convergence of delivery platforms. The Emmy award-winning EA Virtual Sports Playbook was the result of a formal partnership between ESPN and EA Sports, allowing television commentators to provide analysis as they walk among life-sized avatars generated by EA Sports games (Fry 2009; Koranteng 2010; for an example, see ESPN Video 2009). Marketed as an 'augmented reality' technology, this facility enhances the analysis of tactics by match commentators. Initially demonstrated during NFL and NCAA football broadcasts, the Playbook has since been used during the NBA play-offs and the 2010 soccer World Cup in South Africa. The objective of these presentational techniques is, according to EA Sports President Peter Moore, to make gaming technology an accepted part of sports broadcasting:

> There is something about the combination of the real and virtual worlds that captures viewers' imagination, especially the younger demographics; and once they've seen it, it is accepted as normal. (Quoted in Koranteng 2010)

The multiscreen strategy of EA Sports and ESPN during the World Cup was evident in the use of EA Sports' Playbook during the television coverage and the release of a computer game, *2010 FIFA World Cup South Africa*, for the major consoles. This EA Sports title included all the stadiums used during the World Cup and offered online updates to reflect the latest playing squads and advertising hoardings used during the tournament. Game technology was embedded within the World Cup's television coverage, which then referred back to a computer game that simulated and built upon the television experience enjoyed by both viewers and gamers.

Game technologies are also used to enhance the media experience of sports that command sizable resources and fan-bases but marginal television and media attention, and which may not be particularly 'telegenic' or television-friendly. For instance, the distances on the water involved in professional powerboat and yacht racing often prevent close-range television coverage. The challenge of covering races is to communicate the position and movements of boats on the water back to viewers and spectators in real-time. A response to this problem has been the use of gaming technologies to generate a television-like experience for the online computer user. A company called Virtual Spectator has deployed GPS locative media and 3D gaming technologies to present 'realistic' race action as it unfolds offshore. Users are also able to select the 'camera' angle and individual boat that they want to track. Speaking at a media industry event, the promoters of this product describe how they want to create a 'cool, 3D, game-like experience', an effect made possible by 'the convergence of gaming and virtual spectator technology whereby the platforms are near-on identical' (*Sport Business* 2008, p. 33). For audiences, the purchase and use of the latest digital media technologies prevent few barriers to access given the levels of wealth and privilege enjoyed by many members of the nautical racing community (McKay 1991). The Virtual Spectator platform was also used for the 2008–09 edition of the Volvo 'Round the World' Ocean Race, an international yachting event conducted every three years. In addition to the coverage offered by the official website and various online sources, a 3D Race Viewer app was produced for the Apple iPhone that allowed users to check race positions round-the-clock on their mobile handset. This app sat alongside a successful online game that claimed over 60,000 players a day over the course of the event (see Figure 7.1; Sailing Sponsorship Editor 2009). Accessing the map and weather data used by the eight boats in the race, 'virtual captains' raced against their real-life counterparts as they sailed between nine countries over 127 days. A new edition of this game is part of the 2011–12 event. In fashioning an event for the competitor, spectator, and game player, the Ocean Race presents multiple applications for the same digital communications and locational media technologies. These tools are critical for the racing yachts facing changeable and potentially perilous conditions at sea, users interested in tracing the up-to-the-minute progress of boats, and gamers engaged in online competition.

Sportspeople can be gamers too. In particular, many male athletes play the games in which their photo-realistic avatars appear. Their reasons for playing vary, encompassing leisure-time enjoyment, taking (perhaps narcissistic) pleasure in the fact that they appear in a game, and motivation to improve their on-field performance and training. Lauren Silberman (2009) provides examples that highlight the link between the social world of professional football and computer gaming. Returning to the case of *Madden NFL*, each new edition of the game provides updated player rankings

Figure 7.1   Screenshot taken of the Volvo Ocean Race Game website. The copyright for this image is held by *UnitedGames*/Volvo Ocean Race SLU, 2011

measured on a 100-point scale. Many NFL players value a high ranking when it is assigned to their avatar. Defensive end Erasmus James stated in an interview with Silberman that members of his team play *Madden* together regularly, explaining that 'how your player is and how you play in *Madden* is a bragging right' (Silberman 2009, p. 174). Poor rankings are cause for upset, as Isaiah Ekejiuba of the Detroit Lions showed when he received the equal worst player rating of the 1,721 listed in the 2008 version of the game: 'I know my skills. I've played against a lot of guys that I'm better than . . . This really upsets me' (Quoted in Scott 2007, p. 42). Former New York Giant Michael Strahan conveyed the same feeling of disappointment when he described the connection between the limited skills of his on-screen avatar and his motivation to become a better player:

> My character in *Madden* sucked. I was the worst guy on the team . . . but it made me want to work harder. I seriously wanted to get better in real life so I wasn't so bad in *Madden*. (Quoted in Silberman 2009, p. 173)

As Strahan indicates, improved performance statistics over the course of an NFL season are rewarded by a better rating in the next edition of the game. Most of the athletes that Silberman spoke to for her research confirmed that they played 'themselves'. This preference produces another opportunity for public promotion by EA Sports and the NFL. Started in 1995, the *Madden Bowl* event is held on the Super Bowl weekend each year. Streamed live on ESPN3 in 2011, invited NFL footballers play *Madden NFL* against each other in an elimination format tournament, with the winners awarded a trophy and recognition in the next edition of the game (Gaudiosi 2011). Here the deliberate integration of the physical event, athletes and computer game is clearly manifest.

The market dominant sports in Australia also have licensed game titles, including *AFL Live*, *Rugby League 3*, *Wallabies Rugby Challenge*, and *International Cricket 2010*. None of these games rivals the publicity and industry built around the *Madden NFL* franchise, although they report consistently strong sales. A media officer for a football club explained that many of the players own the title that they feature in. The amount of time professional athletes aged in their late teens and 20s spend gaming is a by-product of full-time professionalism. Sportspeople cannot train 'every minute of the day' and many use their 'downtime' to play games:

> The vast majority of them play these games, so they're very savvy in that they know what the games are and how to play them and they enjoy them. (Interview with author)

It is notable that this choice of free-time activity is sport-centered and blurs the boundary between work and play among professional athletes. The media officer chaperoned game development staff when they visited his club to capture the images and movements of players for a forthcoming title. He observed that the footballers appeared enthusiastic about the prospect of appearing in a game and largely uninterested in the issue of remuneration:

> We had the game guys taking the photos at the start of the year— 'Stand this way, wide, tight, raise your arms'. Each player stood there for three or four minutes having photos taken from various angles so they can build these images of them, which was pretty cool to watch . . . so they're [the players] like, 'Great, sweet, no worries', 'Take the photos', and all that sort of stuff. They asked, 'When's the game coming out?' They were told the back end of next year and they were like, 'Sweet, okay cool, no worries'. So they're kind of chuffed [pleased] to be involved. The whole issue of images rights hasn't been around long enough here for it to automatically enter their heads. (Interview with author)

A conspicuous feature of his comments was the lack of player interest in the connection between their avatars, the profits generated by the games industry, and the amount of money that they receive for the use of their likenesses.[7] This attitude contrasts with the US where escalating legal battles over the use of athlete images and statistics in computer games and fantasy sports leagues have occurred (Cianfrone & Baker 2010; Evans 2007–2008). Europe has also witnessed legal action over sports games, including a group of footballers in Belgium who took five games publishers to court over unlicensed use of their names and likenesses (Boyle & Haynes 2004, pp. 91–92).[8] The comparatively small size of the Australian market compared to North America and Europe helps to explain this difference. For instance, the production cycle for an EA Sports title dwarfs that of an Australian rules or rugby union game. EA Sports has hosted the widely publicized 'EA Sports Draft Camp', where basketball players about to enter the annual NBA player draft undertake lengthy motion-capture sessions (Silberman 2009, p. 169).[9] This recording mechanism allows the face, body, and movement of draftees to be captured accurately for the next edition of the console game *NBA Live*. Each new version of *FIFA Soccer* also involves capturing around 150 player moves a day over the course of a regimented five-day period (Stuart 2010). It can be observed that such imaging and surveillance is another means by which the 'technologized' sporting body can be disciplined through intensive monitoring (Magdalinski 2009). By contrast, capturing the visual data for an individual footballer in Australia involves only a 'three or four minute' digital photo and imaging session. The outcome is an in-game likeness that resembles the player, but which falls well short of the accuracy evident in many EA Sports titles.

Sportspeople play computer games for reasons besides having fun, including training and competition preparation. These motives are similar to those of aircraft pilots and members of the military who have long used flight and combat simulators for scenario testing and mission preparation. In the case of war games and first-person shooters, the demand of the defense forces for accurate and immersive battlefield simulations has established and funded a 'military–civilian co-development' process for games (Dyer-Witheford & de Peuter 2009, p. 104), a phenomenon reflecting the military-entertainment complex that gave birth to the games industry (Herz 1997; Kline *et al.* 2003). An early example of co-development occurred in 1981 when a group of retired US Army Generals engaged Atari to produce a version of the tank warfare arcade game, *Battlezone*, for battlefield training purposes (Kent 2001, pp. 153–54).[10] Co-development now sees different versions of a console and PC game like *Full Spectrum Warrior* produced for the consumer entertainment market and specialist military needs. The military version reproduces accurate conflict-zone conditions based upon available intelligence (Dyer-Witheford & de Peuter 2009, pp. 97–122). Military–civilian cooperation has assisted in the pursuit of realism in commercially released games by offering access to information about the specifications of the latest weapons, equipment, and battle scenarios. In return, the military is able to use the games industry to subsidize the cost of innovation, training and recruitment advertising (Kline *et al.* 2003, p. 101). While structured differently, the relationship between EA Sports and a major international sports federation such as FIFA functions according to a similar mutually beneficial logic. Each new edition of a game offers benefits in terms of engagement with sports fans and gamers, creates additional applications for up-to-date statistics and information about players and teams, and increases media and screen exposure for broadcasters, sponsors, and advertisers.

There is growing evidence that the benefits described here are spreading to the preparation of professional athletes for competition, although it should be noted that the uptake of computer games for this purpose is unevenly spread both within and across sports. Games are of greatest use-value for pursuits requiring a high level of familiarity with changing course and track conditions such as golf and motor racing. Playing games enables competitors to gain a sense of the environment that they will experience and allows them to anticipate some of the challenges presented by physical conditions.

The use of simulated digital environments took place in the mid-1990s when the US bobsled team prepared for the 1998 winter Olympics by 'racing' on the track that they would confront at Nagano (Miah 2002, p. 230). At about the same time, Canadian Formula One driver Jacques Villeneuve used a racing simulation as part of his preparation for the Belgian Grand Prix, which he subsequently won (Clarke, McBride & Reece 2002). NASCAR driver, Carl Edwards, has adopted the same strategy, stating that he finds playing the NASCAR video game helpful in approaching tracks that he finds difficult to drive: 'A video game helps you get the rhythm down— helps you find a place where speed is made up and speed is lost' (Quoted in Silberman 2009). In consultation with coaching staff, a convert to Australian football, Israel Folau, plays *AFL Live* on Playstation to improve his positional play and understanding of the code (*Fox Sports* 2011). Simulations have also proven beneficial in sports such as rough water kayaking, where training can involve a significant risk of injury (Clarke *et al.* 2002, p. 220; Fairweather 2002, pp. 241–42). These examples indirectly connect with the routine application of computer aided drafting and digital modeling in the production of sport equipment (Miah 2002, p. 230).

The increasing affordability of computer processing power and memory storage over the past 15 years has meant that the modeling undertaken by computer game manufacturers can reproduce racetracks and golf courses with impressive accuracy. Advances in this regard are conspicuous in golf, where the 18-hole courses available in *Tiger Woods PGA Tour* are built from data collected by ground-based, survey-grade GPS mapping and aerial stereo photography (Clayton 2011). Selected professional PGA competitors have explained how this game helps them prepare for courses including TPC Sawgrass, St Andrews, and Pinehurst, especially if they have not played on them before. After his debut at The Masters, 22-year-old American Rickie Fowler made the following comment:

> When I played Augusta for the first time, I learned that seeing it on the game can teach you quite a bit about the course . . . It's pretty crazy how close they got it to being like it is on the real course. The game helps you with your angles off the tees a bit, and it gives you an overhead view that is very helpful. And the breaks on the greens are pretty true. (Quoted in Clayton 2011)

Fellow PGA professionals Keegan Bradley and Edoardo Molinari concur with this statement. (The fact that these golf players also appear in the game suggests that commercial interest may also relate to the expression of these opinions.) Other game-based orientation strategies include elite college basketball and soccer players who play computer games in order to familiarize themselves with the defensive tactics and playing styles of upcoming opponents (Silberman 2009, pp. 167–69). It should not, however, be assumed from these examples that computer games are a core component of training regimes in high-performance sport. Rather, digital games and simulations have been steadily assimilated into an extensive menu of available training resources from which coaches and athletes can select.

The refashioning of sport and physical activity by game technologies continues through inventive applications for the home television. 'Physical technologies' (Francombe 2010) such as the Nintendo Wii and Microsoft Kinect for Xbox 360 reinscribe the experience of movement, play, and gaming through interactive media technologies, particularly for young people growing up with games (cf. Millington 2009).[11] Games such as *Wii Sports, Wii Fit, Kinect Sports,* and *Fitness Evolved* transcend the distinction made between 'lean back' or 'lean forward' media technologies by encouraging the player to swing, kick, stretch, balance, throw, and jump about in front of a television set. These technologies are an astute response to cultural anxieties about the sedentary and inactive lifestyle habits of children, importing the movement, skill, and exertion of outdoor sport and exercise into the living room (Giddings & Kennedy 2010, p. 167).[12] In the case of the Wii, this dimension of its design and marketing was a central concern, even at the concept phase of its development. In the minds of the Nintendo design team, the console needed to 'endear itself to families' (especially mothers) and be 'approachable for anyone' (Inoue 2010, pp. 38, 45). The Wii's intuitive interface has been created in order to give families the opportunity to play together and to support games such as *Wii Fit* where it is possible to 'really work up a sweat' (Inoue 2010, p. 76). Their inherently sociable characteristics can also be seen as a counter to the individual isolation of some gaming formats. The game-play mechanics of the Wii and Kinect possess uneven correspondence to conventional sports, but they are further evidence that the experience and understanding of sport is increasingly a mediated phenomenon. Speaking from personal experience, it is instructive to witness first-time players of *Wii Sports* or *Kinect Sports* volunteer remarks about the similarities and differences between in-game tennis, golf, or ten-pin bowling and 'the real thing', as well as the immediate smile that these games elicit from a player who hits their first clean shot. *Tiger Woods PGA Tour* for the Wii console demonstrates this comparison by using the remote as a virtual club, simulating head speed and the curve placed on the ball at the point of impact according to the movement of the gamer's hands.

Developments in physical technology and gaming are connected to ongoing experiments in the field of human–computer interaction. Prototype designs of exertion games ('exergames')—large-scale 'computer games that make you sweat' (Mueller 2009)—played a role in the development of the Kinect device, and are representative of an overall design path targeting the structural alignment of sport and screen-based interfaces. The product of internationally funded academic research, exertion games enact the concept of 'sports played over a distance' and include table tennis for three, jogging over a distance, and shadow boxing (Mueller 2009). An objective of this advanced mode of gaming is, according to an interaction design researcher, to bridge the gap between outdoor sport and gaming by 'combining the advantages of both' (Interview with author). He described why playing a game on a Wii console lacks the instantaneous sensory feedback that occurs between competitors in outdoor competition:

> There is a parallel competition between us when we play tennis on the Wii and on the screen there is an offense-defense element. But our movements don't match anymore, so I mean I hit, the ball flies in the virtual world, comes back to your side of the screen and you react

offensively or defensively. But you don't get the immediate feeling that I put exertion in. It's missing feedback. (Interview with author)

Exergames attempt to overcome this sensory deficit. Watching video footage of these games in action (see exertioninterfaces.com) illustrates how they generate the synchronized experience of sport. Participants react instantly and vigorously to each other, but over a distance via screens:

> And that's what makes these things so interesting . . . here all of a sudden we have a parallel physical activity but there are two players that bump into each other, that have a ball and share a ball on the screen. It is that 'match' [between the competitors] that the designer really has to think about. (Interview with author)

In addition to playing a role in commercial game development, the consistent generation of this 'match' is likely to produce games and simulations that are readily useful for sports coaching and training techniques. These developments reflect an overall intensification of the orientation of sport towards screens and digital media devices. As this section has shown, this orientation is widening and subtly reworking the practices and embodied understandings that create the collective meaning and experience of sport and physical activity. This trajectory is driven by both profitable commercial relationships and the spread of games and gaming technologies into everyday media use. The following section examines these developments in relation to the growth of fantasy sports competitions.

FANTASY SPORTS

The popularity of online fantasy sports has mushroomed internationally over the past 10 years, quickly becoming another prominent component of transmedia sport experience. Leagues are available for most major sports, allowing users to assemble a playing roster selected from the full range of athletes competing for each team in a specific competition. Played for prizes, money, and/or prestige among peers, participants perform the role of owner or general manager of their team, selecting and transferring team members who accumulate points based on the statistics and performance of their real-life athlete counterparts (see Lomax 2006). The number of fantasy sports participants in the US and Canada is thought to be in excess of 30 million, with football leagues alone claiming over 20 million players (Dwyer & Kim 2011, p. 71). The money spent on this activity by users is annually around US$800 million (Dwyer & Drayer 2010, p. 207). The appeal of fantasy sports has spread to the UK, with well over one million registered participants competing in the official fantasy game of the EPL alone. Strong participation figures are also evident in Germany, Nordic countries, and several fast-growing markets in the Asia-Pacific, including Australia and Singapore (Fry 2008b). Networked computing, broadband Internet, and the real-time collection and manipulation of statistical data have created a high-powered platform that has transformed fantasy sports from a highly localized pastime played by friends on table-tops with pen and paper to a mass market networked media sport phenomenon.

Fantasy sports are an *attention multiplier*, maximizing the amount of attention paid by participants to sport on television and in the press. Many enthusiasts spend around five to six hours a week managing their team and following the progress of players, draftees, and potential 'bargain buys' through various news media and information sources. The most dedicated fantasy players can spend over 10 hours a week working on their teams, with studies suggesting that 60 percent of participants spend over an hour a day just thinking about their team and 85 percent spend over half-an-hour (Nesbit & King 2010, p. 26). While these figures are contestable, there is no doubt that millions of people spend considerable amounts of time each week—and while in work, educational, and leisure contexts—playing these games and adding to their overall commercial value. These habits were confirmed by a self-confessed fantasy sports 'obsessive' aged in his twenties:

> I was literally just at a friend's house and we spent an hour just talking about it [his 'Dream Team' AFL fantasy league] . . . When the website opened in February, I probably spent about five hours on it just going through everybody, getting to know the pricing and everything. I stay up-to-date with the Internet forums and there are specific sites I read. I just keep up-to-date as much as I can. But it's been funny to see the last few years. It's become cool or normal now to play fantasy sports. In 2002, only the obsessives knew about it, but now literally everybody talks about it. It's getting mainstream advertising and Channel 10 will give you the Dream Team [fantasy] score along with the match stats at quarter time [of the television coverage]. (Interview with author)

The sizable participant base described here has seen the growth of dedicated fantasy sports news, advice and gambling websites such as Rotoworld, ESPN Fantasy and Games, Yahoo! Sports, and Totel Football (see Roy & Goss 2009). Keen participants pursue snippets of valuable information from a diverse range of print, broadcast, and online media in order to gain a competitive advantage. These consumption activities allow participants to indulge their fandom and enlarge the range of media that they regularly consume, including the games that they watch (e.g., some will watch specific games only because members of their fantasy team are competing). Analyzing survey data collected from 25,000 telephone interviews, Todd Nesbit and Kerry King (2010, p. 39) calculated that fantasy baseball players watch between 1.12 and 2.85 more MLB games each week than non-participants. The statistic returned for fantasy football participants was between 0.59 and 1.07 more NFL games. These results are supported by Drayer, Shapiro, Dwyer, Morse & White (2010), who found that fantasy football players used the Internet, television, mobile devices, and a variety of print media at high levels because of their interest in fantasy sports. A committed fantasy NBA participant described the range of media that he consults to maximize his chances of success:

> One thing you do have now is a groundswell of opinion columnists devoted entirely to fantasy sports. They write fantasy opinion. There's also NBA TV, which has a fantasy sports program we don't get in Australia but you can stream it on the Internet . . . Every now and then you get a good columnist. I think Brandon Funston at Yahoo!Sports is quite good . . . I also try to consult the newspapers from the local region I pick my players from. So I always consult the Salt Lake Tribune for the latest info about my players from the Utah Jazz. I always try to go to the local papers to get the best information. (Interview with author)

The specific make-up of his fantasy basketball team influences the media that he consumes, which is noteworthy given that the attention economy at work here is highly competitive and lucrative. Fantasy sports players in the US, for instance, offer the type of attention that advertisers, sponsors, and media outlets covet, especially given the amount of time required to play fantasy sports over the course of a season. The dominant demographic profile for fantasy football (NFL) participation is white, male, aged 18–45 years, and tertiary educated with an average income of between US\$78,000 and \$94,000 (Dwyer & Kim 2011, p. 71; Drayer *et al.* 2010, pp. 130–32; Otto, Metz & Ensmenger 2011, p. 197). Coincidentally, both of the interviewees quoted above roughly fit this profile (outside of the fact that they are Australian citizens). Competition for the user data and time of this engaged group serves further to embed the male dominance that pervades professional sport by valorizing the gaze of men who enjoy watching other men play sport (Miller 2001). This issue is discussed further later in the chapter.

Fantasy sports are now folded into the presentation of live sports television and weekly programming. There are dedicated fantasy sports shows, fantasy sports segments during weekly highlight and panel programs, and fantasy league discussion by commentators during the half time and post-game analysis of live matches. This content and commentary often revolve around the fantasy league either operated or promoted by the host television network. ESPN provides a sophisticated example of how fantasy baseball is part of an overall transmedia strategy (Halverson & Halverson 2008, p. 293). ESPN2 screens an hour-long 'Baseball Tonight Fantasy Baseball Draft Special' at the start of the regular season, offering analysis of different positions, draft strategies, and rookie players. This program promotes the ESPN Fantasy Baseball league, directs viewers to resources and fantasy blogs available via the ESPN website, connects to an ESPN Fantasy Baseball mobile app, and highlights the 'Fantasy Focus Baseball' podcast that participants can subscribe to via Apple iTunes. Variations of this strategy are evident across sports in the US and other countries, and live fantasy statistics are increasingly inserted into the live coverage of matches, with updates on both the greater and lesser performances of players.

The movement of fantasy sports into the routine format of sports television in Australia has been noticeable in recent years. Broadcasts of the various football codes feature commentators boasting about the performance of their fantasy team or lamenting their inability to select a successful team. This development contributed to a display of crass insensitivity by a rugby league commentator after a player was knocked unconscious and removed from the field for the rest of the game. The commentator was criticized for complaining that his fantasy team's performance had been negatively affected ('Terrible alright. He's in my Dream Team!'), rather than expressing concern for an athlete who was in distress because of a head clash with an opponent.[13] Disregarding such tactlessness, this example shows how the perspective of a fantasy sports participant can shift when viewing a match. An investment in the performance of a specific athlete (or selected athletes) creates a game within a game, as is explained by the fantasy NBA enthusiast cited earlier:

> There's nothing more fun than watching your players playing live and keeping track of their stats . . . And it's funny, I've got this player who makes all these great moves. You find yourself not watching the game. You find yourself watching your player as he makes his cut. You think, 'That's a good cut, you're going to get the ball there', and he gets the ball, so you really become a strategist. (Interview with author)

This explanation indicates how fantasy games add an additional layer to the narrative structure of television sport that exists beyond the score line, a team's performance, or the general flow of play. Contrasted with the collective address of broadcast commentary, fantasy sports produce an individualized narrative generated by the correspondence between on-field athlete performance and the team selection choices of the fantasy sports player.

The value attributed to fantasy leagues is measurable in different ways. For those licensed and/or run by sports organizations, leagues are, as already mentioned, a method through which to capture the lasting fan attention that can be sold to advertisers and sponsors. The websites where fans manage their teams enable the harvesting of user data, as well as linkage to stories and footage in other sections of an online portal. Yet a communications manager for a national sport explained that fantasy competitions are about more than extracting an immediately calculable financial return. They are, he claims, an 'educational tool' that has the potential to turn 'casual followers into ardent fans' (Interview with author). Once treated as little more than an 'interesting add-on' to a website, fantasy sports have become a mechanism that encourages participants to engage more deeply with a sport. For a participant to be competitive in their league, they must grasp the intricacies of athlete valuation, the roles of different positions on a field or court, and the importance of various moves and actions in defeating an opponent. The fantasy points awarded to athletes in multiple sports for 'saves', 'rebounds', 'sacks', 'steals', 'run-outs', 'hitouts', and 'try assists' emphasize why particular players are regarded as highly skilled:

> Fantasy games make people want to follow the sport closely . . . You learn about the players. You know which player has got the best moves or who is the best in that position, and so I have got to have him in my team. It teaches us. Things like that are educational tools, which should be a core part of our business. (Interview with author)

This realization dawned for this manager only after repeated discussions with fans, and observations of the growing amount of time participants spent on fantasy sports websites each season. This fan 'education' through gaming is not just directed at acquiring knowledge of the relative capabilities of players, but extends to a fuller appreciation of the many ways of engaging with sport and availing oneself of its commercial goods and services.

The increasing popularity of fantasy leagues has sparked fierce competition to own and run them. The primary unit of value in this market is data and the real-time statistics that create extensive databases. Fantasy sports and computer games have provided additional and profitable uses for the exhaustive data collected on player performance by teams and leagues for training and coaching purposes. The control and use of these data have been the source of vigorous legal battles in the US over how much of this information is privately owned and subject to copyright pre-emption by corporations, and how much is freely available for use in the public domain as fair dealing.[14] A source of confusion in this matter is the point at which the public reporting and reproduction of freely available sports statistics crosses over into the active manipulation of data and infringement of the intellectual property rights contained in privately owned databases. As became apparent during discussion with the CEO of a media company, the corporations and organizations that collect data advocate a predictably conservative position on this issue and the protection of 'their product'. His company holds contracts to collect athlete performance data for selected professional teams and competitions, which is on-sold to video game developers and used to run several fantasy leagues. Reflecting the trade in digital data across national and regional borders (Maxwell 2003), his company also purchases the 'official data' for overseas sports in order to run additional fantasy leagues:

We've been running fantasy games for about four years and we've got about 250,000 players, which is pretty good . . . Importantly, you need to have a reliable source of data. We collect the data ourselves so we have the rights to use it. Alternatively, we buy official data . . . The legal side of it is that once it is published in the public domain you can generally use the data and you can use player names for instance. But you can't use images or intellectual property like team jerseys and things like that—so there are rules. But we're running four or five games at the moment and they are good fun and bring people back to the website, so it works. (Interview with author)

Access to reliable and comprehensive data is central to market power. This CEO's company has used the data that it controls to develop and refine fantasy sports software packages that are purchased by companies operating leagues in overseas markets. The ready availability of these packages is of benefit to those sports possessing the fan-base, capital, and staff to establish appealing fantasy sports competitions. As Chapter 3 indicated, however, such online tools are of little use to minor codes and leagues that cannot afford to collect data across the full spectrum of their competitions and so be in a position to set up viable fantasy games. As the following, concluding comments contend, the impediments to institutional sporting progress caused by inherited discrimination and disadvantage means that the masculine privilege historically perpetuated by sport is arguably exacerbated by—and is certainly to date little challenged by—sports computer games.[15]

GENDER AND SPORTS GAMING

The remediation process described in this chapter is corrosive for gender equity because it perpetuates a double-layer of exclusion. Sport has long been a site of institutionalized discrimination against women (Hargreaves 1994). Computer games and fantasy leagues compound this problem by awarding even greater attention to men's professional sport, and continuously reward gamers and fantasy sports participants for their dedication to them (Davis & Duncan 2006). Apologists for this heavy concentration on male sport assert that console golf games feature a small number of female professionals (e.g., Anna Sorenstam and Natalie Gulbis), and *Virtua Tennis* displays current figures on the women's world tour, including Venus Williams, Maria Sharapova, and Ana Ivanovic. But men remain the overwhelming focus of adulation in the form and content of both elite sport and computer games. For instance, Taylor, Jenson & de Castell (2009) persuasively argue that the genealogy of 'booth babes'—scantily clad models hired to promote new computer game titles at interactive entertainment industry tradeshows—can be traced to the performance of cheerleaders.

In each case, women are rendered visible for sexualized consumption by men and made invisible in terms of active participation and social power. This inequitable gender order can also be discerned among computer game and television sport texts. Catering to a core market demographic of heterosexual teenage boys, sections of the games industry continue to attract attention through titles such as *Dead or Alive Xtreme Volleyball*, *BMX XXX*, and various fighting games that depict anatomically absurd female characters with 'micro-thin' waists, 'voluminous, pneumatic breasts' and 'ultra-long legs' (Cassell & Jenkins 1998a, p. 8; Richard & Zaremba 2005, p. 294). Male gamers use these characters to compile online lists of the 'hottest video game babes' and dissect their attributes in frequently crass terms in online forums. These activities continue despite the expanding number of female gamers and mounting evidence of the enjoyment experienced by women who choose to play computer games (Bryce & Rutter 2005; Royse, Lee, Undrahbuyan, Hopson & Consalvo 2007; Brand, Borchard & Holmes 2008; Cassell and Jenkins 1998b). The hyper-sexualization of female game characters is matched by the fetishization of the 'eye-candy' shown on the sports television screen and in online and print media. Examples here include the NBA's Los Angeles 'Laker Girls', the Lingerie Football League (tagline: 'true fantasy football'), *Sports Illustrated* swimwear models, UFC 'ring girls', and the 'grid girls' who parade at the start of many motor races. Recent years have also seen the rise of 'WAGS', or wives and girlfriends of famous sportsmen (called 'SCRUMMIES' in punning fashion in rugby union), in the modeling industry and gossip media. On screen and off, men dominate positions of wealth and opportunity, and women perform as objects of male desire or are relegated to support roles.

New social practices and cultural forms are generated by the material integration of sport and media (Hutchins 2008, p. 852). The latest of these is e-sport, or professional competitive computer gaming; an activity that excites both curiosity and disappointment. The first response relates to the observation of intense rivalries and action set in an unfamiliar competitive digital gaming environment. The second reaction occurs when it is realized that female competitors are almost non-existent in this increasingly popular pursuit. E-sport tournaments are staged throughout North America, Europe, and Asia and are sponsored by multinational information technology and media companies. 'Cyber-athletes' compete individually and in teams in games such as *FIFA Soccer*, *Forza Motorsport*, *Tekken*, *Starcraft*, and *Counter-Strike*, with in-game action displayed on giant screens to spectators and streamed live for online audiences (Jonasson & Thiborg 2010). The World Cyber Games (WCG) is arguably the most prestigious international e-sport tournament, drawing competitors from around 60 nations competing for a prize pool valued at almost US$500,000. The WCG is modeled explicitly on the Olympics and includes a host-city selection process, national teams, opening and closing ceremonies, medal ceremonies, and an e-sport 'hall of fame'. These Games also boast an idealistic quasi-philosophy that recalls the flawed principles of Olympism (Hutchins 2008; Hoberman 1995). Much like the Olympic Movement at the turn of the 20th century, females are absent from the WCG grand final as competitors. Women are, instead, present as booth babes available for photographs with male gamers and spectators.[16] The presence of these paid models affirms a hierarchical gender order that ties technological competence to hetero-sexual masculinity (Taylor *et al.* 2009, pp. 248–49). This association is reflected in the composition of professional cyber-athlete teams in South Korea, a country where the e-sport market is estimated to be worth around US$120 million a year (Jin 2010, p. 67). In a study of Korea's online gam-ing culture, Dal Yong Jin (2010, p. 89) identified just three females among 763 registered professional gamers in 2007. This is a problematic under-representation given the prominence of e-sport in Korea, with events staged in 500-seat arenas and shown on two cable television channels that claim audiences of between 1.5 and 4 million viewers (pp. 72–73). The young men that manage to reach the pinnacle of e-sport competition also repli-cate the media performances of male sport stars, marrying 'supermodels', publishing autobiographies in their early to mid-twenties, making regular media appearances, and forming fan clubs that claim membership numbers of well over half-a-million fans (pp. 60, 92).

The objectionable situation surveyed here informs how female gamers negotiate the playing of sports titles and the competitive dimensions of online games. T.L. Taylor (2006b, pp. 106–09) writes of the approach taken by female gamers to the sport-like dimensions of team work in the MMOG *Everquest*, referring to the sophisticated ways in which they approach in-game violence and use their avatars to combat gender ste-reotypes and express themselves as 'powerful active agents within the game' (p. 107). The first ever sport MMOG, *Empire of Sports*, is also trying to attract a female player base in order to make its multi-sport game design appealing enough to sustain a sizable online community. In the case of fantasy sports, an experienced female fantasy sports player acknowledged during a research interview that her sex/gender is consis-tently commented on in her league's online message forum. As an ardent supporter of teams in two different professional sports, she has estab-lished casual friendships with other female participants in the midst of a male dominated environment. These relationships have become easier to establish as increasing numbers of women have started playing over the past five years (Otto *et al.* 2011, p. 197). These developments have helped to dispel unwelcome gender stereotypes: 'The idea that women don't like fantasy sports is like saying that women don't like sports, which is a gross exaggeration' (Interview with author). Fantasy leagues also offer an opportunity to experience a subject position that few women ever get to occupy outside the realms of an online game—the ownership of a professional men's team:

It's the notion of women in ownership roles of sporting teams and management positions in professional sport. It's still a breakthrough thing, but it is that sense that women can be in the CEO role. In fantasy sports you're managing the team. In some ways you're associating with the power structure of sport, even if you're not associating with the athletes . . . It's also a little bit like playing the stock market without any of the risk, watching the numbers move and working out how long to stay with a player that isn't doing well. (Interview with author)

Currently improbable aspirations of material ownership and control of sport are, then, 'imaginable' for women through fantasy league participation. Moreover, while the players traded are almost always men, the rules and scores are, at the level of statistical calculation at least, gender neutral for the women who choose to play.

A thread running through the course of this chapter is that the collection of player and team performance data in professional men's sport is used for manifold purposes, including computer games and fantasy sports. Other uses include coaching analysis, training simulations, sport science, television commentary, and programming. As discussed in the opening of this book, the use of locational and biometric data is also filtering down to recreational pursuits, as is evidenced by cheap mobile apps for runners and cyclists that combine timing, location mapping, cadence sensors, and heart-rate monitoring. The diffusion of these techniques hints at a shift in the historical development of sport, particularly if sport is viewed as the outcome of large-scale interaction between social practices, cultural values, and prevailing technologies. As detailed in *From Ritual to Record: The Nature of Modern Sports* (2004 [1978]), Allen Guttmann's much debated Weberian analysis identified the peculiarly modern characteristics of sport, including rationalization, specialization, quantification, and record-keeping, that distinguished it from 'cultic' and ritualistic ancient and pre-modern physical contests. The application of these characteristics to sport under modernity produced the codification of rules and standardization of playing conditions that have become a taken-for-granted feature of sport. Following Guttmann's example, this chapter (and book) point to a number of crucial characteristics flowing from the interpenetration of sport and media that is profoundly altering the fabric of sport. The rise of the network society and the information technology paradigm since the 1970s (Castells 2000a) is characterized by mediatization, networked communications, digitization, content proliferation, and the 'data-isation of human endeavour' at work, home, and in public space (Hunter 2003, p. 150).[17] This chapter has established that the multiple applications of sport data collection and processing, and the remediating effects of computer games and fantasy sports leagues, supply firm evidence of change in the presentation, practice, and economics of sport. Yet, as the final section of this chapter has argued, it should not be assumed that these transformations equate with either cultural democratization or equitable gender politics. The conclusion to the book continues this line of argument, discussing how the media sport content economy is set to operate over the next decade, and reinforcing why an understanding of media sport is necessary for anyone wishing to understand the wider sphere of contemporary media markets and culture.

8 The Future
Networks, Telecoms, and Access

In concluding this book, we consider how some recent developments in the communication of sport presage a future that is, sometimes vividly and sometimes hazily, coming into view. The most recent evidence of how the media sport content economy operates emphasizes the continuing value of television, the delivery of digital media through different interlocking screens, and the growing significance of transmedia sport experience. One major event in 2011, the Rugby World Cup (RWC), and three media rights deals signed in the early months of the same year demand attention given the issues raised throughout this volume. Each demonstrates how media sport is presently packaged, communicated, and experienced, and the strategies adopted to balance the control and access of content in broadcast and online media.

The RWC was played across New Zealand during the months of September and October. Sanctioned by the International Rugby Board (IRB), the promotion and coverage of this quadrennial international tournament highlighted the transmedia dimensions of media sport at the highest levels of competition. Matches were broadcast into multiple international markets on free-to-air and subscription television. Authorized and unauthorized Internet streams were available for the event. An official website and YouTube channel promoted the event in the lead-up to the first game and housed highlights from previous World Cup tournaments. Casual online games, a mobile app game, and an IRB endorsed Playstation and Xbox 360 console game, *Rugby World Cup 2011*, were released. Twitter, Facebook, and mobile media were used to disseminate information about ticketing and promotional events, and generated feedback from fans. Three months prior to the event, promoters boasted about already having one million fans on Facebook, over 26,000 followers on Twitter, and 1.5 million views on YouTube (Snedden 2011). The technical team employed to create and manage this content was extensive, involving specialist video producers and editors, graphic and digital designers, photographers, Web producers, and social network managers.[1] These workers produced and managed extensive online content, highlights, and commentary to command the attention of those fans following particular teams. Much like the coverage of the

Olympics, this approach aimed to ensure that those accessing Internet and mobile media platforms consumed more of the RWC than those who only watched broadcast television. In addition to staging an entertaining rugby union tournament, the multiplatform coverage of the RWC confirmed the substantial financial and human resources needed to deliver *reliably* engaging digital content. Viewed in this light, the success of the RWC inadvertently revealed the ongoing resource and coverage challenges confronted by poorly resourced minor sports, including the promotional difficulties faced by the comparatively ignored Women's Rugby World Cup. Furthermore, the escalating media market value attached to major men's sports leagues exacerbates this imbalance, as is indicated by the size of the coverage rights deals discussed below.

Capitalizing on audience growth over several years, the North American National Hockey League (NHL) sold its media rights for an entire decade (up to the 2020–21 season) to NBC and cable television channel, Versus. Reportedly worth a record US$2 billion (Podell 2011), the deal includes a platform neutral dimension with the NBC Sports Group controlling digital rights across all broadcast and digital platforms for the games that it televises. Returning to the arguments detailed earlier in the book, these arrangements stymie the progress of specialist Internet providers by locking away the rights to NHL games for many years, and announce, in the face of claims of accelerating decline, that the financial might of the television networks is undiminished (see various contributions to Katz & Scannell 2009). For a league such as the NHL, the promise of plentiful rights income outweighed the potential benefits of experimenting with new self-funded online and digital media distribution models (although ice hockey teams may attempt to pursue independent media operations). A 10-year period also affords NBC and Versus the time to refine their own online services that cater for the needs of NHL fans while attempting to increase revenue streams from online media. The duration of the deal with NBC and Versus complements the stability of the commercial relationship that exists between the NHL and EA Sports, which has produced *NHL* game titles for the past 21 years.

Another deal signed in early 2011 was an extraordinary 20-year agreement between Time Warner Cable and the NBA's LA Lakers for regional broadcast rights in Southern California; that is, for games not telecast on a national basis. The exact value of the contract was not disclosed, but the intense competition for these regional rights produced rumors that it was worth close to US$3 billion (Flint 2011a). Basketball is the beneficiary of a regionally targeted programming strategy, reflecting a movement away from the valuation of fans and audiences in terms of national reach and 'one size fits all' broadcast strategies. Time Warner is in this instance using Lakers' games to drive subscriptions for two newly established regional sport channels, one an English language service and the other Spanish (Flint 2011b). This investment represents a concerted effort to secure the viability of a subscription television business, and creates related opportunities for Time Warner Cable to sell broadband, telephone, wireless, and digital video recorder products to subscribers. Paying 'one of the highest local TV rights fees in professional sports' is a gamble that the investment can be recouped over several years, not least by overcoming the obstacle of around 620,000 homes in Southern California not currently subscribing to pay television (Flint 2011a). Regional sport networks are also among the most expensive for cable channel distributors, suggesting that fans unwilling to pay for Lakers games may be tempted by illicit Internet streams. Nonetheless, this 20-year deal demonstrates how established media capital is responding to the challenges of a changing technology and media content market. Rather than developing significant new properties or investing in lower-tier sport, companies such as Time Warner are pouring large amounts of money into 'blue-chip' sporting properties—established and popular male teams and leagues.

The final coverage rights deal is arguably the most important of the three discussed in this section, showing how sport is subject both to television 'network-era practices *and* post-network realities' (Johnson 2009, p. 116; emphasis added). The AFL may run a sport with limited appeal beyond the shores of Australia, but its coverage rights model and the financial success of the league that it runs is attracting international attention. The terms of the unprecedented AUD$1.25 billion deal signed for the 2012–16 period[2] (Kermond & Battersby 2011) balance the mass audience exposure made available by free-to-air television, the competing commercial power exercised by pay-for-view television networks, and the growing influence of the telecommunications sector, digital media operators, and computer game console manufacturers.

The multiple access points for content provided by the AFL and its media partners acknowledge that audiences are interested in more than a single audiovisual medium for live sport. The principal value of the coverage rights contract resides in free-to-air and subscription television, with Channel Seven showing four live matches each week nationally, and pay television operator, Foxtel, telecasting all nine games in each round on a new 24-hour AFL channel. The transmedia dimension of the deal is built on an investment by the largest telecommunications carrier in the country, Telstra, which spent AUD$140 million for online and mobile phone rights (Masters 2011).[3] Telstra will stream live match footage to mobile phones and tablet computers for customers using their network, as well as through their recently launched IPTV service, the T-Box (*Telstra* 2011). The additional feature of AFL coverage in the new 2012–16 contract is eight live games available in each round for Microsoft Xbox 360 game console owners who, as the last chapter indicated, can already play the computer game, *AFL Live*. Foxtel programming is streamed through the Xbox Live service, providing an additional way to access television sport through the Internet.[4] This coverage option consolidates the marketing and operation of consoles as a home entertainment media hub, and allows a pay-for-view television network to reach users who enjoy 'flipping' between computer games and television on the same screen.

This flexible range of broadcast and online consumption options enriches Australian rules football as a media sport experience and positions the code to capitalize on one of the biggest government sponsored infrastructure projects undertaken in Australian history, the National Broadband Network (NBN). Expected to cost around AUD$43 billion[5] and scheduled for ultimate completion in 2021, the NBN rollout promises optical fiber network access to over 90 percent of Australian homes and guaranteed speeds of up to 100 megabits per second (Mbps) (cf. Barr 2008; Given 2009; Cunningham 2011). The connection of the first homes and businesses started in 2010 and will be extended across most of Australia's large landmass through a system of networks and hubs. In conjunction with privately run wireless Internet services, the NBN is set to support a wide range of existing and emergent online options for users. This network will almost certainly change the way in which many Australian fans access sport. At present, downloading music requires a speed of around 2 Mbps and multichannel IPTV needs 25 Mbps (Barr 2008, p. 3). Connection to the NBN will, therefore, allow the ready availability of high-quality live streaming of sport and other video content for those Australian households willing to pay for access. This fact is well understood by technology analysts and the Chairman of Google, Eric Schmidt, who has publicly praised the NBN as a 'wonderful' initiative (*ABC News* 2011). Left unspoken in Schmidt's endorsement is that his company is a potential beneficiary of the NBN as it develops, markets, and promotes its interactive viewing platform, Google TV.

A compelling point made by communications analyst, Trevor Barr, about the operation and feasibility of the NBN is that 'broadband is not Internet' (Barr 2008, p. 3). Internet services are a key part of broadband, but many more modes of communication are enabled by broadband technology. Broadcasters can also deliver content via broadband networks; a point underlined by watching AFL games on Telstra's T-Box or an Xbox console. As Internet providers and services continue to grow and compete for sports rights in order to attract subscribers, so will the offensive and defensive responses of television networks as they promote their rival content offerings. To restate an argument presented in Chapter 2, television is repositioned and redefined by its relationship to the Internet, Web, and mobile media (Lotz 2007, p. 6). This process will continue as the NBN is activated in Australian cities and towns, and similar telecommunications infrastructure investments and advances are made in other countries around the world. Understood in the context of these developments, the AFL's media rights deal for 2012–16 deserves recognition for more than its record value. The combination of free-to-air and pay television, online and mobile media, and IPTV and gaming console content is a rehearsal for the next round of rights negotiations (for 2017–21), when the NBN will have become a functional reality for many households. The most recent deal enables a sense of how different digital media technologies might work together when faster broadband speeds are more widely available. However, the history of media and communications teaches, as we have shown in this book, that there are also certain to be various unanticipated arrangements and uses.

The power of telecommunications companies is relevant whenever the future of network infrastructure is discussed (Goggin 2011, p. 14). The AFL's Internet and mobile rights deal with Telstra, and the notable role played by Telstra-owned infrastructure in the NBN rollout, are telling signs that telecommunications companies will increasingly control and transmit media sport in the coming years.[6] For instance, the global mobile media company Hutchison Whampoa, which trades as '3', has expanded its operations in a number of markets internationally by offering dedicated sports programming on mobile handsets (Goggin 2011, p. 20). Other rights deals have seen France Telecom's Orange take control of IPTV and mobile rights for French Ligue 1 soccer (Ovum analysts 2008), Singtel acquire the Internet rights for Italy's Serie A soccer (*Sport Business International* 2008), and Vodafone Essar stream live matches from the 2011 Cricket World Cup on mobile phones via ESPN Mobile TV (Cutler 2011d). The upsurge in control of IPTV, Internet, and mobile coverage rights by telecommunications operators has provoked open conflict with and among news media, television broadcasters, and sports organizations over who has the right to replay and archive match highlights and photographs online (see Chapter 6; Hutchins & Rowe 2010). These disagreements reflect both the unpredictable flow of content across and between platforms in a convergent media environment, and the growing commercial influence of the telecommunications sector.

Television broadcasters are watchful as telecommunications carriers extend their operations beyond fixed-line and mobile telephony, and network construction and management. As more people access content through the Internet and mobile handsets, telecommunications companies increasingly produce, package, and/or distribute entertainment content such as sport. Telstra was, for example, repositioned deliberately by its former Chief Executive Officer, Sol Trujillo, as a 'new kind of company'—'a media communications company'—that could respond effectively to technological convergence by competing in the content and applications marketplace (Sainsbury 2006). Trujillo's controversial tenure at Telstra (2005–09) coincided with a spike in the purchase of exclusive online sports rights for the AFL, rugby league, and motor racing. However, firm conclusions about the long-term success of many telecoms as entertainment media enterprises are difficult to reach. Many companies are still developing the necessary expertise, corporate cultures, and stable relationships with content owners needed to be successful consistently in the supply of media sport. But impressive annual revenues are available to bankroll the fostering of these strengths, as is indicated by the most recent report on social and economic infrastructure produced by the Productivity Commission (2009) in Australia. Telecommunications carriers reported annual revenues of AUD$25.2 billion in the 2006–07 financial year, approaching four times that of the broadcast and subscription television sector (AUD$6.9 billion) (p. 130). The obvious capacity of carriers to purchase exclusive rights to content, and to offer it to their customers alone, raises concerns about public access to sport that require consideration.

VIEWING RIGHTS?

Citizen access to popular sport is set to become a pressing political issue over the next decade. Several of the rights deals and media arrangements described here involve the privatization and locking away of content in subscription based services for television, the Internet, and mobile media. If a sizable audience can be guaranteed, elite sports leagues are increasingly in favor of moving their most popular matches or events behind pay walls in order to attract the highest possible financial return. This free market trajectory overturns the valuable historical role played by public service media in the development of sports broadcast technologies and markets, and undercuts the capacity of public broadcasters to source programming of widespread appeal and significance to national publics (Rowe 2004b, 2004c). It also contradicts the pronouncements of major sports organizations that frequently invoke the 'public interest' when shamelessly soliciting taxpayer funds to build stadiums and training facilities, as well as to subsidize their competition and operating costs (Crompton 2001; Hutchins 2009).

There are two main factors that presently preserve the 'viewing rights' of citizens (Rowe 2004c, 2011b), particularly in relation to national teams, mega-events, and league finals. The first is anti-siphoning legislation in Australia, Europe, and in other parts of the globe, which ensures that listed sporting events considered to be of national or cultural significance are telecast on free-to-air television (see Rowe 2004a; Scherer & Rowe 2012 forthcoming; Smith 2010). Many sports officials argue that these lists restrict their capacity to maximize media rights income, conveniently ignoring the role played by the public, and often public service media, in elevating their popularity and profitability in the first place. Second, industry regulators monitor media companies that purchase exclusive rights to multiple sports. This purchasing tactic asserts their dominance in the marketplace and obstructs the entry of new competitors through such practices as the 'hoarding' of mediated sports content. According to a spokesperson for an industry regulator, the length of many rights deals risks stifling both competition and public access to media sport:

It will all mean nothing if we have vigorous competition in the market for customer access to a media platform and then suddenly find that all the valuable content has been tied up by a big gorilla, [company name]. So one of the things we have got to be watching is who is actually doing the deals. Keep in mind that these deals are for five years sometimes, even 10-year deals with first and last options to renew. A five-year deal starts to significantly step into the NBN rollout. And the last thing we want is a position where a company says to consumers, 'Look, I will supply you with your high-speed, 100 megabit service. But you're going to have to sign on for two or three years because I'm the only one that can give you all the best sport'. We've got to make sure that the sporting bodies don't fall for the lure of the short-term 'sugar hit', so to speak; the high sum of money that locks them in for five years, with the operator also having the right of first and last refusal on the next contract. We will then suddenly find that the open access market regime meant to be delivered by the NBN counts for naught because all of the content's been locked up. It goes back to both distribution channels and who controls access to content. (Interview with author)

However, the determination of national regulatory bodies (or supranational as in the case of the European Union) and governments to provide oversight is also undermined if they do not possess the requisite resources and legislative power to act. The intricacies of Internet and broadband regulation pose additional challenges. Whereas broadcast licenses issued by national governments conventionally contain community obligations and standards of various kinds that must be followed, the rules applying to online operators are not as developed and vary markedly according to the legislative and legal norms applying within and across different territories. Debates occurring internationally about net neutrality[7] and universal service obligations applying to ISPs both reflect and complicate these matters (Butt 2006).

A vital question will be answered over the next 10 years: what are the networked media services, content, and standards that citizens rightfully can expect to access and experience free-of-charge or at minimal cost? The response to this question will determine whether the value of sport as a social experience and cultural good is further diminished at the expense of untrammeled commodification and marketization. The many democratic states that primarily address their subjects as self-governing consumers, rather than as engaged citizens, give little cause for optimism in this regard (Miller 2007). In the case of sport, this state of affairs suggests that those people with sufficient wealth will enjoy the extensive range of consumer technologies and digital content required to experience the excitement of media sport spectacle. Those unable to afford premium sports content and the latest digital technologies—the 'flawed consumers' (Bauman 1998)—will be comparatively neglected by the major sports and clubs with which they have an affinity. Those left behind will likely express their collective frustration through unauthorized online media and/or message boards, deploring the inequities of hyper-commodified media sport while still emotionally investing in the outcomes of premierships and championships (Ruddock *et al.* 2010). Other aficionados may turn their attention to the lower levels of competition to search for different meanings and experiences of sport, much like the MyFootballClub experiment and its nostalgic appeal to grassroots soccer (see Chapter 5). A small number of fans may walk away from sport altogether, feeling little connection with distant spectacles that are unable to satisfy their urge for social connection and community. Given their lack of disposable income, they are unlikely to be missed by the titans of media sport capital who insist that everyone must pay a price that includes a healthy profit margin. If current trends continue, those setting the prices will lack the imagination and vision to see that the cultural and social deficits flowing from their limited horizons cannot be measured by ratings, website hits, or financial statements. Each of these scenarios reflects differing conceptions of connection and disconnection in a conflicted world of media forms, communications technologies, and large-scale media institutions.

THE SIGNIFICANCE OF MEDIA SPORT

It has been said that some people take sport too seriously, and others not quite seriously enough (see Haigh 2008, p. ix). Considered reflection on this statement is necessary when analyzing the current state of the media industries, the evolution of networked digital communications, and the interaction between broadcast and online environments. Sport is foremost among the appealing and valuable forms of content pursued by many global media and technology corporations, including News Corporation, ESPN, NBC-Universal, Time Warner, Google, Electronic Arts, and Microsoft, in the quest for large-scale profit. Yet, if much of the available scholarship on media, communications, and technology is taken as a guide, the attentive reader could be forgiven for remaining unaware of this fact. A timely 'comment' (by omission) on this deficit is the otherwise excellent volume, the *International Handbook of Internet Research* (Hunsinger, Klastrup & Allen 2010), a comprehensive edited collection spanning over 30 chapters and 600 pages that manages to mention sport in just a handful of passing observations.

Lacunae of this kind lead to the question of why sport struggles to receive the attention that it needs. Inattention stems from many sources, including the personal preferences of many scholars and commentators. The physicality and anti-intellectualism of many sporting cultures, combined with the widely publicized indiscretions of well-paid athletes, hold little fascination for those who consider themselves to be serious thinkers, and whose media habits may, in fact, involve the determined avoidance of sport. This attitude blinds them to the importance of sport in online cultures and practices and the sociological significance of the media sports cultural complex. There are also those who openly admit their hostility to sport because of unpleasant formative experiences or justified resentment that so much popular attention is awarded to pursuits that 'crowd out' other cultural forms while often perpetuating inequality and discrimination in relation to gender, race, and class. For others, sport is an activity enjoyed for relaxation and fun, deliberately compartmentalized to create temporary distance from 'weightier matters' of politics, economics, and culture that occupy their intellectual energies, or from the more mundane but crucial demands of quotidian life. Occasionally, there are figures whose love of sport overwhelms their capacity to offer the sort of sustained, reflexive critique that is necessary to place it in meaningful context for themselves and for (un)interested others. Thankfully, a slowly growing community of scholars and critics insist that sport be included in broader research agendas and public debates that enrich collective wisdom both in and outside the academy.

Our position corresponds with the opening sentence of this section. Sport is of consequence in different ways and to varying degrees depending on the historical period and prevailing circumstances. The emergence of networked media sport offers immense potential for critical analysis of the operation of media and power at the current conjuncture (Wilson, B. 2007, p. 468), and with regard to the range of possible, contending futures that it foreshadows. It is playing a pivotal role in the evolution of markets, culture, and everyday life in the network society, and supplies a crucial form of content that informs how the movement from analogue-broadcast to digital-convergent media systems is unfolding. For anyone wanting to understand how the game is played in capitalist systems, global communications, and the digital technology marketplace, the field of media sport is a vibrant theatre of the triumphant and the defeated, as well as the exhilarated and the despondent. The idea of 'sport beyond television' also consciously contains the seeds of its own critique because sport, though profoundly influenced by it, could never be completely contained and controlled by television and the wealthy corporations that deliver programming. This is not only because, as our sub-title signals, the Internet, digital media and networked media sport are re-shaping the place of broadcast television—and, indeed, what we *understand* by television. Beyond sport and television are the vast array of social and cultural structures, struggles, relations, practices, and meanings that have given both of them life in the ceaseless movement of human history. Our analysis calls for an appropriate recognition of the significance of media sport, while demonstrating its utility in facilitating a wider inquiry into the dynamics of social life, media transformation, technological change, and cultural flux that extends far beyond it. The proliferation of platforms and screens tracked in this book demands knowledgeable, inquisitive viewers and users who engage with and analyze the unfolding drama that is contemporary media sport.

Notes

NOTES TO CHAPTER 1

1. There are different versions of IPTV in terms of services provided. Kim (2009, p. 536) offers a useful definition that allows for these variations when he states that 'IPTV refers to the delivery of video and interactive information and communication services over landline networks by the telcos [telecommunications companies]'.
2. While these are impressive figures, it should be noted that the distribution of users across countries and continents is uneven. The highest concentrations of Internet users are located in developed economies. There is also strong evidence of a growing range of languages used online in addition to English (26.8 percent of users), with Chinese (24.2 percent) and Spanish (7.8 percent) ranked second and third respectively (*Internet World Stats* 2011).
3. The cinema screen is excluded from this specific formulation because live sports coverage has rarely occurred at the cinema (except in the case of boxing matches), although the spread of 3D cinema and the proliferating use of cinemas as 'live sites', as occurred internationally during the 2010 FIFA World Cup, are changing this situation.
4. Manuel Castells' theory of the network society explains the broader conditions of media sport in contemporary society, and provides an effective, albeit often implicit, context for the analysis and presentation of empirical evidence throughout this book. Direct consultation of Castells is recommended for a full explanation of his theory (2000a, 2000b, 2002, 2004a, 2004b, 2009).
5. All project participants are fully de-identified in accordance with requirements mandated by the Monash University Human Research Ethics Committee.
6. STATS SportVU provides an example of such a service. See http://www.stats.com/sportvu/index.asp
7. Ironically, the coin had to be tossed twice before the 2011 World Cup cricket final between India and Sri Lanka. The Mumbai crowd's noise prevented the match referee, standing a short distance away, from hearing whether Sri Lankan captain Kumar Sangakkara had called 'heads' or 'tails'. It can be safely assumed that a technological solution to this audio problem will be available at the next cricket World Cup in Australia and New Zealand in 2015.
8. There has been recent debate about the relative value of the terms mediatization and mediation in the study of communication and media. Couldry (2008), Livingstone (2009) and Hesmondhalgh and Toynbee (2008) provide useful insights into how claims about the mediation of the social world should be analyzed and investigated. The term mediatization has been used deliberately here because it best captures the annexation of professional sport by

media conglomerates, technologies, and formats over the past 50 years (see Hutchins & Mikosza 2010).
9. It is worth noting that Jimmy Sanderson has developed a methodology for the analysis of cultural identity in online media sport in a series of articles (Sanderson 2008a, 2008b, 2009a, 2009b; 2010).

NOTES TO CHAPTER 2

1. This is not to say that such activities by 'mini-creators' (Kawashima 2010) do not occur in relation to sport, as a cursory search on YouTube will testify to the existence of fan dedication videos (fanvids) in particular. Rather, the point being made is that 'ripping, mixing, and burning' are far more commonplace activities in online fan communities that form around fictional television and film popular culture texts (Lessig 2002; Jenkins 2006a).
2. Kreiss, Finn & Turner (2011) offer an incisive critique of claims made about the cultural democratization and egalitarianism resulting from widespread digitally enabled peer production. The example of sport adds to this critique.
3. In fairness to those scholars who use such terms, which includes (on occasion) one of the authors of this book, they are useful conceptual devices with which to think through processes of media transformation and change.
4. Other less prominent categories include in-flight and ship-at-sea rights.
5. The American-Russian billionaire, Len Blavatnik, owns a 58 percent share in Perform.
6. Hulu revenue has climbed from US$108 million in 2009 to US$263 million in 2010, and expects to pass one million subscribers during 2011. These figures have not, however, been achieved without conflict between the CEO of Hulu, Jason Kilar, and the broadcast joint venture between Disney, News Corporation, and NBC-Universal that funds Hulu's operation (Appelo 2011). This conflict is centred upon a compelling memo written by Kilar, in which he lays out his vision for a future of television where online distribution, video on demand, fewer advertisements, and lower margins are all dominant features (Kilar 2011).
7. Ananda Krishnan supports Fetch. He is a Malaysian billionaire who has interests spanning an array of sectors, including telecommunications, pay television, satellite systems, construction, and shipping.
8. An amusing and effective spoof of the scare tactics deployed in anti-piracy advertising campaigns was broadcast by British comedy *The IT Crowd*. See http://www.youtube.com/watch?v=ALZZx1xmAzg.
9. A number of online sports betting sites like Unibet and Bet365 also offer access to streams if the user registers for a small fee.
10. Many streams claim user numbers in the dozens rather than the hundreds or thousands.
11. The cautionary tale of the rock band Metallica's poor publicity after taking action against fan users of Napster is often referred to in this regard (Garofalo 2003).
12. The World Marathon Majors consists of the Boston, London, Berlin, Chicago, and New York marathons.
13. Digital piracy is actually a signpost that selected sports leagues have achieved a key strategic objective—penetration into Asian markets (see Manzenreiter & Horne 2004). While actual viewer figures are unreliable, reports indicate that Asian countries and China in particular are hubs for unauthorized live streams (NetResult 2008; Gibson 2009b; Dunne 2011c).

14. A different example of this pattern occurred in 2011. A super-injunction brought down by a British court to prevent the news reporting of Manchester United footballer Ryan Giggs' extramarital affair was the subject of a widespread breach online (*BBC* 2011).
15. Lloyd *et al.* (2009, p. 6) present these perspectives as a continuum, acknowledging that there is no such thing as a completely open or closed system. Rather, the two axes alert the observer to 'extreme alternatives'.
16. This figure was created by the team of researchers responsible for the 'Outside the Box—The Future of Television' Project (Lloyd-James, Gibson, Bell, Pattinson, Goldsmith, Chandler & McKay 2009). This Project was funded by an Australian Research Council (ARC) Linkage grant (LP0775364).

NOTES TO CHAPTER 3

1. Online statistics are regularly subject to disagreement and variation. The point to note here is that these numbers are consistently sizable and continue to grow.
2. For instance, after the completion of an interview, one of the authors was asked a series of pointed questions by the interviewee—a communications manager for a club—about how to redress the scepticism of the club's owners about the need to monitor closely activity on their website. The connection between investing in the operation of a website and assessing its value as an 'attention generator' had not at that point been established at the club.
3. 'Unique browsers': each user visiting a site has a unique cookie ID assigned to their browser to help determine browser uniqueness. This metric displays the number of unique browsers which visited a site owned by a publisher. A 'page impression' is recorded each time a page is displayed in a browser window, whether the page is served directly from the Web server, from a proxy, or from the browser's cache.
4. 'Average daily unique browsers' refers to the average number of unique browsers each day for a website over a reporting period. 'Average user session duration' records a period of user activity on a website, provided that there is not more than 30 minutes inactivity between consecutive events for the same user.
5. Of course, that a user opens a webpage does not mean that it is being actively regarded, but the act of opening is necessary for it to be so.
6. An area requiring further investigation is the fact that the type of fan targeted by these multiplatform strategies must have the necessary disposable income to enjoy them.
7. These walled gardens contrast with open source platforms and communities built around the likes of the Linux operating system and the creative activities of many hackers (not malicious crackers) using it (Himanen 2001).
8. Again raising the specter of clubs breaking away from the EPL, Liverpool FC recently declared that they want a 'debate' about whether they should have the right to negotiate their own media rights deals separate from the rest of the League when playing in matches overseas (Hunter 2011).
9. This argument does not extend to the level of the league or competition itself as an economic entity. High-profile leagues aggressively pursue and achieve monopoly status.
10. Internazionale Milano ('Inter') and Juventus have won seven of 11 championships contested since the 2000–01 season. Only Milan and Roma have managed to break this dominance.

11. These are Swellnet (www.swellnet.com.au) and Coastal Watch (www.coast-alwatch.com).
12. Challenges of this kind are also reported in UK labor movement organizations that have struggled to 'afford interactivity' on YouTube and Facebook because of time and human resource shortfalls (Fenton & Barassi 2011, p. 187).
13. The trials and travails of the cricket club in question are described in Gideon Haigh's light-hearted 2002 book, *The Vincibles*.
14. This point is reinforced by studies of social cohesion and sport. Government departments demand—at least when they are not already convinced of a course of action—evidence-based outcomes. This need can create problems when a worthwhile project objective is difficult to deliver, requires repeated attempts to find the right approach, is a poor fit for the relevant funding criteria, or is inherently difficult to affirm in performative terms (Hutchins 2007).
15. The figures mentioned were actually modest, especially when divided between different state and territory branches of the sport across Australia. But the difference between the canvassed government grant and those previously obtained was notable.

NOTES TO CHAPTER 4

1. This was at the time of writing (mid-2011). The other four sites were search engine portals that increasingly incorporate user-generated content and features (Alexa Internet 2011b).
2. Social software possesses design characteristics that build 'expectations about the social interactions that the software will facilitate' (Benkler 2006, p. 373).
3. Ferriter (2009) provides a study of how fans use Wikipedia to augment public narratives about sport.
4. Web 2.0 is a contentious term that is the subject of debate (Goggin 2011; Goggin & Hjorth 2009; Allen 2009). This term does, however, serve to categorise a range of technical, content, user, and Internet traffic developments that distinguish it from earlier iterations of the Web (Cormode & Krishnamurthy 2008). The cultural discourses surrounding Web 2.0, which overwhelmingly legitimate 'entrepreneurial, advanced capitalism' (Allen 2009, p. 8), have nonetheless contributed to an increased popular awareness about the changing features of user participation and interaction in online environments (Valtysson 2010; Kawashima 2010; Spurgeon 2008).
5. danah boyd and Nicole Ellison (2007, p. 211) provide a useful definition of social networking sites, explaining that they are web-based services that 'allow individuals to (1) construct a public or semi-public profile within a bounded system, (2) articulate a list of other users with whom they share a connection, and (3) view and traverse their list of connections and those made by others within the system'.
6. A regular feature of online activity in Internet-connected societies worldwide, blogging is most popular at present in China, South Korea, India, and Malaysia (Smith 2011).
7. These figures have not translated into obvious commercial success for the company that owns the platform, Automattic.
8. The president and co-founder of Team Darfur, Olympic gold-medal winning US speed skater, Joey Cheek, had his visa revoked by Chinese authorities prior to the Olympics for undisclosed reasons. The group's activism was then

given further impetus by the choice of Team Darfur member, former Sudanese refugee and 1500-meter runner Lopez Lomong, as the flag bearer for the US team during the Opening Ceremony.

9. The Pan-American Games is a major multi-sports event that has a long and instructive history. Held for the first time in Brazil in 1951, countries throughout the Americas are eligible to participate, although most interest in the event is concentrated in South America. Held in Rio de Janeiro, the 2007 events featured over 5,000 athletes from 42 countries and underscored major inequalities in wealth, power and social status in the host city (Curi, Knijnik & Mascarenhas 2011).

10. Exceptions to this statement are those sports journalists who come solely to praise sport and lionize athletes, or who only 'delight in trivial controversy' (Boyle, Rowe & Whannel 2010).

11. Sadly, Jeret Peterson passed away in July 2011, aged 29-years.

12. Algorithmic trading reportedly accounts for around 70 percent of trades on US markets and 30 percent in Australia. This form of trading has been linked to the 'flash crash' of 6 May 2010 that saw the Dow Jones lose and recover 900 points within minutes (Background Briefing 2010c).

13. He has since transferred to Aston Villa.

14. The impersonation of baseball player and Milwaukee Brewer, Nyjer Morgan, on Twitter demonstrates that such activities are not uniformly malicious or mischievous. In this case, Morgan even welcomed his impersonator, tweeting that 'da tweetz is brilliant and I got nothing but love for him!' (Albert 2011).

15. Also known as social marketing intelligence firms.

16. Barton spent 11 weeks in prison for common assault and affray. The amount paid to Barton for his image rights was reported to be in excess of those of his teammates (White 2009).

17. A parallel example of such a commodification has already unfolded around Australian sporting icon, cricketer Don Bradman (1908–2001). In 2000, the Bradman Foundation claimed ownership of the domain name bradman.com.au after court action. The name had been registered by a New South Wales property developer, Bradman Corporation, which also agreed to cease trading under the name. The Federal Government then intervened in October of the same year to amend Corporations Law Regulations in order to protect the Bradman name from unauthorized exploitation, thereby ensuring that the commercial activities and merchandizing of the Bradman Foundation could continue unhindered (Hutchins 2002, pp. 93–100).

18. It should also be noted that only a small minority of successful athletes actually benefit significantly from these developments.

19. The AOC recently advised athletes that it was not legally liable for any message posted on an athlete's personal profile (Halloran 2011).

NOTES TO CHAPTER 5

1. Howe's book was developed from his essay that initially appeared in *Wired* (2006).

2. MySpace was purchased in 2011 by Specific Media and Justin Timberlake for US$35 million, only a little over 6 percent of the reported US$580 million that News Corporation paid for it in 2005.

3. Readers interested in this argument should also consult Dunning and Rojek (1992). Henry Jenkins (2007) supplies an engaging contemporary analysis of wrestling as masculine melodrama that draws upon Elias and Dunning.

Although in a very different theoretical tradition, it would be remiss of us not to mention Roland Barthes' (1973, p. 23) brilliant seminal essay on wrestling and social mythology, and its culturally conditioned split between American wrestling's 'mythological fight between Good and Evil' and the French construction of 'a highly moral image: that of the perfect "bastard"'.

4. The term 'supporter' is used interchangeably with 'fan' in this chapter. Giulianotti (2002) explains, however, that the difference between terms such as supporters, followers, and fans is worth acknowledging (without, though, diverting discussion into taxonomy in every instance).

5. The similarities and differences between sports fandom and fan practices in other areas of popular culture is a subject that has received modest attention (Gantz, Wang, Bryant & Potter 2006; Gray, Sandvoss & Harrington 2007; Rowe 1995; Schimmel, Harrington & Bielby 2007). The available literature suggests that distinctions include the types and intensity of media use, and levels of emotional involvement. There are also evident disciplinary differences, which are reflected in the journals likely to publish articles on sport compared to other areas of popular culture.

6. The wealthiest clubs and leagues can afford the personnel required to house and monitor these forums. An example is the award-winning 'The Shed' section of Chelsea FC's Website, which is moderated by the club.

7. A media manager explained that he still received emails from supporters complaining about the termination of his club's official message board over a year after the decision had been taken (Interview with author).

8. This access parallels an approach taken by some computer game developers when dealing with the enthusiasm, creative energies, and contrasting opinions of their user community (Humphreys, Fitzgerald, Banks & Suzor 2005, pp. 18–19).

9. Our thanks to Andy Ruddock for his insight into how this concept can be best understood.

10. He also mentioned that this investment of time caused friction with his wife.

11. Current challengers to this dominance are Cricbuzz and Cricketnext.

12. MFC was forced to launch a 'save our squad' donation campaign. Around £40,000 was required to avoid losing members of the playing squad.

13. As well as winning the FA Trophy, Ebbsfleet United claimed the Kent Senior Cup in the same season. Clubs that have gone into receivership during the period discussed include Luton Town, Portsmouth, Plymouth Argyle, Southampton, Chester City, Northwich Victoria, Salisbury City, and Crystal Palace.

14. Norton featured in the production and release of a FA Trophy Cup Final song, 'Beat the Weather'. An accompanying video was placed on YouTube in late April 2008 and also made available for purchase on iTunes (for 79 pence, with profits going to the club). The first purchase with the proceeds, according to the MFC e-newsletter, 'will be a new fertilizer distributor for Peter. We have already sent the MyFC podcast to No1 in the charts. Can we do the same for our groundsman?' The exercise was quite successful, with 'Beat the Weather' reaching number 21 on the UK iTunes dance chart on April 30, 2008. This campaign, in seeking to transform an elderly, grass mower-riding groundsman into a cult media celebrity, deployed the kind of quirky viral marketing that has become common in online environments (Schmitt, Rogers & Vrotsos 2004).

15. The US has supplied the largest proportion of overseas MFC members. Some of these members have explained that they are attracted by MFC's

democratic membership ethos, which contrasts with the private franchise ownership model that dominates North American professional sport.

16. These issues are discussed in-depth by Hutchins *et al.* (2009), Ruddock *et al.* (2010) and Rowe *et al.* (2010).

17. *Championship Manager* and *Football Manager* are among the most enduring and successful game franchises of all time in the UK (Crawford 2006).

18. The latest attempt at establishing a 'football fan democracy' is also based in the UK, www.RunTheFootballClub.com.

19. The globalization of media sport and televisual flows has seen Western sports leagues focus heavily on expansion into East and South Asian countries, where commercial opportunities have arisen from rapidly expanding economies, increased media capital, and growing levels of affluence among rising middle-class populations (Manzenreiter & Horne 2004; Rowe & Gilmour 2008).

20. It should be noted that Dayan & Katz (1992) are also concerned about the capacity of sport related communitas to spark urban disorder.

NOTES TO CHAPTER 6

1. The anti-siphoning scheme refers to federal government legislation that ensures that selected major sports events are shown on free-to-air television because of their 'national importance' and/or 'cultural significance' (Rowe 2004a, 2004c). These events presently include major football code finals and international cricket matches played in Australia involving the national men's team. The list guarantees these events can be watched free of charge by the general public.

2. Attempting to emphasize a commitment to community welfare, COMPS recently changed its name to the Coalition of Major Professional and Participation Sports (COMPPS).

3. The problem for the journalist on the ground is also replicated at the organizational level, including conflicting taxonomies within major media companies. As an online sports editor for a major broadsheet newspaper observed, 'We've been told on several occasions when we try and do things that, "We're a print company so therefore your request is not valid". We've maintained the argument, "No, we're not a print company . . . we are in the process of becoming a digital media company".' (Interview with author)

4. One interviewee recounted a vivid anecdote about racing to make a deadline during an Indian cricket tour in 1986, which involved a desperate search on rickshaws for a functioning telex machine.

5. It should be acknowledged that this critical observation also applies to other reporting rounds.

6. This is an inevitable question for synthetic media. For example, when television augmented broadcast sound with moving, visual imagery, it became necessary to overcome the static visual protocols associated with the 'talking heads' that had populated radio studios.

7. Mentioned in Chapter 3, the Crawford review of sport relates to the proposed blueprint for the future funding and structure of elite and mass participation sport in Australia (Australian Government Independent Sports Panel 2010).

8. This section of the Australian Trade Practices Act empowers government to regulate the conduct of participants in an industry. The purpose of such a code would be to reduce the level of conflict between sports organizations and news media companies by formally regulating their conduct towards each other.

NOTES TO CHAPTER 7

1. The concept of remediation has also been applied in games studies to understand the incorporation of 'retro' game and movie aesthetics in independent
game development (Camper 2009).
2. This motto has since been revised to, 'It's in the game!', which presents a
suggestive claim about the degree to which computer games are embedded
within the culture and practice of professional sports.
3. Bird's rivalry with the Los Angeles Lakers' Earvin 'Magic' Johnson was so
newsworthy in basketball that it became the subject of a 1984 Converse
basketball shoe advertisement in which they both appeared in appropriately
'cartoonish' enmity.
4. John Madden was also a head coach in the NFL between 1969 and 1978.
5. NASCAR recently ended its 12-year relationship with EA Sports in response
to the diversification of gaming platforms and a desire to target new demographics in the marketplace.
6. This studio is responsible for the hit-game *L.A. Noire*.
7. Players receive a small amount of money for their participation in the creation of these games through a collective bargaining agreement signed with
league authorities.
8. They were later persuaded by a player's union to drop the case.
9. Waters (2003, p. 5) outlines how these sessions involve the digital capture of
players in motion and translation into a computer game. A series of cameras
tracks the motion of reflective balls attached to a lycra jumpsuit worn by
the athlete. Several balls are placed on their body, including the head, feet,
hands, elbows, and knees. Footage of this process in action can be found at:
http://www.youtube.com/watch?v=oi2jVCJ4Nmg.
10. Atari produced *Military Battlezone*, a more realistic version of the arcade
release. The lead programmer, Ed Rotberg, disliked the use of his game for
battlefield training. Given his counter-culture sympathies, he was uncom-
fortable that his creation was used to 'train people to kill' (Kent 2001, pp.
153–54).
11. The Wii remote functions as a handheld pointing device. A sensor bar placed
in front of the television detects the movement of the remote. Microsoft's
Kinect is a peripheral device that connects to the Xbox 360 console. The
Kinect sensor device uses 3D scanning technology to track gestures and
movements and allows the gamer to play and interact with the console without a remote.
12. Another game seeking to leverage the opportunity created by these lifestyle
issues is 'FunGoPlay', which is staffed by former employees of Nickelodeon,
Disney, and Sesame Workshop (Kessler 2011). Designed for children aged
between six and 11 and featuring 26 games, this online sports world provides an actual soccer ball or flying disc to subscribers. A chip is inserted into
these objects, registering when they are played with and thereby activated.
Operating across the boundary of physical and online play, subscribers are
offered rewards in the game for using the ball or disc offline.
13. In responding to criticism the commentator stated that he was unaware that
his microphone was 'live' at the time.
14. Consultation with the relevant legal analyses is recommended for those readers interested in this aspect of fantasy sports (e.g., Grady 2007; Evans 2007–
2008; Cianfrone & Baker 2010, pp. 59–63).
15. There is also a significant intersection between masculinity and race that
is often ignored in the examination of sports games (Leonard 2005, 2006;
Oates 2009).

16. An amusing and perceptive critique of the relationship between booth babes and young male gamers is available from the blog, *Demonbaby* (2006).
17. Marshall McLuhan foreshadowed the last of these processes when he wrote of private and corporate lives as 'information processes' (2001 [1964], p. 57).

NOTES TO CHAPTER 8

1. The range of staff detailed here was described by the Manager of Online and Communications Projects for the RWC, Clare Wolfensohn. She spoke at the 2011 Digital Sports Summit held at the Melbourne Cricket Ground on 8 June.
2. This figure represents a significant increase on the previous multi-year deal, valued at AUD$780 million for the 2007–2011 period.
3. This is more than double the AUD$60 million figure secured for online and mobile rights in the previous deal.
4. A deal signed in the same year saw Playstation 3 console owners in the US given the option of watching live NFL matches streamed via Direct TV.
5. The Federal government's commitment is approximately AUD$26 billion of the total figure. The remaining money is expected to come from revenue generated by the NBN and the private debt of NBN Co., the company charged with building and operating the network.
6. These rights are obtained either by direct purchase from a sports organization, or from another media company that on-sells mobile and Internet coverage rights parcels from the overall 'platform neutral' package they control (see Chapter 2).
7. Net neutrality references a complex set of technical and legislative debates occurring in the US. Industry, policy, and media commentators around the world closely monitor these debates. The term refers to the right of ISPs and telecommunications carriers to 'prioritise certain traffic or charge differential rates for different kinds of content' (Butt 2006, p. 14).

References

AAP 2010, 'I Want You to Know How Sorry I Am: Tearful Rice', *Sydney Morning Herald*, 8 September. Online. Available http://www.smh.com.au/sport/swimming/i-want-you-to-know-how-sorry-i-am-tearful-rice-20100908–150s3.html?autostart=1 (accessed 8 September 2010).

ABC News 2011, 'Google Boss Praises NBN', 20 February. Online. Available http://www.abc.net.au/news/stories/2011/02/19/3143457.htm (accessed 23 February 2011).

ACCC (Australian Competition and Consumer Commission) 2006, *Media Mergers*, Dickson, ACT: ACCC.

ACMA (Australian Communications and Media Authority) 2010, *IPTV and Internet Video Services in Australia: The IPTV and Internet Video Market in Australia*, Canberra: ACMA.

Adams, P.C. 2009, *Geographies of Media and Communication,* Malden, MA: Blackwell.

Adler, D. 2011, 'Mission Impossible', *Sport Business International*, No. 165, March, p. 14.

Albert, J. 2011, 'Being Tony Plush', *Slate*, 12 August. Online. Available http://www.slate.com/id/2301477/ (accessed 17 August 2011).

Albury, K., Funnell, N. & Noonan, E. 2010, 'The Politics of Sexting: Young People, Self-Representation and Citizenship', in *Media, Democracy and Change: Refereed Proceedings of the Australian and New Zealand Communication Association Conference 2010.*

Alexa Internet 2011a, 'wikipedia.org'. Online. Available http://www.alexa.com/siteinfo/wikipedia.org# (accessed 17 January 2011).

Alexa Internet 2011b, 'Top Sites'. Online. Available http://www.alexa.com/topsites (accessed 3 January 2011).

Alexander, J.C. 1990, 'Introduction: Understanding the "Relative Autonomy" of Culture', in J.C. Alexander & S. Seidman (eds), *Culture and Society: Contemporary Debates*, New York: Cambridge University Press, pp. 1–27.

Al Jazeera 2007, 'Cricket Australia Lockout Media: Restrictions are Imposed on the Media for Australia's Test Series against Sri Lanka', 9 November. Online. Available http://english.aljazeera.net/sport/2007/11/2008526105019908392.html (accessed 20 August 2011).

Allan, S. 2006, *Online News: Journalism and the Internet*, Maidenhead, UK: Open University Press.

Allan, S. (ed) 2010, *Routledge Companion to News and Journalism Studies*, London: Routledge.

Allan, S. & Thorsen, E. (eds) 2009, *Citizen Journalism: Global Perspectives*, New York: Peter Lang.

Allen, M. 2009, 'Tim O-Reilly and Web 2.0: The Economics of Mimetic Liberty and Control', *Communication, Politics & Culture*, 42(2), pp. 6–23.

Anderson, C. 2004, 'The Long Tail', *Wired* 12(10), October. Online. Available http://www.wired.com/wired/archive/12.10/tail.html (accessed 4 April 2008).

Anderson, N. 2010, 'Any Use of the Article Without the NFL's Express Written Consent is Prohibited', *ars technica*, 15 February. Online. Available http://arstechnica.com/tech-policy/news/2010/02/challenging-copyright-at-the-nfl.ars# (accessed 22 February 2011).

Andrejevic, M. 2007, *iSpy: Surveillance and Power in the Interactive Era*, Lawrence, KA: University Press of Kansas.

Andrejevic, M. 2008, 'Watching Television Without Pity: The Productivity of Online Fans', *Television & New Media*, 9(1), pp. 24–46.

Andrejevic, M. 2009, 'The Twenty-First Century Telescreen', in G. Turner & J. Tay (eds), *Television Studies After TV: Understanding Television in the Post-Broadcast Era*, London: Routledge, pp. 31–40.

Andrejevic, M. 2011, 'The Work that Affective Economics Does', *Cultural Studies*, 25(4–5), pp. 604–20.

Andrews, D.L. 2006, *Sport-Commerce-Culture: Essays on Sport in Late Capitalist America*, New York: Peter Lang.

Andrews, D.L. & Jackson, S.J. (eds) 2001, *Sports Stars: The Cultural Politics of Sporting Celebrity*, London: Routledge.

AOC (Australian Olympic Committee) 2008, 'Schedule 6 Media Guidelines. 2008 Australian Olympic Team', *2008 Australian Olympic Team Membership Agreement—Athletes*, St Leonards, NSW: AOC.

AP (Associated Press) 2011, 'Tweet Record Smashed by Women's World Cup', *Sydney Morning Herald*, 19 July. Online. Available http://www.smh.com.au/technology/technology-news/tweet-record-smashed-by-womens-world-cup-20110719-1hm4z.html (accessed 19 July 2011).

Appelo, Y. 2011, 'The Aftermath of Hulu CEO's Bad Boy Memo', *The Hollywood Reporter*, 18 February. Online. Available http://www.hollywoodreporter.com/news/aftermath-hulu-ceos-bad-boy-101517 (accessed 21 February 2011).

Apple 2008, 'Apple Reports Fourth Quarter Results', Data Summary, 21 October. Online. Available http://www.apple.com/pr/library/2008/10/21results.html (accessed February 2010).

Arceneaux, N. & Weiss, A.S. 2010, 'Seems Stupid Until You Try It: Press Coverage of Twitter, 2006–9', *New Media & Society*, 12(8), pp. 1262–279.

Arsenault, A. & Castells, M. 2008, 'Switching Power: Rupert Murdoch and the Global Business of Media Politics', *International Sociology*, 23(4), pp. 488–513.

Askew, K. & Wilk, R.R. (eds) 2002, *The Anthropology of Media: A Reader*, Malden, MA: Blackwell.

Australian Athletes' Alliance 2009, Submission to the Inquiry into the Reporting of Sports News and the Emergence of Digital Media, *Senate Standing Committee on Environment, Communications and the Arts*, Canberra: Parliament of Australia.

Australian Government Independent Sport Panel 2010, *The Future of Sport in Australia*, Commonwealth of Australia.

Australian Press Council 2009, Submission to the Inquiry into the Reporting of Sports News and the Emergence of Digital Media, *Senate Standing Committee on Environment, Communications and the Arts*, Canberra: Parliament of Australia.

Background Briefing 2010a, 'Why is James Murdoch So Angry?' *ABC Radio National*, 31 October. Online. Available http://www.abc.net.au/rn/background-briefing/stories/2010/3048341.htm (accessed 1 November 2010).

Background Briefing 2010b, 'Social Media and Sentiment Mining', *ABC Radio National*, 27 June. Online. Available http://www.abc.net.au/rn/background-briefing/stories/2010/2933391.htm (accessed 27 June 2010).

Background Briefing 2010c, 'The Flash Crash', *ABC Radio National*, 29 August. Online. Available http://www.abc.net.au/rn/backgroundbriefing/stories/2010/2991685.htm (accessed 29 August 2010).

Baerg, A. 2007, '*Fight Night 2*: Mediating the Body and Digital Boxing', *Sociology of Sport Journal*, 24(3), pp. 325–45.

Bagchi, R. 2011, 'Sponsor to Show Ascot United v Wembley FC FA Cup Tie on Facebook', *The Guardian*, 17 August. Online. Available http://www.guardian.co.uk/football/2011/aug/17/ascot-united-wembley-budweiser-facebook (accessed 17 August 2011).

Balnaves, M. & O'Regan, T. 2002, 'The Ratings in Transition: The Politics and Technologies of Counting', in M. Balnaves, T. O'Regan & J. Sternberg (eds), *Mobilising the Audience*, St Lucia, Brisbane: University of Queensland Press, pp. 29–64.

Barlow, A. 2008, *Blogging America: The New Public Sphere*, Westport, CT: Praeger.

Barr, T. 2008, 'Forgotten Agendas: Broadband Services for Australians', Submission to the *Select Committee on the National Broadband Network*, Canberra: Parliament of Australia.

Barthes, R. 1973, 'The World of Wrestling', *Mythologies*, London: Paladin, pp. 15–25.

Battersby, L. 2011, 'AFL Takes Optus to Court Over Rights', *The Age*, 27 September. Online. Available http://www.theage.com.au/entertainment/tv-and-radio/afl-takes-optus-to-court-over-rights-20110926–1ktnr.html (accessed 27 September 2011).

Bauman, Z. 1998, *Work, Consumerism and the New Poor*, Buckingham, UK: Open University Press.

Bauman, Z. 2000, *Liquid Modernity*, Cambridge, UK: Polity Press.

Bauman, Z. 2001, *Community: Seeking Safety in an Insecure World*, Cambridge, UK: Polity Press.

BBC 2008, 'Bristol City Complete Akinde Deal', Sport: Football, 1 September. Online. Available http://news.bbc.co.uk/sport2/hi/football/teams/b/bristol_city/7590208.stm (accessed 11 September 2008).

BBC 2009a, 'Bent Move "Aided" by Twitter Rant', Sport: Football, 6 August. Online. Available http://news.bbc.co.uk/sport2/hi/football/teams/s/sunderland/8186921.stm (accessed 9 August 2009).

BBC 2009b, 'Bell a Victim of Twitter Hoaxer', Sport: Cricket, 12 August. Online. Available http://news.bbc.co.uk/sport2/hi/cricket/8196649.stm (accessed 13 August 2009).

BBC 2010, 'Google Changes Search Service to Prevent Online Piracy', Technology, 2 December. Online. Available http://www.bbc.co.uk/news/technology-11900347 (accessed 2 December 2010).

BBC 2011, 'Injunctions Doubt as Footballer Ryan Giggs Named by MP', News, 24 May. Online. Available http://www.bbc.co.uk/news/uk-13516941 (accessed 6 June 2011).

Beal, B. & Wilson, C. 2004, '"Chicks Dig Scars": Commercialisation and the Transformation of Skateboarders' Identities', in B. Wheaton (ed), *Understanding Lifestyle Sports: Consumption, Identity and Difference*, London: Routledge, pp. 31–54.

Beck, H. 2008, 'The Real O'Neal Puts His Cyber Foot Down', *The New York Times*, 20 November. Online. Available http://www.nytimes.com/2008/11/20/sports/basketball/20shaq.html (accessed 1 February 2009).

Beck, U. 2005, *Power in the Global Age: A New Global Political Economy*, Cambridge, UK: Polity Press.

Beck, U. & Lau, C. 2005, 'Second Modernity as a Research Agenda: Theoretical and Empirical Explorations in the "Meta-Change" of Modern Society', *British Journal of Sociology*, 56(4), pp. 525–57.

Benkler, Y. 2006, *The Wealth of Networks: How Social Production Transforms Markets and Freedom*, New Haven, CT: Yale University Press.

Berg, K.A. & Harthcock, A. 2008, '"Let the Domination Begin": Sports Fans' Construction of Identity in Online Message Boards', in L.W. Hugenberg, P.M. Haridakis & A.C. Earnheardt (eds), *Sports Mania: Essays on Fandom and the Media in the 21ˢᵗ Century*, North Carolina: McFarland and Co., pp. 203–17.

Bignall, C. 2009, 'Diminishing Returns', *Sport Business International*, No. 143, March, p. 13.

Bingemann, M. & Chessell, J. 2010, 'Foxtel Chief Warns of Piracy', *The Australian*, 22 December. Online. Available http://www.theaustralian.com.au/business/industry-sectors/foxtel-chief-warns-of-piracy/story-e6frg9hx-1225974683646 (accessed 22 December 2010).

Birmingham, J. & David, M. 2011, 'Live-Streaming: Will Football Fans Continue to be More Law Abiding than Music Fans?' *Sport in Society*, 14(1), pp. 69–80.

Bollmer, G. 2010, 'Not Understanding the Network? A Review of Four Contemporary Works', *The Communication Review*, 13(3), pp. 243–60.

Bolter, J.D. & Grusin, R. 1999, *Remediation: Understanding New Media*, Cambridge, MA: The MIT Press.

Born, G. 2004, *Uncertain Vision: Birt, Dyke and the Reinvention of the BBC*, London: Vintage.

Bourdieu, P. 2005, 'The Political Field, the Social Science Field, and the Journalistic Field', in R. Benson & E. Neveu (eds), *Bourdieu and the Journalistic Field*, Cambridge, UK: Polity Press, pp. 29–47.

boyd, d. & Ellison, N. 2007, 'Social Network Sites: Definition, History, and Scholarship', *Journal of Computer-Mediated Communication*, 13(1), pp. 210–30.

Boyle, R. 2004, 'Mobile Communication and the Sports Industry: The Case of 3G', *Trends in Communication*, 12(2), pp. 73–82.

Boyle, R. 2006, *Sports Journalism: Context and Issues*, London: Sage.

Boyle, R. & Haynes, R. 2000, *Power Play: Sport, Media & Popular Culture*, Harlow, England: Pearson Education.

Boyle, R. & Haynes, R. 2004, *Football in the New Media Age*, London: Routledge.

Boyle, R., Rowe, D. & Whannel, G. 2010, '"Delight in Trivial Controversy?" Questions for Sports Journalism', in S. Allan (ed), *Routledge Companion to News and Journalism Studies*, London: Routledge, pp. 245–55.

Boyle, R. & Whannel, G. 2010a, 'Editorial: Sport and the New Media', *Convergence*, 16(3), pp. 259–62.

Boyle, R. & Whannel, G. 2010b, 'Three Interviews', *Convergence*, 16(3), pp. 355–68.

Brand, J.E., Borchard, J. & Holmes, K. 2008, *IA9: Interactive Australia 2009*, Gold Coast: The Centre for New Media Research.

brianlevine 2009, 'The Dangers of Realtime Weather', *EA Sports Forums*, 14 August. Online. Available http://forum.ea.com/eaforum/posts/list/282145.page (accessed 2 July 2010).

Briton, D. 2010, 'The Virtual Expanses of Canadian Popular Culture', in B. Beaty, D. Briton, G. Filax & R. Sullivan (eds), *How Canadians Communicate III: Contexts of Canadian Popular Culture*, Edmonton, Alberta: Athabasca University, pp. 319–52.

Broersma, M. 2010, 'Journalism as Performative Discourse: The Importance of Form and Style in Journalism', in V. Rupar (ed), *Journalism and Sense-Making: Reading the Newspaper*, Cresskill, NJ: Hampton Press, pp. 15–35.

Brookes, R. 2002, *Representing Sport*, London: Arnold.

Bruns, A. 2005, *Gatewatching: Collaborative Online News Production*, New York: Peter Lang.

Bruns, A. 2008, *Blogs, Wikipedia, Second Life, and Beyond: From Production to Produsage*, New York: Peter Lang.

Bruns, A. & Jacobs, J. (eds) 2006, *Uses of Blogs*, New York: Peter Lang.

Bryant, J. & Cummins, R.G. 2010, 'The Effects of Outcome of Mediated and Live Sporting Events on Sport Fans' Self- and Social Identities', in H.L. Hundley & A.C. Billings (eds), *Examining Identity in Sports Media*, Thousand Oaks, CA: Sage, pp. 217–38.

Bryant, N. 2007, 'Australian Athlete Blogs Banned', *BBC News*, 9 February. Online. Available http://news.bbc.co.uk/2/hi/asia-pacific/6345085.stm (accessed 7 June 2008).

Bryce, J. & Rutter, J. 2005, 'Gendered Gaming in Gendered Space', in J. Raessens & J. Goldstein (eds), *Handbook of Computer Game Studies*, Cambridge, MA: The MIT Press, pp. 300–10.

Burgess, J. & Green, J. 2009, *YouTube: Online Video and Participatory Culture*, Cambridge, UK: Polity Press.

Butt, D. 2006, 'Net Neutrality: No Easy Answers', *Media International Australia*, No. 120, pp. 14–17.

Callow, J. 2010, 'Thoughts for Manchester United: How Other Clubs are Owned', *The Guardian*, 2 March. Online. Available http://www.guardian.co.uk/football/2010/mar/02/manchester-united-ownership-models (accessed 4 April 2010).

Cammaerts, B. 2011, 'The Hegemonic Copyright Regime vs the Sharing Copyright Users of Music?' *Media, Culture & Society*, 33(3), pp. 491–502.

Camper, B. 2009, 'Retro Reflexivity: *La-Mulana*, an 8-Bit Period Piece', in B. Perron & M.J.P. Wolf (eds), *The Video Game Theory Reader 2*, New York: Routledge, pp. 169–95.

Carey, J.W. 2005, 'Historical Pragmatism and the Internet', *New Media & Society*, 7(4), pp. 443–55.

Carey, J.W. & Quirk, J.J. 1992, 'The Mythos of the Electronic Revolution', in J. Carey, *Communication as Culture: Essays on Media and Society*, New York: Routledge, pp. 113–41.

Carpentier, N. 2011, 'New Configurations of the Audience? The Challenges of User-Generated Content for Audience Theory and Media Participation', in V. Nightingale (ed), *The Handbook of Media Audiences*, Oxford: Blackwell, pp. 190–212.

Casey, P.R. 2010, 'Interview with Nick Maywald, CEO and Founder of SportingPulse', *The Huffington Post*, 19 March. Online. Available http://www.huffingtonpost.com/peter-robert-casey/interview-with-nick-maywa_b_505912.html (accessed 24 January 2011).

Cash, J. & Damousi, J. 2009, *Footy Passions*, Sydney: University of New South Wales Press.

Cashman, R. 2010, *Paradise of Sport: The Rise of Organized Sport in Australia*, revised edition, Sydney: Walla Walla Press.

Cashman, R. & Darcy, S. 2008, *Benchmark Games: The Sydney 2000 Paralympic Games*, Sydney: Wall Walla Press.

Cashmore, E. 2004, *Beckham*, 2nd edition, Cambridge, UK: Polity Press.

Cassell, J. & Jenkins, H. 1998a, 'Chess for Girls? Feminism and Computer Games', in J. Cassell & H. Jenkins (eds), *From Barbie to Mortal Kombat: Gender and Computer Games*, Cambridge, MA: The MIT Press, pp. 2–45

Cassell, J. & Jenkins, H. (eds) 1998b, *From Barbie to Mortal Kombat: Gender and Computer Games*, Cambridge, MA: The MIT Press.

Castells, M. 2000a, *The Rise of the Network Society*, 2nd edition, Oxford: Blackwell.

Castells, M. 2000b, *End of Millennium*, 2ⁿᵈ edition, Oxford: Blackwell.

Castells, M. 2002, *The Internet Galaxy: Reflections on the Internet, Business, and Society*, Oxford: Oxford University Press.

Castells, M. 2004a, *The Power of Identity*, 2ⁿᵈ edition, Oxford: Blackwell Publishers.

Castells, M. (ed) 2004b, *The Network Society: A Cross-Cultural Perspective*, Cheltenham, UK: Edward Elgar.

Castells, M. 2009, *Communication Power*, Oxford: Oxford University Press.

Castells, M., Fernandez-Ardevol, M., Qiu, J.L. & Sey, A. 2007, *Mobile Communication and Society: A Global Perspective*, Cambridge, MA: The MIT Press.

Castronova, E. 2005, *Synthetic Worlds: The Business and Culture of Online Games*, Chicago, IL: University of Chicago Press.

Chandler, J.M. 1988, *Television and National Sport: The United States and Britain*, Urbana, IL: University of Illinois Press.

Church-Sanders, R. 2008, 'Online Sports Piracy: Is Prevention Better Than Cure?' *Sport Media Technology*, March, pp. 10–11.

Church-Sanders, R. 2010, 'To Tweet, or Not to Tweet', *Sport Business International*, No. 153, February, pp. 20–21.

Cianfrone, B.A. & Baker, T.A. 2010, 'The Use of Student-Athlete Likenesses in Sport Video Games: An Application of the Right of Publicity', *Journal of the Legal Aspects of Sport*, 20(1), pp. 35–74.

Cisco 2011, 'Cisco Visual Networking Index: Forecast and Methodology, 2010–2015'. Online. Available http://www.cisco.com/en/US/solutions/collateral/ns341/ns525/ns537/ns705/ns827/white_paper_c11–481360_ns827_Networking_Solutions_White_Paper.html (accessed 19 May 2011).

Clark, N. 2011, 'Perform Plans Public Listing in London', *The Independent*, 11 March. Online. Available http://www.independent.co.uk/news/business/news/perform-plans-public-listing-in-london-2238558.html (accessed 12 March 2011).

Clarke, T.L., McBride, D.K. & Reece, D. 2002, 'All But War is Simulation', *Sport Technology: History, Philosophy and Policy*, 21, pp. 215–24.

Clayton, W. 2011, 'Video Game Helps with PLAYERS Preparation', *Yahoo!Sports*, 11 May. Online. Available http://sports.yahoo.com/golf/pga/news?slug=pgatour_com-ea-sports-practice-20110511&print=1 (accessed 12 May 2011).

Cleland, J. 2011, 'The Media and Football Supporters: A Changing Relationship', *Media, Culture & Society*, 33(2), pp. 299–315.

Close, P., Askew, D. & Xin, X. 2007, *The Beijing Olympiad: The Political Economy of a Sporting Mega-Event*, London: Routledge.

Coakley, J., Hallinan, C., Jackson, S. & Mewett, P. 2009, *Sports in Society: Issues and Controversies in Australia and New Zealand*, Sydney: McGraw Hill.

Cohen, S. 1980 [1972], *Folk Devils and Moral Panics: The Making of Mods and Rockers*, Oxford: Martin Robertson.

Consalvo, M. 2009, 'There is No Magic Circle', *Games and Culture*, 4(4), pp. 408–17.

Conway, S. 2010, '"It's in the Game" and Above the Game: An Analysis of the Users of Sports Videogames', *Convergence*, 16(3), pp. 334–54.

Coombe, R.J. 1998, *The Cultural Life of Intellectual Properties: Authorship, Appropriation, and the Law*, Durham, NC: Duke University Press.

Cormode, G. & Krishnamurthy, B. 2008, 'Key Differences Between Web 1.0 and Web 2.0', *First Monday*, 13(6), http://firstmonday.org/htbin/cgiwrap/bin/ojs/index.php/fm/article/view/2125/1972 (accessed 4 December 2008).

Couldry, N. 2003, *Media Rituals: A Critical Approach*, London: Routledge.

Couldry, N. 2006, *Listening Beyond the Echoes: Media, Ethics, and Agency in an Uncertain World*, Boulder, CO: Paradigm Publishers.

Couldry, N. 2008, 'Mediatization or Mediation? Alternative Understandings of the Emergent Space of Digital Storytelling', *New Media & Society*, 10(3), pp. 373–91.

Couldry, N. 2010, *Why Voice Matters: Culture and Politics After Neoliberalism*, London: Sage.

Couldry, N., Livingstone, S. & Markham, T. 2007, *Media Consumption and Public Engagement: Beyond the Presumption of Attention*, Basingstoke, Hampshire: Palgrave Macmillan.

Couldry, N. & McCarthy, A. (eds) 2004, *Mediaspace: Place, Scale and Culture in a Media Age*, London: Routledge.

Coyle Media 2011, 'Digital Business Development'. Online. Available http://www.coylemedia.com/ (accessed 14 January 2011).

Crawford, G. 2004, *Consuming Sport: Fans, Sport and Culture*, London: Routledge.

Crawford, G. 2006, 'The Cult of Champ Man: The Culture and Pleasures of Championship Manager / Football Manager Games', *Information, Communication & Society*, 9(4), pp. 496–514.

Crawford, G. 2008, '"It's in the Game": Sports Fans, Film and Digital Gaming', *Sport in Society*, 11(2–3), pp. 130–45.

Crawford, G. & Gosling, V.K. 2009, 'More Than A Game: Sports-Themed Video Games and Player Narratives', *Sociology of Sport Journal*, 26(1), pp. 50–66.

Crawford, K. 2005, 'Adaptation: Tracking the Ecologies of Music and Peer-to-Peer Networks', *Media International Australia*, No. 114, pp. 30–39.

Crawford, K. 2009, 'These Foolish Things: On Intimacy and Insignificance in Mobile Media', in G. Goggin & L. Hjorth (eds), *Mobile Technologies: From Telecommunications to Media*, New York: Routledge, pp. 252–65.

CRI 2008, 'Netizens Incensed Over Tibet Album on iTunes', *China.org.cn*. Online. Available http://www.china.org.cn/china/national/2008–08/08/content_16161481.htm (accessed 16 August 2008).

Cricinfo Staff 2007, 'ESPN Acquires Cricinfo', *ESPN Cricinfo*, 11 June. Online. Available http://www.espncricinfo.com/ci/content/current/story/297655.html (accessed 4 January 2010).

Cricket Australia 2009, Submission to the Inquiry into the Reporting of Sports News and the Emergence of Digital Media, *Senate Standing Committee on Environment, Communications and the Arts*, Canberra: Parliament of Australia.

Crompton, J.L. 2001, 'Public Subsidies to Professional Team Sport Facilities in the USA', in C. Gratton & I.P. Henry (eds), *Sport in the City*, London: Routledge, pp. 15–34.

Crossley, R. 2010, 'Female Count of UK Dev Workforce "Falls to 4%"', *Develop*, 8 September. Online. Available http://www.develop-online.net/news/35806/Female-count-of-UK-dev-workforce-falls-to-4 (accessed 10 January 2011).

Cubitt, S., Hassan, R. & Volkmer, I. 2011, 'Does Cloud Computing Have a Silver Lining?' *Media, Culture & Society*, 33(1), pp. 149–58.

Cummins, R.G. 2006, 'Sports Fiction: Critical and Empirical Perspectives', in A.A. Raney & J. Bryant (eds), *Handbook of Sports and Media*, Mahwah, NJ: Lawrence Erlbaum Associates, pp. 185–204.

Cunningham, S. 2011, 'Broadband, the NBN and Screen Futures', *Media International Australia*, No. 140, pp. 16–21.

Curi, M., Knijnik, J. & Mascarenhas, G. 2011, 'The Pan American Games in Rio de Janeiro 2007: Consequences of a Sport Mega-Event on a BRIC Country', *International Review for the Sociology of Sport*, 46(2), pp. 140–56.

Curran, J. 2011, *Media and Democracy*, London: Routledge.

Cutler, M. 2011a, 'You Tube to Expand Live Sports Portfolio with Copa America Coverage', *Sport Business.com*, 16 June. Online. Available http://www.

sportbusiness.com/news/183792/youtube-to-expand-live-sports-portfolio-with-copa-america-coverage (accessed 16 June 2011).

Cutler, M. 2011b, 'FA Announce Twitter Crackdown', *Sport Business.com*, 14 February. Online. Available http://www.sportbusiness.com/news/183025/fa-announces-twitter-crackdown (accessed 14 February 2011).

Cutler, M. 2011c, 'Chelsea Maintains Asian Vision', *Sport Business.com*, 16 March. Online. Available http://www.sportbusiness.com/news/183257/chelsea-maintains-asian-vision (accessed 20 April 2011).

Cutler, M. 2011d, 'Vodafone Essar to Stream Cricket World Cup Matches', *Sport Business.com*, 14 February. Online. Available http://www.sportbusiness.com/news/183026/vodafone-essar-to-stream-cricket-world-cup-matches (accessed 14 February 2011).

Cyclingnews.com 2011, 'About Cyclingnews'. Online. Available http://autobus.cyclingnews.com/adpage/about.php (accessed 16 March 2011).

Dart, J.J. 2009, 'Blogging the 2006 FIFA World Cup Finals', *Sociology of Sport Journal*, 26(1), pp. 107–26.

Dart, T. 2007, 'Fans Pick the Team as Computer Games Turn Fantasy Into Reality', *Times Online*, 25 October. Online. Available http://www.timesonline.co.uk/tol/sport/football/article2733559.ece (accessed 3 December 2007).

David's Blog 2011, Online. Available http://www.davidbeckham.com/news (accessed 1 July 2011).

Davis, N.W. & Duncan, M.C. 2006, 'Sports Knowledge is Power: Reinforcing Masculine Privilege Through Fantasy Sport League Participation', *Journal of Sport and Social Issues*, 30(3), pp. 244–64.

Dayan, D. 2008, 'Beyond Media Events: Disenchantment, Derailment, Disruption', in M.E. Price & D. Dayan (eds), *Owning the Olympics: Narratives of the New China*, Ann Arbor, MI: University of Michigan Press, pp. 391–401.

Dayan, D. & Katz, E. 1992, *Media Events: The Live Broadcasting of History*, Cambridge, MA: Harvard University Press.

Demonbaby 2006, 'E3 Ramblings and Xbox Live Terrorism', 17 May. Online. Available http://www.demonbaby.com/blog/2006/05/e3-ramblings-and-xbox-live-terrorism.html (accessed 2 May 2007).

Department of Broadband, Communications and the Digital Economy 2010a, *Sport on Television: A Review of the Anti-Siphoning Scheme in the Contemporary Digital Environment*, Australian Government.

Department of Broadband, Communications and the Digital Economy 2010b, *Code of Practice for Sports News Reporting (Text, Photography and Data)*, Australian Government.

Denton, S. (ed) 2008, *the fleet@wembley: Ebbsfleet United—FA Trophy Winners 2008*, Shrewsbury, UK: Jam Book Publishing.

Derober 2008, '8 Athletes Who Blog (and 2 That Shouldn't)', 10 July. Online. Available http://derober.com/?s=athletes+who+blog (accessed 2 August 2008).

Deuze, M. 2007, *Media Work*, Cambridge, UK: Polity Press.

Deuze, M. 2009, 'Media Industries, Work and Life', *European Journal of Communication*, 24(4), pp. 467–80.

Deuze, M. 2011, 'Media Life', *Media, Culture & Society*, 33(1), pp. 137–48.

Deuze, M. & Marjoribanks, T. 2009, 'Newswork', *Journalism: Theory, Practice and Criticism*, 10(5), pp. 555–61.

deZwart, M. 2009, 'The Panel Case', in A. Kenyon, M. Richardson & S. Ricketson (eds), *Landmarks in Australian Intellectual Property Law*, Port Melbourne: Cambridge University Press, pp. 251–63.

Dittmer, J. 2009, 'Football's New Forms', *FlowTV*, 10(10), http://flowtv.org/?p=4423 (accessed 18 October 2009).

Drayer, J., Shapiro, S.L., Dwyer, B., Morse, A.L. & White, J. 2010, 'The Effects of Fantasy Football Participation on NFL Consumption: A Qualitative Analysis', *Sport Management Review*, 13(2), pp. 129–41.

du Gay, P., Hall, S., Janes, L., Mackay, H. & Negus, K. 1997, *Doing Cultural Studies: The Story of the Sony Walkman*, London: Sage.

Dumitrescu, A. 2008, 'Peter Moore Talks About Madden NFL 2009', *Softpedia*, 10 September. Online. Available http://news.softpedia.com/news/Peter-Moore-Talks-About-Madden-NFL-2009–93308.shtml (accessed 12 December 2010).

Dunne, F. 2011a, 'Language Key to Future Rights Values in Kolkott ECJ Opinion', *Sport Business International*, No. 165, March, pp. 50–51.

Dunne, F. 2011b, 'The Road Ahead', *Sport Business International*, No. 165, March, pp. 38–39.

Dunne, F. 2011c, 'Asian Engine Room', *Sport Business International*, No. 165, March, pp. 40–41.

Dunning, E. & Rojek, C. (eds) 1992, *Sport and Leisure in the Civilizing Process: Critique and Counter-Critique*, Toronto: University of Toronto Press.

Dwyer, B. & Drayer, J. 2010, 'Fantasy Sport Consumer Segmentation: An Investigation into the Differing Consumption Modes of Fantasy Football Participants', *Sport Marketing Quarterly*, 19(4), pp. 207–16.

Dwyer, B. & Kim, Y. 2011, 'For Love or Money: Developing and Validating a Motivational Scale for Fantasy Football Participation', *Journal of Sport Management*, 25(1), pp. 70–83.

Dyer-Witheford, N. & de Peuter, G. 2009, *Games of Empire: Global Capitalism and Video Games*, Minneapolis, MN: University of Minnesota Press.

ea_spouse 2004, 'EA: The Human Story', *Live Journal*, 10 November. Online. Available http://ea-spouse.livejournal.com/274.html (accessed 22 October 2008).

Eckersley, O. & Benton, N. 2002, 'The Venue Versus the Lounge Room', *Australasian Leisure Management*, No. 35, pp. 20–23.

eCoinToss Sports Display 2010, 'The eCoinToss Sports Display Technology'. Online. Available http://ecointoss.com/technology.php (accessed 1 June 2010).

Economic Times (India) 2007, 'Football Gathers Crowd Through Web', 7 September. Online. Available http://economictimes.indiatimes.com/Infotech/Internet_/Football_gathers_crowd_through_web/articleshow/msid-2345508,curpg-2.cms (accessed 2 December 2007).

Edwards, R. 2008, 'Does the Current MyFC Model Have a Future?' *MyFootballClub.co.uk*, 13 April. Online. Available http://members.myfootballclub.co.uk/item/does-the-current-myfc-model-have-a-future-31601 (accessed 13 April 2008).

Ehrlich, B. 2011, 'Sports Fans Could Soon Tune in to Games Live on YouTube', *Mashable*, 22 February. Online. Available http://mashable.com/2011/02/22/youtube-live-sports/ (accessed 2 March 2011).

Electronic Arts 2010, 'Electronic Arts Updates Fiscal Year Outlook 2010', 11 January. Online. Available http://investor.ea.com/releasedetail.cfm?ReleaseID=436876 (accessed 14 February 2011).

Elias, N. & Dunning, E. 1986, *Quest for Excitement: Sport and Leisure in the Civilizing Process*, Oxford: Blackwell.

Elliott, A. & Urry, J. 2010, *Mobile Lives*, London: Routledge.

Elmer, G. 2004, *Profiling Machines: Mapping the Personal Information Economy*, Cambridge, MA: The MIT Press.

Eltham, B. 2011, 'The Copyright Lobby's Loose Facts', *Crikey*, 18 March. Online. Available http://www.crikey.com.au/2011/03/18/the-copyright-lobby-why-you-cant-believe-what-you-read/ (accessed 20 March 2011).

Epstein, R.A. 2005, 'The Creators Own Ideas', *Technology Review*, June, pp. 57–60.

ESPN Video 2009, 'Virtual Playbook', 19 May. Online. Available http://espn. go.com/video/clip?id=4178973 (accessed 11 February 2010).

Evans, S. 2007–2008, 'Whose Stats are they Anyway? Analyzing the Battle Between Major League Baseball and Fantasy Game Sites', *Texas Review of Entertainment and Sports Law*, 9(2), pp. 335–51.

Evens, T. & Lefever, K. 2011, 'Watching the Football Game: Broadcasting Rights for the European Digital Television Market', *Journal of Sport and Social Issues*, 35(1), pp. 33–49.

Evens, T., Lefever, K., Valcke, P., Schuurman, D. & De Marez, L. 2011, 'Access to Premium Content on Mobile Television Platforms: The Case of Mobile Sports', *Telematics and Informatics*, 28(1), pp. 32–39.

Fairweather, N.B. 2002, 'Disembodied Sport: Ethical Issues in Virtual Sport, Electronic Games and Virtual Leisure', *Sport Technology: History, Philosophy and Policy*, 21, pp. 235–49.

Farman, J. 2010, 'Mapping the Digital Empire: Google Earth and the Process of Postmodern Cartography', *New Media & Society*, 12(6), pp. 869–88.

Fenton, N. & Barassi, V. 2011, 'Alternative Media and Social Networking Sites: The Politics of Individuation and Political Participation', *The Communication Review*, 14(3), pp. 179–96.

Ferriter, M.M. 2009, '"Arguably the Greatest": Sports Fans and Communities at Work on Wikipedia', *Sociology of Sport Journal*, 26(1), pp. 127–54.

Flew, T. 2005, *New Media: An Introduction*, Melbourne: Oxford University Press.

Flint, J. 2011a, 'Time Warner Cable, Lakers Strike 20-Year Deal', *Los Angeles Times*, 14 February. Online. Available http://articles.latimes.com/2011/feb/14/ sports/la-sp-0215-lakers-time-warner-20110215 (accessed 20 May 2011).

Flint, J. 2011b, 'Time Warner Cable's Lakers Deal is Bad news for Other Pay-TV Distributors', *Los Angeles Times*, 16 February. Online. Available http://latimes-blogs.latimes.com/entertainmentnewsbuzz/2011/02/time-warner-cables-laker-deal-is-bad-news-for-other-pay-tv-distributors.html (accessed 20 May 2011).

Florian, E. 2004, 'Six Lessons from the Fast Lane', *Fortune Magazine*, 6 September. Online. Available http://money.cnn.com/magazines/fortune/fortune_ archive/2004/09/06/380342/index.htm (accessed 10 August 2010).

Foran, M. 2008, 'One Nation Under Madden', *Nielsen Wire*, 3 November. Online. Available http://blog.nielsen.com/nielsenwire/sports/one-nation-under-madden-how-the-madden-video-game-franchise-became-bigger-than-john-madden/ (accessed 3 September 2009).

Foucault, M. 1991, 'Governmentality', in G. Burchell, C. Gordon & P. Miller (eds), *The Foucault Effect: Studies in Governmentality*, Chicago, IL: University of Chicago Press, pp. 87–104.

Four Corners 2009, 'Code of Silence', 11 May. Online. Available http://www.abc. net.au/4corners/content/2009/s2565007.htm (accessed 12 May 2009).

Fox Sports 2011, 'Former NRL Star and Greater Western Sydney Code-Crosser Israel Folau Uses Playstation to Learn AFL', 1 June. Online. Available http:// www.foxsports.com.au/afl/afl-premiership/former-nrl-star-and-greater-western-sydney-code-crosser-israel-folau-uses-playstation-to-learn-afl/story-e6frf3e3-1226067017977 (accessed 1 June 2011).

Francombe, J. 2010, '"I Cheer, You Cheer, We Cheer": Physical Technologies and the Normalized Body', *Television & New Media*, 11(5), pp. 350–66.

Freeman, J. 2011, 'Local E-Government: Politics and Civic Participation,' unpublished PhD thesis, Monash University.

Friedman, J. 2008, 'Ebbswhat?' in S. Denton (ed), *the fleet@wembley: Ebbsfleet United—FA Trophy Winners 2008*, Shrewsbury, UK: Jam Book Publishing, pp. 38–49.

Friedman, M. 2008, '5 Minute World Wide Fire Works', *Mike Friedman: Jelly Belly / Kenda Pro Cycling Team*, 6 August. Online. Available http://www.mike-friedman.missingsaddle.com/2008/08/06/5-minute-world-wide-fire-works/ (accessed 6 August 2008).

Frost & Sullivan 2011, 'Australian Online General and Mobile Advertising Market 2010', Sydney: Frost & Sullivan.

Fry, A. 2008a, 'In Defiance of the Downturn', *Sport Business International,* No. 139, October, pp. 34–39.

Fry, A. 2008b, 'Fantasy Gaming Comes of Age', *Sport Business International,* No. 135, June, pp. 22–25.

Fry, A. 2009, 'New Dimension', *Sport Business International,* No. 145, May, pp. 32–33.

Fry, A. 2010, 'Measuring the Media', *Sport Business International,* No. 156, May, pp. 20–21.

Gane, N. 2004, *The Future of Social Theory*, London: Continuum.

Gane, N. 2006, 'Speed Up or Slow Down? Social Theory in the Information Age', *Information, Communication & Society*, 9(1), pp. 20–38.

Gantz, W., Wang, Z., Bryant, P. & Potter, R.F. 2006, 'Sports Versus All Comers: Comparing TV Sports Fans With Fans of Other Programming Genres', *Journal of Broadcasting & Electronic Media*, 50(1), pp. 95–118.

Garofalo, R. 2003, 'I Want My MP3: Who Owns Internet Music?' in M. Cloonan & R. Garofalo (eds), *Policing Pop*, Philadelphia, PA: Temple University Press, pp. 30–45.

Gates, K. 2006, 'Will Work for Copyrights: The Cultural Policy of Anti-Piracy Campaigns', *Social Semiotics*, 16(1), pp. 57–73.

Gaudiosi, J. 2011, 'EA Sports' Madden Bowl XVII Video Game Tournament Goes Live on ESPN3.com', *Hollywood Reporter*, 2 February. Online. Available http://www.hollywoodreporter.com/news/ea-sports-madden-bowl-xvii-95812 (accessed 12 April 2011).

Gibson, O. 2009a, 'Online Broadcaster Defends Decision Only to Show England Match on Web', *The Guardian*, 5 October. Online. Available http://www.guardian.co.uk/media/2009/oct/05/ukraine-england-football-perform-online (accessed 5 October 2009).

Gibson, O. 2009b, 'Premier League Goes to War on Internet Pirates', *The Guardian*, 22 January. Online. Available http://www.guardian.co.uk/football/2009/jan/21/premier-league-cracks-down-on-illegal-broadcasts (accessed 22 January 2009).

Giddings, S. & Kennedy, H.W. 2010, '"Incremental Speed Increases Excitement": Bodies, Space, Movement, and Televisual Change', *Television & New Media*, 11(3), pp. 163–79.

Gillespie, T. 2007, *Wired Shut: Copyright and the Shape of Digital Culture*, Cambridge, MA: The MIT Press.

Gillespie, T. 2009, 'Characterizing Copyright in the Classroom: The Cultural Work of Antipiracy Campaigns', *Communication, Culture & Critique*, 2(3), pp. 274–318.

Gilmour, R. 2009, 'Ukraine v England: Internet Match Attracts 500,000 Web Viewers', *The Telegraph*, 11 October. Online. Available http://www.telegraph.co.uk/sport/football/teams/england/6298446/Ukraine-v-England-internet-match-attracts-500000-web-viewers.html (accessed 11 October 2009).

Giulianotti, R. 1999, *Football: A Sociology of the Global Game*, Cambridge, UK: Polity Press.

Giulianotti, R. 2002, 'Supporters, Followers, Fans, and *Flaneurs*: A Taxonomy of Spectator Identities in Football', *Journal of Sport and Social Issues*, 26(1), pp. 25–46.

Giulianotti, R. & Robertson, R. 2009, *Globalization and Football*, London: Sage.

Given, J. 2009, 'Bothering About Broadband: Review Essay', *Media International Australia*, No. 132, pp. 118–32.

Glendinning, M. 2009, 'Follow the Leader: Serie A', *Sport Business International*, No. 148, August, p. 33.

Goffman, E. 1990 [1959], *The Presentation of Self in Everyday Life*, Harmondsworth, London: Penguin.

Goggin, G. 2006, *Cell Phone Culture: Mobile Technologies in Everyday Life*, London: Routledge.

Goggin, G. 2011, *Global Mobile Media*, London: Routledge.

Goggin, G. & Hjorth, L. 2009, 'Waiting to Participate Introduction', *Communication, Politics & Culture*, 42(2), pp. 1–5.

Goggin, G. & Newell, C. 2000, 'Crippling Paralympics? Media, Disability and Olympism', *Media International Australia*, No. 97, pp. 71–83.

Goggin, G. & Spurgeon, C. 2007, 'Premium Rate Culture: The New Business of Mobile Interactivity', *New Media & Society*, 9(5), pp. 753–70.

Goldlust, J. 1987, *Playing for Keeps: Sport, The Media and Society*, Melbourne: Longman Cheshire.

Goldsmith, B. 2009, '"Outside the Box: Television 2018" Project Background, Research Questions, and Critical Uncertainties', *Record of the Communications and Policy Research Forum 2009*, Sydney: Network Insight Institute, pp. 176–78.

Grady, J. 2007, 'Fantasy Stats Case Tests Limits of Intellectual Property Protection in the Digital Age', *Sport Marketing Quarterly*, 16(4), pp. 203–31.

Gray, J., Sandvoss, C. & Harrington, C. (eds) 2007, *Fandom: Identities and Communities in a Mediated World*, New York: New York University Press.

Gregg, M. 2011, *Work's Intimacy*, Cambridge, UK: Polity Press.

Groshell, W. 2008, 'Linfield Keeper's Trophy Final Day', in S. Denton (ed), *the fleet@wembley: Ebbsfleet United—FA Trophy Winners 2008*, Shrewsbury, UK: Jam Book Publishing, pp. 82–90.

Grossman, L. 2006, 'You—Yes, You—are TIME's Person of the Year', *Time* magazine, 13 December. Online. Available http://www.time.com/time/magazine/article/0,9171,1569514,00.html (accessed 10 March 2011).

Gruneau, R. & Whitson, D. 1993, *Hockey Night in Canada: Sport, Identities and Cultural Politics*, Toronto: Garamond Press.

Gurak, L., Antonijevic, S., Johnson, L.A., Ratliff, C. & Reyman, J. (eds) 2004, *Into the Blogosphere: Rhetoric, Community and Culture of Weblogs*, Minneapolis, MN: University of Minnesota.

Guttmann, A. 2002, *The Olympics: A History of the Modern Games*, Urbana, IL: University of Illinois Press.

Guttmann, A. 2004 [1978], *From Ritual to Record: The Nature of Modern Sports*, New York: Columbia University Press.

Haigh, G. 1993, *The Cricket War*, Melbourne: Text Publishing.

Haigh, G. 2002, *The Vincibles: A Suburban Cricket Season*, Melbourne: Text Publishing.

Haigh, G. 2006, *Silent Revolutions: Writings on Cricket History*, Melbourne: Black Inc.

Haigh, G. 2008, *Inside Out: Writings on Cricket Culture*, Melbourne: Melbourne University Press.

Haigh, G. 2010, *Sphere of Influence: Writings on Cricket and its Discontents*, Melbourne: Victory Books.

Halloran, J. 2010, 'Australian Commonwealth Games Athletes Handed Twitter, Facebook Ban', *Fox Sports*, 4 October. Online. Available http://www.foxsports.com.au/other-sports/australian-commonwealth-games-athletes-handed-twitter-facebook-ban/story-e6frf57c-1225933667743 (accessed 4 October 2010).

Halloran, J. 2011, 'Australian Olympic Committee Designs Workshops to Teach Athletes Safe Use of Social Media', *Fox Sports*, 20 February. Online. Available http://www.foxsports.com.au/other-sports/australian-olympic-committee-designs-workshops-to-teach-athletes-safe-use-of-social-media/story-e6frf56c-1226008884990 (accessed 21 February 2011).

Halverson, E.R. & Halverson, R. 2008, 'Fantasy Baseball: The Case for Competitive Fandom', *Games and Culture*, 3(3–4), pp. 286–308.

Hamil, S., Walters, G. & Watson, L. 2010, 'The Model of Governance at FC Barcelona: Balancing Member Democracy, Commercial Strategy, Corporate Social Responsibility and Sporting Performance', *Soccer & Society*, 11(4), pp. 475–504.

Hammervold, R. & Solberg, H.A. 2006, 'TV Sport Programs—Who is Willing to Pay to Watch', *Journal of Media Economics*, 19(3), pp. 147–62.

Harambam, J., Aupers, S. & Houtman, D. 2011, 'Game Over? Negotiating Modern Capitalism in Virtual Game Worlds', *European Journal of Cultural Studies*, 14(3), pp. 299–319.

Hargreaves, J. 1994, *Sporting Females: Critical Issues in the History and Sociology of Women's Sport*, London: Routledge.

Harvell, B. 2011, 'We'll Be Much Bigger Than Twitter', *Benharvell.com*, 3 May. Online. Available http://www.benharvell.com/journal/2011/5/3/well-be-much-bigger-than-twitter-an-interview-with-tout-ceo.html (accessed 2 June 2011).

Harvey D. 2005, *A Brief History of Neoliberalism*, Oxford: Oxford University Press.

Hassan, R. 2011, 'The Speed of Collapse: The Space-Time Dimensions of Capitalism's Great Crisis of the 21st Century', *Critical Sociology*, 37(4), pp. 385–402.

Hawthorne, M. 2010, 'News Gags its Storm Website Critics', *The Age*, 27 July. Online. Available http://www.theage.com.au/rugby-league/league-news/news-gags-its-storm-website-critics-20100726–10soh.html (accessed 27 July 2010).

Hawthorne, M. 2011, 'Storm Boss Threatens to Sue Club Fan', *The Age*, 20 January. Online. Available http://www.smh.com.au/rugby-league/league-news/storm-boss-threatens-to-sue-club-fan-20110119–19wnw.html (accessed 20 January 2011).

Haynes, R. 1995, *The Football Imagination: The Rise of Football Fanzine Culture*, Aldershot, UK: Arena.

Haynes, R. 1998, 'A Pageant of Sound and Vision: Football's Relationship with Television, 1936–60', *International Journal of the History of Sport*, 15(1), pp. 211–26.

Haynes, R. 2004, 'The Fame Game: The Peculiarities of Sports Image Rights in the United Kingdom', *Trends in Communication*, 12(2), pp. 101–16.

Heinrichs, P. 2007, 'Rush to Block Web Broadcast of Soccer Final', *The Age*, 18 February. Online. Available http://www.theage.com.au/news/soccer/rush-to-block-web-broadcast-of-soccer-final/2007/02/17/1171405502827.html (accessed 18 February 2007).

Hellekson, K. & Busse, K. 2006, *Fan Fiction and Fan Communities in the Age of the Internet*, Jefferson, NC: McFarland and Co.

Hermes, J. 2006, 'Citizenship in the Age of the Internet', *European Journal of Communication*, 21(3), pp. 295–309.

Hermida, A. 2010, 'Twittering the News: The Emergence of Ambient Journalism', *Journalism Practice*, 4(3), pp. 297–308.

Herz, J.C. 1997, *Joystick Nation: How Videogames Ate Our Quarters, Won Our Hearts, and Rewired Our Minds,* Boston, MA: Little, Brown and Co.

Herz, J.C. 2005, 'Harnessing the Hive', in J. Hartley (ed), *Creative Industries*, Malden, MA: Blackwell, pp. 327–41.

Hesmondhalgh, D. & Toynbee, J. 2008, 'Why Media Studies Needs Better Social Theory', in D. Hesmondhalgh & J. Toynbee (eds), *The Media and Social Theory*, London: Routledge, pp. 1–24.

Hill, C. 1992, *Olympic Politics*, Manchester: Manchester University Press.

Hills, M. 2002, *Fan Cultures*, London: Routledge.

Himanen, P. 2001, *The Hacker Ethic and the Spirit of the Information Age*, New York: Random House.

Hiscock, G. 2011, 'Media Giant Wins IPL Cricket Rights', *The Australian*, 22 March. Online. Available http://www.theaustralian.com.au/business/in-depth/media-giant-wins-ipl-cricket-rights/story-e6frgaho-1226026145815 (accessed 23 March 2011).

Hoberman, J. 1995, 'Toward a Theory of Olympic Internationalism', *Journal of Sport History*, 22(1), pp. 1–37.

Holt, R. 1989, *Sport and the British: A Modern History*, Oxford: Oxford University Press.

Hornby, N. 1992, *Fever Pitch*, London: Victor Gollancz.

Horne, D. 1964, *The Lucky Country*, Ringwood, Victoria: Penguin Books.

Horne, J. 2006, *Sport in Consumer Culture*, Basingstoke, UK: Palgrave Macmillan.

Horne, J. & Whannel, G. 2010, 'The "Caged Torch Procession": Celebrities, Protesters and the 2008 Olympic Torch Relay in London, Paris and San Francisco', *Sport in Society*, 13(5), pp. 760–70.

Howe, J. 2006, 'The Rise of Crowdsourcing', *Wired* 14.6, June. Online. Available http://www.wired.com/wired/archive/14.06/crowds.html (accessed 13 March 2007).

Howe, J. 2008, *Crowdsourcing: How the Power of the Crowd is Driving the Future of Business*, London: Random House.

Huizinga, J. 1955, *Homo Ludens: A Study of the Play Element in Culture*, Boston, MA: Beacon.

Humphreys, L. & Finlay, C.J. 2008, 'New Technologies, New Narratives', in M.E. Price & D. Dayan (eds), *Owning the Olympics: Narratives of the New China*, Ann Arbor, MI: The University of Michigan Press, pp. 284–306.

Humphreys, S., Fitzgerald, B., Banks, J. & Suzor, N. 2005, 'Fan-Based Production for Computer Games: User-Led Innovation, the "Drift of Value" and Intellectual Property Rights', *Media International Australia*, No. 114, pp. 16–29.

Hunsinger, J., Klastrup, L. & Allen, M. (eds) 2010, *International Handbook of Internet Research*, London: Springer.

Huntemann, N. 2010, 'Irreconcilable Differences: Gender and Labor in the Video Game Workplace', *FlowTV,* 11(6): http://flowtv.org/2010/01/irreconcilable-differences-gender-and-labor-in-the-video-game-workplace-nina-b-huntemann-suffolk-university/ (accessed 4 February 2010).

Hunter, A. 2011, 'Liverpool Threatens Breakaway from Premier League's TV Rights Deal', *The Guardian*, 11 October. Online. Available http://www.guardian.co.uk/football/2011/oct/11/liverpool-breakaway-tv-deal (accessed 11 October 2011).

Hunter, M. 2003, 'McLuhan's Pendulum: Reading Dialectics of Technological Distance', in *Sarai Reader: Shaping Technologies*, Delhi: The Sarai Programme, pp. 144–56.

Hutcheon, S. 2008a, 'Masked Cyclist: "I'd Do It Again"', *The Age*, 8 August. Online. Available http://www.theage.com.au/news/off-the-field/masked-cyclist-id-do-it-again/2008/08/08/1218139043975.html (accessed 8 August 2008).

Hutcheon, S. 2008b, 'Dalai Lama Muso Didn't Mean to Hit iTunes', *Sydney Morning Herald*, 22 August. Online. Available http://www.smh.com.au/news/technology/creator-shocked-at-china-itunes-ban/2008/08/22/1219262492497.html (accessed 22 August 2008).

Hutchins, B. 2002, *Don Bradman: Challenging the Myth*, Melbourne: Cambridge University Press.

Hutchins, B. 2007, 'The Problem of Sport and Social Cohesion,' in J. Jupp & J. Nieuwenhuysen with E. Dawson (eds), *Social Cohesion in Australia*, Melbourne: Cambridge University Press, pp. 170–81.

Hutchins, B. 2008, 'Signs of Meta-Change in Second Modernity: The Growth of e-Sport and the World Cyber Games,' *New Media & Society*, 10(6), pp. 851–69.

Hutchins, B. 2009, '26 January 1981. The Opening of the Australian Institute of Sport: The Government Takes Control of the National Pastime', in D. Roberts & M. Crotty (eds), *Turning Points in Australian History*, Sydney: University of New South Wales Press, pp. 198–210.

Hutchins, B. 2011, 'The Acceleration of Media Sport Culture: Twitter, Telepresence and Online Messaging', *Information, Communication & Society*, 14(2), pp. 237–57.

Hutchins, B. & Mikosza, J. 2010, 'The Web 2.0 Olympics: Athlete Blogging, Social Networking and Policy Contradictions at the 2008 Beijing Games', *Convergence*, 16(3), pp. 279–97.

Hutchins, B. & Rowe, D. 2009a, 'From Broadcast Rationing to Digital Plenitude: The Changing Dynamics of the Media Sport Content Economy', *Television & New Media*, 10(4), pp. 354–70.

Hutchins, B. & Rowe, D. 2009b, '"A Battle Between Enraged Bulls": The 2009 Australian Senate Inquiry into Sports News and Digital Media', *Record of the Communications Policy & Research Forum 2009*, Sydney: Network Insight Institute, pp. 165–75.

Hutchins, B. & Rowe, D. 2010, 'Reconfiguring Media Sport for the Online World: An Inquiry Into "Sports News and Digital Media"', *International Journal of Communication*, vol. 4, pp. 696–718.

Hutchins, B., Rowe, D. & Ruddock, A. 2009, '"It's Fantasy Football Made Real": Networked Media Sport, the Internet, and the Hybrid Reality of MyFootballClub', *Sociology of Sport Journal*, 26(1), pp. 89–106.

IGDA (International Game Developers Association) 2005, *Game Developer Demographics: An Exploration of Workforce Diversity*, San Francisco: IGDA.

Indvik, L. 2011, 'Twitter Set New Tweets Per Second Record During Super Bowl', *Mashable*, 9 February. Online. Available http://mashable.com/2011/02/09/twitter-super-bowl-tweets/ (accessed 9 February 2011).

Informa 2010, 'Sports Broadcasting Summit 2010'. Online. Available http://www.informa.com.au/conferences/business/media/sports-broadcasting-summit-2010-P10I17 (accessed 21 May 2010).

Inoue, O. 2010, *Nintendo Magic: Winning the Video Game Wars*, New York: Vertical.

International Television Expert Group 2009, 'IPTV Global Forecast (2008–2013)', November. Online. Available http://www.international-television.org/tv_market_data/global-iptv-forecast-2009–2013.html (accessed 17 June 2010).

Internet World Stats 2011, Online. Available http://www.internetworldstats.com/stats.htm (accessed 31 March 2011).

IOC (International Olympic Committee) 2007, *Olympic Charter*, Lausanne, Switzerland: IOC.

IOC 2008a, *IOC Internet Guidelines for the Written Press and Other Non-Rights Holding Media, Games of the XXIX Olympiad, Beijing 2008*, Lausanne, Switzerland: IOC.

IOC 2008b, *IOC Blogging Guidelines for Persons Accredited at the Games of the XXIX Olympiad, Beijing 2008*, Lausanne, Switzerland: IOC.

IOC 2009a, *The Olympic Movement in Society: 121ˢᵗ IOC Session & XIII Olympic Congress*, 5 October, Copenhagen, Denmark.

IOC 2009b, Submission to the Inquiry into the Reporting of Sports News and the Emergence of Digital Media, *Senate Standing Committee on Environment, Communications and the Arts*, Canberra: Parliament of Australia.

IOC 2010, *IOC Blogging Guidelines for Persons Accredited at the XXI Olympic Winter Games, Vancouver 2010*, Lausanne, Switzerland: IOC.

IOC 2011, *IOC Social Media, Blogging and Internet Guidelines for Participants and Other Accredited Persons at the London 2012 Olympic Games*, Lausanne, Switzerland: IOC.

Jacka, E. 1994, 'Researching Audiences: A Dialogue Between Cultural Studies and Social Science', *Media Information Australia*, No. 73, pp. 93–98.

Jackson, G., Walter, B. & Prichard, G. 2009, 'Mat Bites Off More Than He Can Chew', *Sydney Morning Herald*, 21 August. Online. Available http://www.smh.com.au/rugby-league/league-news/mat-bites-off-more-than-he-can-chew-20091123-j1tm.html (accessed 21 August 2009).

Jansen, J. 2010, *65% of Internet Users Have Paid for Online Content*, Washington, DC: Pew Internet & American Life Project.

Jenkins, H. 1992, *Textual Poachers: Television Fans and Participatory Culture*, New York: Routledge.

Jenkins, H. 2003, 'Curt Schilling, Media Theorist?' *Technology Review*, 20 December. Online. Available http://www.technologyreview.com/blog/post.aspx?bid=293&bpid=15720 (accessed 27 August 2007).

Jenkins, H. 2005, 'Games, the Lively New Art', in J. Raessens & J. Goldstein (eds), *Handbook of Computer Game Studies*, Cambridge, MA: The MIT Press, pp. 175–89.

Jenkins, H. 2006a, *Convergence Culture: Where Old and New Media Collide*, New York: New York University Press.

Jenkins, H. 2006b, *Fans, Bloggers, and Gamers: Exploring Participatory Culture*, New York: New York University Press.

Jenkins, H. 2007, 'Never Trust a Snake: WWF Wrestling as Masculine Melodrama', in H. Jenkins, *The Wow Climax: Tracing the Emotional Impact of Popular Culture*, New York: New York University Press, pp. 75–101.

Jhally, S. 1984, 'The Spectacle of Accumulation: Material and Cultural Factors in the Evolution of the Sports/Media Complex', *The Insurgent Sociologist*, 12(3), pp. 41–57.

Jin, D.Y. 2010, *Korea's Online Gaming Empire*, Cambridge, MA: The MIT Press.

Johns, J. 2006, 'Video Games Production Networks: Value Capture, Power Relations and Embeddedness', *Journal of Economic Geography*, 6(2), pp. 151–80.

Johnson, V.E. 2009, 'Everything New Is Old Again: Sport Television, Innovation, and Television for a Multi-Platform Era', in A.D. Lotz (ed), *Beyond Prime Time: Television Programming in the Post-Network Era*, New York: Routledge, pp. 114–37.

Jonasson, K. & Thiborg, J. 2010, 'Electronic Sport and its Impact on Future Sport', *Sport in Society*, 13(2), pp. 287–99.

Jones, S. & Fox, S. 2009, *Generations Online in 2009*, Washington, DC: Pew Internet & American Life Project.

Joshi, S. 2007, 'Virtually There: Cricket, Community, and Commerce on the Internet', *International Journal of the History of Sport*, 24(9), pp. 1226–241.

Justin 2010, 'Official PR—EA Sports FIFA Soccer Franchise Sales Top 100 Million Units Lifetime', *Gamer Investments*, 4 November. Online. Available http://gamerinvestments.com/video-game-stocks/index.php/2010/11/04/official-pr-ea-sports-fifa-soccer-franchise-sales-top-100-million-units-lifetime/ (accessed 3 January 2011).

Karaganis, J. (ed) 2011a, *Media Piracy in Emerging Economies*, New York: Social Science Research Council.

Karaganis, J. 2011b, 'Introduction: Piracy and Enforcement in Global Perspective', in J. Karaganis (ed), *Media Piracy in Emerging Economies*, New York: Social Science Research Council, pp. i–vi.

Karaganis, J. 2011c, 'Rethinking Piracy', in J. Karaganis (ed), *Media Piracy in Emerging Economies*, New York: Social Science Research Council, pp. 1–75.

Katz, E. & Scannell, P. (eds) 2009, 'The End of Television? Its Impact on the World (So Far)', Special Issue of *The Annals of the American Academy of Political and Social Science*, 625(1), pp. 6–236.

Kawashima, N. 2010, 'The Rise of "User Creativity"—Web 2.0 and a New Challenge for Copyright Law and Cultural Policy', *International Journal of Cultural Policy*, 16(3), pp. 337–53.

Keane, J. 1991, *The Media and Democracy*, Cambridge, UK: Polity Press.

Keane, J. 2009, *The Life and Death of Democracy*, Sydney: Pocket Books.

Kelso, P. 2003, 'Footballer's Agent Threatens to Sue Over Rape Case Rumours', *The Guardian*, 2 October. Online. Available http://www.guardian.co.uk/uk/2003/oct/02/ukcrime.football (accessed 4 January 2010).

Kent, S.L. 2001, *From Pong to Pokemon and Beyond . . . The Ultimate History of Video Games. The Story Behind the Craze that Touched Our Lives and Changed the World*, New York: Three Rivers Press.

Kermond, C. 2010, 'Internet Numbers to Get More Solid', *The Age*, 8 October. Online. Available http://www.theage.com.au/business/media-and-marketing/internet-numbers-to-get-more-solid-20101007–169ts.html (accessed 8 October 2010).

Kermond, C. & Battersby, L. 2011, 'Online Spoils Go to Telstra in AFL's $1.2b Broadcast Rights Deal', *Sydney Morning Herald*, 29 April, Online. http://www.smh.com.au/business/media-and-marketing/online-spoils-go-to-telstra-in-afls-12b-broadcast-rights-deal-20110428–1dz3t.html (accessed 5 June, 2011).

Kessler, S. 2011, 'Virtual World Launches for Kids With Free Offline Sporting Equipment', *Mashable*, 15 June. Online. Available http://mashable.com/2011/06/15/fungoplay-launch/ (accessed 19 June 2011).

Kilar, J. 2011, 'Stewart, Colbert, and Hulu's Thoughts About the Future of TV', *Hulu Blog*, 2 February. Online. Available http://blog.hulu.com/2011/02/02/stewart-colbert-and-hulus-thoughts-about-the-future-of-tv/ (accessed 21 February 2011).

Kim, P. 2009, 'Internet Protocol TV in Perspective: A Matrix of Continuity and Innovation', *Television & New Media*, 10(6), pp. 536–45.

King, G. & Krzywinska, T. 2006, *Tomb Raiders and Space Invaders: Videogame Forms and Contexts,* London: I.B. Tauris.

Kiss, J. 2008, 'Olympics: NBC Hails Multimedia "Phenomenon" in Games Coverage', *The Guardian*, 14 August. Online. Available http://www.guardian.co.uk/media/2008/aug/14/olympicsandthemedia.digitalmedia (accessed 15 August 2008).

Kiss, J. 2011, 'Twitter Reveals it Has 100m Active Users', *The Guardian*, 8 September. Online. Available http://www.guardian.co.uk/technology/pda/2011/sep/08/twitter-active-users (accessed 9 September 2011).

Kline, S., Dyer-Witheford, N. & de Peuter, G. 2003, *Digital Play: The Interaction of Technology, Culture, and Marketing*, Montreal: McGill-Queen's University Press.

Koranteng, J. 2010, 'Virtually There', *Sport Business International*, No. 157, June, pp. 20–21.

Kreiss, D., Finn, M. & Turner, F. 2011, 'The Limits of Peer Production: Some Reminders from Max Weber for the Network Society', *New Media & Society*, 13(2), pp. 243–59.

Kruger, C. 2005, 'Telstra Broadband Unlocks Revenue from Music and Video', *The Age*, 19 December. Online. Available http://www.theage.com.au/articles/2005/12/18/1134840741250.html (accessed 19 December 2005).

Kuhn, K.L. 2009, 'The Market Structure and Characteristics of Electronic Games', in N. Pope, K. Kuhn & J. Forster (eds), *Digital Sport For Performance Enhancement and Competitive Evolution*, Hershey, PA: Information Science Reference, pp. 257–85.

Kuhn, J. 2007, 'Crowdsourcing Soccer in the UK', *Wired: Tech Biz*, 13 July. Online. Available http://www.wired.com/techbiz/media/news/2007/07/crowdsourcing_soccer (accessed 2 December 2007).

Kumar, S. 2010, 'Google Earth and the Nation State: Sovereignty in the Age of New Media', *Global Media and Communication*, 6(2), pp. 154–76.

Lane, D. 2010, '"Beeker Shark" was Cronulla Web Critic', *Sydney Morning Herald*, 25 July. Online. Available http://www.smh.com.au/rugby-league/league-news/beeker-shark-irvine-was-cronulla-web-critic-20100724–10phe.html (accessed 25 July 2010).

Lanham, R.A. 2006, *The Economics of Attention: Style and Substance in the Age of Information*, Chicago, IL: University of Chicago Press.

Lash, S. 2002, *Critique of Information*, London: Sage.

Latour, B. 1993, *We Have Never Been Modern*, Cambridge, MA: Harvard University Press.

Latour, B. 1999, *Pandora's Hope: Essays on the Reality of Science Studies*, Cambridge, MA: Harvard University Press.

Lee, D. 2010, 'What Happened to MyFootballClub and Ebbsfleet United?' *BBC London*, 6 September. Online. Available http://news.bbc.co.uk/local/london/hi/front_page/newsid_8967000/8967067.stm (accessed 7 October 2010).

Lee, J. 2010, 'Content is King But Social Media Provide the Court Jesters', *The Age*, 5 February. Online. Available http://www.smh.com.au/business/content-is-king-but-social-media-provide-the-court-jesters-201002 04-ngc7.html (accessed 5 February 2010).

Lenhart, A. 2009, *Teens and Sexting*, Washington, DC: Pew Internet & American Life Project.

Leonard, D. 2005, 'To the White Extreme: Conquering Athletic Space, White Manhood, and Racing Virtual Reality', in N. Garrelts (ed), *Digital Gameplay: Essays on the Nexus of Game and Gamer*, North Carolina: McFarland and Company, pp. 110–29.

Leonard, D. 2006, 'Not a Hater, Just Keepin' It Real: The Importance of Race- and Gender-Based Game Studies', *Games and Culture*, 1(1), pp. 83–88.

Lessig, L. 2002, *The Future of Ideas: The Fate of the Commons in a Collective World*, New York: Vintage Books.

Lessig, L. 2005, 'The People Own Ideas!' *Technology Review*, June, pp. 46–53.

Levinson, P. 1999, *Digital McLuhan: A Guide to the Information Age*, London: Routledge.

Leyshon, A., Webb, P., French, S., Thrift, N. & Crewe, L. 2005, 'On the Reproduction of the Musical Economy After the Internet,' *Media, Culture & Society*, 27(2), pp. 177–209.

Liedtke, M. 2010, 'Viacom Loses to YouTube in Landmark Copyright Case', *The Huffington Post*, 23 June. Online. Available http://www.huffingtonpost.com/2010/06/23/youtube-viacom-lawsuit-se_n_623256.html (accessed 4 July 2010).

Livingstone, S. 2009, 'On the Mediation of Everything: ICA Presidential Address 2008', *Journal of Communication*, 59(1), pp. 1–18.

Lloyd-James, A., Gibson, R., Bell, P., Pattinson, H., Goldsmith, B., Chandler, A. & McKay, C. 2009, *Outside The Box—Future of Television Dossier*, Outside the Box Researchers, October.

Lomax, R.G. 2006, 'Fantasy Sports: History, Game Types, and Research', in A.A. Raney & J. Bryant (eds), *Handbook of Sports and Media*, Mahwah, NJ: Lawrence Erlbaum Associates, pp. 383–92.

Lotz, A.D. 2007, *The Television Will be Revolutionized*, New York: New York University Press.

Lotz, A.D. (ed) 2009a, *Beyond Prime Time: Television Programming in the Post-Network Era*, New York: Routledge.

Lotz, A.D. 2009b, 'Introduction', in A.D. Lotz (ed), *Beyond Prime Time: Television Programming in the Post-Network Era*, New York: Routledge, pp. 1–13.

Lumby, C., Caple, H. & Greenwood, K. 2009, *Towards a Level Playing Field: Sport and Gender in Australian Media*, Canberra: Australian Sports Commission.

McClusky, M. 2010a, 'Athletes Confused by Social Media Rules', *Wired: Epicenter*, 5 February. Online. Available http://www.wired.com/epicenter/2010/02/athletes-confused-by-olympic-social-media-rules/ (accessed 6 February 2010).

McClusky, M. 2010b, 'Golden Games for Social Media', *Playbook: The Wired World of Sports*, 25 February. Online. Available http://www.wired.com/playbook/2010/02/golden-games-for-social-media/ (accessed 25 February 2010).

McCullagh, K. 2009a, 'Piracy Battle Hotting Up', *Sport Business International*, No. 144, April, p. 18.

McCullagh, K. 2009b, 'Creating Social Networks', *Sport Business International*, No. 146, June, pp. 18–19.

McCullagh, K. 2010, 'Premier League's Case Against YouTube Thrown Out of Court', *Sport Business.com*, 25 June. Online. Available http://www.sportbusiness.com/news/178216/premier-leagues-case-against-youtube-thrown-out-of-court (accessed 1 August 2010).

McCullagh, K. 2011, 'Elusive Value', *Sports Business International*, No. 165, March, pp. 46–47.

McKay, J. 1991, *No Pain, No Gain? Sport and Australian Culture*, Sydney: Prentice Hall.

McKay, J., Messner, M.A. & Sabo, D. (eds) 2000, *Masculinities, Gender Relations, and Sport*, Thousand Oaks, CA: Sage.

McLuhan, M. 2001 [1964], *Understanding Media: The Extensions of Man*, London: Routledge Classics.

McMillen, A. 2011, 'Why Did L.A. Noire Take Seven Years to Make?' *IGN*, 24 June. Online. Available http://au.xbox360.ign.com/articles/117/1179020p1.html (accessed 29 June 2011).

McRobbie, A. 2005, 'Clubs to Companies', in J. Hartley (ed), *Creative Industries*, Malden MA: Blackwell, pp. 375–90.

Macur, J. 2008, 'U.S. Cyclists Are Masked, and Criticism is Not', *New York Times*, 6 August. Online. Available http://www.nytimes.com/2008/08/06/sports/olympics/06masks.html (accessed 6 August 2008).

Magdalinski, T. 2009, *Sport, Technology and the Body: The Nature of Performance*, Oxon, UK: Routledge.

Maguire, J. 1999, *Global Sport: Identities, Societies, Civilizations*, Cambridge, MA: Polity Press.

Majumdar, B. 2011, 'The Indian Premier League and World Cricket', in A. Bateman & J. Hill (eds), *The Cambridge Companion to Cricket*, Cambridge, MA: Cambridge University Press, pp. 173–86.

Malec, M.A. 1995, 'Sports Discussion Groups on the Internet', *Journal of Sport and Social Issues*, 19(1), pp. 108–14.

Malone, M. 2007, 'User-Generated Soccer', *Portfolio.com*, 15 October. Online. Available http://www.portfolio.com/culture-lifestyle/culture-inc/sports/2007/10/15/Will-Brooks-Fan-Ownership-Model (accessed 2 December 2007).

Mandle, W.F. 1976, 'Cricket and Australian Nationalism in the Nineteenth Century', in T.D. Jaques & G.R. Pavia (eds), *Sport in Australia: Selected Readings in Physical Activity*, Sydney: McGraw-Hill, pp. 46–72.

Manzenreiter, W. & Horne, J. (eds) 2004, *Football Goes East: Business, Culture and The People's Game in China, Japan and South Korea*, London: Routledge.

Margalit, A. 2008, '"You'll Never Walk Alone": On Property, Community, and Football Fans', *Theoretical Inquiries in Law*, 10(1), pp. 217–40.

Marshall, P.D. 1997, *Celebrity and Power*, Minneapolis, MN: University of Minnesota Press.

Marshall, P.D. 2009, 'Screens: Television's Dispersed "Broadcast"', in G. Turner & J. Tay (eds), *Television Studies After TV: Understanding Television in the Post-Broadcast Era*, London: Routledge, pp. 41–50.

Marshall, P.D., Walker, B. & Russo, N. 2010, 'Mediating the Olympics', *Convergence*, 16(3), pp. 263–78.

Marvin, C. 1988, *When Old Technologies Were New*, New York: Oxford University Press.

Marwick, A.E. & boyd, d. 2011, 'I Tweet Honestly, I Tweet Passionately: Twitter Users, Context Collapse, and the Imagined Audience', *New Media & Society*, 13(1), pp. 114–33.

Masters, R. 2011, 'Footy Deal Scores Well for Viewers and Codes', *Sydney Morning Herald*, 29 April. Online. Available http://www.smh.com.au/afl/afl-news/footy-deal-scores-well-for-viewers-and-codes-20110428–1dyxj.html (accessed 29 April 2011).

Maxwell, R. 2003, 'The Marketplace Citizen and the Political Economy of Data Trade in the European Union', in J. Lewis & T. Miller (eds), *Critical Cultural Policy Studies: A Reader*, Malden, MA: Blackwell, pp. 149–60.

Mean, L.J. 2010, 'Making Masculinity and Framing Femininity: FIFA, Soccer, and World Cup Web Sites', in H.L. Hundley & A.C. Billings (eds), *Examining Identity in Sports Media*, Thousand Oaks, CA: Sage, pp. 65–86.

Messner, M.A. 2007, *Out of Play: Critical Essays on Gender and Sport*, Albany, NY: State University of New York Press.

MFC (MyFootballClub) Podcast 2007–2009. Online. Available http://members.myfootballclub.co.uk/category/myfc-podcast/ (accessed between 23 December 2007—26 April 2009).

Miah, A. 2002, 'Immersion and Abstraction in Virtual Sport', *Sport Technology: History, Philosophy and Policy*, 21, pp. 225–33.

Miah, A., Garcia, B. & Zhihui, T. 2008, '"We are the Media": Non-Accredited Media and Citizen Journalists at the Olympic Games', in M.E. Price & D. Dayan (eds), *Owning the Olympics: Narratives of the New China*, Ann Arbor, MI: The University of Michigan Press, pp. 320–45.

Mikosza, J. 1997, *Inching Forward: Newspaper Coverage and Portrayal of Women's Sport in Australia*, ACT: Womensport Australia.

Miller, A. 2009, 'Twittering Cricketers', *ESPNcricinfo*, 30 July. Online. Available http://www.espncricinfo.com/engvaus2009/content/story/417068.html (accessed 1 July 2011).

Miller, D. & Slater, D. 2000, *The Internet: An Ethnographic Approach*, Oxford: Berg.

Miller, T. 2001, *Sportsex*, Philadelphia, PA: Temple University Press.

Miller, T. 2006, 'Gaming for Beginners', *Games and Culture,* 1(1), pp. 5–12.

Miller, T. 2007, *Cultural Citizenship: Cosmopolitanism, Consumerism, and Television in a Neoliberal Age*, Philadelphia, PA: Temple University Press.

Miller, T. 2009, 'Approach With Caution and Proceed With Care: Campaigning for the US Presidency "After" TV', in G. Turner & J. Tay (eds), *Television Studies After TV: Understanding Television in the Post-Broadcast Era*, London: Routledge, pp. 75–82.

Miller, T. 2010a, 'The Cognitariat', *Occasional Links and Commentary on Economics, Culture & Society*, 3 August. Online. Available http://anticap.wordpress.com/2010/08/03/the-cognitariat/ (accessed 4 August 2010).

Miller, T. 2010b, 'A Future for Media Studies', in B. Beaty, D. Briton, G. Filax & R. Sullivan (eds), *How Canadians Communicate III: Contexts of Canadian Popular Culture*, Edmonton, Alberta: Athabasca University, pp. 35–53.

Miller, T., Lawrence, G., McKay, J. & Rowe, D. 2001, *Globalization and Sport: Playing the World*, London: Sage.

Miller, T., Rowe, D., McKay, J. & Lawrence, G. 2003, 'The Over-Production of US Sports and the New International Division of Cultural Labor', *International Review for the Sociology of Sport*, 48(4), pp. 427–40.

Millington, B. 2009, 'Wii Has Never Been Modern: "Active" Video Games and the "Conduct of Conduct"', *New Media & Society*, 11(4), pp. 621–40.

Mirghani, S. 2011, 'The War on Piracy: Analyzing the Discursive Battles of Corporate and Government-Sponsored Anti-Piracy Media Campaigns', *Critical Studies in Media Communication*, 28(2), pp. 113–34.

Monbiot, G. 2008, 'How Can the Rich Still be Buying Our Silence with this 13th-Century Law?' *The Guardian*, 17 September. Online. Available http://www.guardian.co.uk/commentisfree/2008/sep/17/matthiasrath.medialaw (accessed 13 November 2009).

Mosco, V. 2004, *The Digital Sublime: Myth, Power, and Cyberspace*, Cambridge, MA: The MIT Press.

Mueller, F. 2009, 'Digital Sport: Merging Gaming with Sports to Enhance Physical Activities such as Jogging', in N. Pope, K. Kuhn & J. Forster (eds), *Digital Sport For Performance Enhancement and Competitive Evolution*, Hershey, PA: Information Science Reference, pp. 150–66.

Mulholland, W. 2007, 'Just Who Controls the Rights to a Sporting Star's Image? Behind the Leo Barry/AFL/Tabcorp Image Rights Stoush', *The ANZSLA Commentator*, 69 (21 March), pp. 3–5.

NBC 2008, 'NBC's Complete Olympics', *nbcolympics.com*, 9 July. Online. Available http://www.nbcolympics.com/newscenter/news/newsid=148556.html (accessed 7 November 2008).

Neale, W.C. 1964, 'The Peculiar Economics of Professional Sports: A Contribution to the Theory of the Firm in Sporting Competition and in Market Competition', *The Quarterly Journal of Economics*, 78(1), pp. 20–33.

Nesbit, T.M. & King, K.A. 2010, 'The Impact of Fantasy Sports on Television Viewership', *Journal of Media Economics*, 23(1), pp. 24–41.

NetResult 2008, *Background Report on Digital Piracy of Sporting Events*, Cambridge, UK: Envisional Ltd and NetResult Ltd.

Nicita, A. & Rossi, M.A. 2008, 'Access to Audio-Visual Contents, Exclusivity and Anticommons in New Media Markets', *Communications and Strategies*, 71(3), pp. 79–102.

Nieborg, D. & van der Graaf, S. 2008, 'The Mod Industries? The Industrial Logic of Non-Market Game Production', *European Journal of Cultural Studies*, 11(2), pp. 177–95.

Nielsen 2010, '14% Multi-Tasked and Got Social on the Web During Super Bowl', *Nielsen Wire*, 12 February. Online. Available http://blog.nielsen.com/nielsen-wire/online_mobile/14-multi-tasked-and-got-social-on-the-web-during-super-bowl/ (accessed 12 February 2010).

Nielsen 2011, 'Super Bowl XLV Most Viewed Telecast in U.S. Broadcast History', *Nielsen Wire*, 7 February. Online. Available http://blog.nielsen.com/nielsen-wire/media_entertainment/super-bowl-xlv-most-viewed-telecast-in-broadcast-history (accessed 22 March 2011).

Nielsen NetRatings 2008–2010, *Market Intelligence Domestic Sports*, The Nielsen Company.

Nissenbaum, H. 2004, 'Hackers and the Contested Ontology of Cyberspace', *New Media & Society*, 6(2), pp. 195–217.

Novak, M. 1976, *The Joy of Sports: End Zones, Bases, Baskets, Balls and the Consecration of the American Spirit*, New York: Basic Books.

Oates, T.P. 2009, 'New Media and the Repackaging of NFL Fandom', *Sociology of Sport Journal*, 26(1), pp. 31–49.

OECD (Organisation for Economic Co-operation and Development) 2007, Working Party on Communications Infrastructure and Services Policy, *IPTV: Market Developments and Regulatory Treatment*, Unclassified, DSTI/ICCP/CISP2006,5/FINAL.

Oriard, M. 1993, *Reading Football: How the Popular Press Created an American Spectacle*, Chapel Hill, NC: The University of North Carolina Press.

Otto, J., Metz, S. & Ensmenger, N. 2011, 'Sports Fans and Their Information-Gathering Habits: How Media Technologies Have Brought Fans Closer to Their Teams Over Time', in W. Aspray & B.M. Hayes (eds), *Everyday Information: The Evolution of Information Seeking in America*, Cambridge, MA: The MIT Press, pp. 185–216.

Ourand, J. 2010, 'Fox' Hill Warns Leagues' Streaming Efforts Could Turn Off Nets', *Street & Smith's Sports Business Daily*, 12 May. Online. Available http://www.sportsbusinessdaily.com/article/139268 (accessed 24 August 2010).

Ovum analysts 2008, 'The Future's Bright', *Sport Business International*, No. 134, May, p. 22.

Pandaram, J. 2010, 'Top for Tweets', *Sydney Morning Herald*, 4 August. Online. Available http://www.smh.com.au/sport/speedster-blake-triggers-fourway-bidding-war-20100803-115ir.html (accessed 4 August 2010).

Parkins, W. & Craig, G. 2006, *Slow Living*, Sydney: University of New South Wales Press.

Parliament of Australia Environment, Communications, Information Technology and the Arts References Committee 2006, *About Time! Women in Sport and Recreation in Australia,* Commonwealth of Australia.

Parliament of Australia Senate Standing Committee 2009, *The Reporting of Sports News and the Emergence of Digital Media*, Commonwealth of Australia.

Paul, P. 2010, 'Men's Hockey Final Most-Watched Television Event in Canadian History', *Toronto Examiner*, 1 March. Online. Available http://www.examiner.com/headlines-in-toronto/men-s-hockey-final-most-watched-television-event-canadian-history (accessed 1 March 2011).

Pells, E. 2010, 'The Social Olympics: Twitter, Facebook Get the Message Out', *The Bismarck Tribune*, 14 February. Online. Available http://www.bismarck-tribune.com/news/national/article_dc4c6f10–16ce-11df-8c16–001cc4c03286.html (accessed 14 February 2010).

Phillips, A. 2010, 'Old Sources: New Bottles', in N. Fenton (ed), *New Media, Old News: Journalism and Democracy in the Digital Age*, London: Sage, pp. 87–101.

Phillips, M.G. 1997, *An Illusory Image: A Report on the Media Coverage and Portrayal of Women's Sport in Australia*, Canberra: Australian Sports Commission.

Pierik, J. 2010, 'St Kilda Chief Backs Riewoldt After Scandal', *Sydney Morning Herald*, 21 December. Online. Available http://www.smh.com.au/afl/afl-news/st-kilda-chief-backs-riewoldt-after-scandal-20101220–1936j.html (accessed 21 December 2010).

Pierik, J. 2011, 'In Pay Battle, Image is Everything', *The Age*, 2 September. Online. Available http://www.theage.com.au/afl/afl-news/in-pay-battle-image-is-everything-20110901–1jo8y.html (accessed 2 September 2011).

Pleyers, G. 2010, *Alter-Globalization: Becoming Actors in the Global Age*, Cambridge, UK: Polity Press.

Plunkett Research 2010, 'Sports Industry Overview'. Online. Available http://www.plunkettresearch.com/sports%20recreation%20leisure%20market%20research/industry%20statistics (accessed 27 July 2010).

Plymire, D.C. 2009, 'Remediating Football for the Posthuman Future: Embodiment and Subjectivity in Sport Video Games', *Sociology of Sport Journal*, 26(1), pp. 17–30.

Plymire, D.C. & Forman, P.J. 2000, 'Breaking the Silence: Lesbian Fans, the Internet, and the Sexual Politics of Women's Sport', *International Journal of Sexuality and Gender Studies*, 5(2), pp. 141–53.

Podell, I. 2011, 'NHL Inks 10-Year Deal with NBC, Versus for Rights', *Huffington Post*, 19 April. Online. Available http://www.huffingtonpost.com/2011/04/19/nhl-inks-10year-deal-with_n_851131.html (accessed 20 May 2011).

Poor, N. 2006, 'Playing Internet Curveball with Traditional Media Gatekeepers: Pitcher Curt Schilling and Boston Red Sox Fans', *Convergence*, 12(1), pp. 41–53.

Price, M.E. 2008, 'On Seizing the Olympic Platform', in M.E. Price & D. Dayan (eds), *Owning the Olympics: Narratives of the New China*, Ann Arbor, MI: The University of Michigan Press, 86–114.

PricewaterhouseCoopers 2007, *Global Entertainment and Media Outlook 2007–2011*, PricewaterhouseCoopers International Limited.

PRLog 2008, 'Olympic Athletes Worldwide Download "Songs For Tibet" Wearing a iPod Symbolizing Freedom', 6 August. Online. Available http://www.prlog.org/10100238-olympic-athletes-worldwide-download-songs-for-tibet-wearing-ipod-symbolizing-freedom.html (accessed 8 August 2008).

Productivity Commission 2009, *Annual Review of Regulatory Burdens on Business: Social and Economic Infrastructure Services*, Commonwealth of Australia.

Proof Committee Hansard 2009, *The Reporting of Sports News and the Emergence of Digital Media*, 15–16 April, 29 April. Senate Standing Committee on Environment, Communications and the Arts, Commonwealth of Australia.

Puijk, R. 2004, 'Television Sport on the Web: The Case of Norwegian Public Service Television', *Media, Culture & Society*, 26(6), pp. 883–92.

Qing, L. & Richeri, G. 2011, *Encoding the Olympics: The Beijing Olympic Games and the Communication Impact Worldwide*, London: Routledge.

Qiu, J.L. 2009, *Working-Class Network Society: Communication Technology and the Information Have-Less in Urban China*, Cambridge, MA: The MIT Press.

Read, A. 2010, *The Essential Guide to Grass Roots Sports and Social Media*, FundSport.

Redhead, S. 2007, 'Those Absent from the Stadium are Always Right: Accelerated Culture, Sport Media, and Theory at the Speed of Light', *Journal of Sport and Social Issues*, 31(3), pp. 226–41.

Rehak, B. 2003, 'Playing at Being: Psychoanalysis and the Avatar', in M.J.P. Wolf & B. Perron (eds), *The Video Game Theory Reader*, New York: Routledge, pp. 103–27.

Rettberg, J.W. 2008, *Blogging*, Cambridge, UK: Polity Press.

Reuters 2011, 'Internet Ad Revenue Hits High in '10', 13 April. Online. Available http://uk.reuters.com/article/2011/04/13/us-internetadvertising-idUK-TRE73C6R420110413 (accessed 18 April 2011).

Rheingold, H. 2002, *Smart Mobs: The Next Social Revolution*, Cambridge, MA: Basic Books.

Richard, B. & Zaremba, J. 2005, 'Gaming With Girls: Looking for Sheroes in Computer Games', in J. Raessens & J. Goldstein (eds), *Handbook of Computer Game Studies*, Cambridge, MA: The MIT Press, pp. 283–300.

Roberts, K. 2009, 'The View from the Top', *Sport Business International*, No. 142, February, pp. 26–28.

Robertson, C. 2004, 'A Sporting Gesture? BSkyB, Manchester United, Global Media, and Sport', *Television & New Media*, 5(4), pp. 291–314.

Roche, M. 2000, *Mega-Events and Modernity: Olympics and Expos in the Growth of Global Culture*, London: Routledge.

Rockstar Spouse 2010, 'Wives of Rockstar San Diego Employees Have Collected Themselves', *Gamastura*, 7 January. http://www.gamasutra.com/blogs/RockstarSpouse/20100107/4032/Wives_of_Rockstar_San_Diego_employees_have_collected_themselves.php (accessed 22 January 2010).

Rodzvilla, J. (ed) 2002, *We've Got Blog. How Weblogs are Changing Our Culture*, Cambridge, MA: Perseus Publications.

Rojek, C. 2010, *The Labour of Leisure: The Culture of Free Time*, London: Sage.

Ross, A. 2009, *Nice Work If You Can Get It: Life and Labor in Precarious Times*, New York: NYU Press.

Ross, S.M. 2008, *Beyond the Box: Television and the Internet*, Oxford: Blackwell.

Rowe, D. 1995, *Popular Cultures: Rock Music, Sport and the Politics of Pleasure*, London: Sage.

Rowe, D. 2004a, *Sport, Culture and the Media: The Unruly Trinity*, 2nd edition, Berkshire, UK: Open University Press.

Rowe, D. 2004b, 'Fulfilling the "Cultural Mission": Popular Genre and the Public Remit', *European Journal of Cultural Studies*, 7(3), pp. 381–400.

Rowe, D. 2004c, 'Watching Brief: Cultural Citizenship and Viewing Rights', *Sport in Society*, 7(3), pp. 385–402.

Rowe, D. 2005, 'Fourth Estate or Fan Club? Sports Journalism Engages the Popular', in S. Allan (ed), *Journalism: Critical Issues*, Maidenhead, UK: Open University Press, pp. 125–36.

Rowe, D. 2007, 'Sports Journalism: Still the "Toy Department" of the News Media?' *Journalism: Theory, Practice & Criticism*, 8(4), pp. 385–405.

Rowe, D. 2011a, 'Sports Media: Beyond Broadcasting, Beyond Sports, Beyond Societies?' in A. Billings (ed), *Sports Media: Transformation, Integration, Consumption*, New York: Routledge, pp. 94–113.

Rowe, D. 2011b, *Global Media Sport: Flows, Forms and Futures*, London: Bloomsbury Academic.

Rowe, D. 2011c, 'Sport and its Audiences', in V. Nightingale (ed), *Handbook of Media Audiences*, Oxford: Blackwell, pp. 509–26.

Rowe, D. & Gilmour, C. 2008, 'Contemporary Media Sport: De- or Re-Westernization?' *International Journal of Sport Communication*, 1(2), pp. 177–94.

Rowe, D. & McKay, J. 2012, 'Torchlight Temptations: Hosting the Olympics and the Global Gaze', in J. Sugden & A. Tomlinson (eds), *Watching the Games:*

Politics, Power and Representation in the London Olympiad, London: Routledge, pp. 122–37

Rowe, D., Ruddock, A. & Hutchins, B. 2010, 'Cultures of Complaint: Online Fan Message Boards and Networked Digital Media Sport Communities,' *Convergence*, 16(3), pp. 298–315.

Roy, D.P. & Goss, B.D. 2009, 'A League of Our Own: Empowerment of Sports Consumers Through Fantasy Sports Participation', in N. Pope, K. Kuhn & J. Forster (eds), *Digital Sport For Performance Enhancement and Competitive Evolution*, Hershey, PA: Information Science Reference, pp. 178–93.

Royse, P., Lee, J., Undrahbuyan, B., Hopson, M. & Consalvo, M. 2007, 'Women and Games: Technologies of the Gendered Self', *New Media & Society*, 9(4), pp. 555–76.

Ruddock, A. 2001, *Understanding Audiences*, London: Sage.

Ruddock, A., Hutchins, B. & Rowe, D. 2010, 'Contradictions in Media Sport Culture: The Reinscription of Football Supporter Traditions through Online Media', *European Journal of Cultural Studies*, 13(3), pp. 323–39.

Ryan, J. 2010, *A History of the Internet and the Digital Future*, London: Reaktion Books.

Sailing Sponsorship Editor 2009, 'Volvo Ocean Race Media Figures Show Importance of Digital', *Yachtsponsorship.com*, 12 November. Online. Available http://www.yachtsponsorship.com/2009/11/volvo-ocean-race-media-figures-show-importance-of-digital/ (accessed 2 April 2010).

Sainsbury, M. 2006, 'Telstra Gets a Media Makeover', *The Australian*, 1 July. Online. Available http://www.theaustralian.com.au/news/telstra-gets-a-media-makeover/story-e6frgal6–1111112127927 (accessed 20 April 2008).

Sanderson, J. 2008a, '"You Are the Type of Person That Children Should Look up to as a Hero": Parasocial Interaction on 38pitches.com', *International Journal of Sport Communication*, 1(3), pp. 337–60.

Sanderson, J. 2008b, 'The Blog is Serving Its Purpose: Self-Presentation Strategies on 38pitches.com', *Journal of Computer-Mediated Communication*, 13(4), pp. 912–36.

Sanderson, J. 2009a, 'Professional Athletes' Shrinking Privacy Boundaries: Fans, Information and Communication Technologies, and Athlete Monitoring', *International Journal of Sport Communication*, 2(2), pp. 240–56.

Sanderson, J. 2009b, '"Thanks for Fighting the Good Fight": Cultivating Dissent on Blogmaverick.com', *Southern Communication Journal*, 74(4), pp. 390–405.

Sanderson, J. 2010, 'Weighing in on the Coaching Decision: Discussing Sports and Race Online', *Journal of Language and Social Psychology*, 29(3), pp. 301–20.

Sandvoss, C. 2003, *A Game of Two Halves: Football, Television and Globalization*, London: Routledge.

Sanna, D. 2008, 'Northerners on Tour', in S. Denton (ed), *the fleet@wembley: Ebbsfleet United—FA Trophy Winners 2008*, Shrewsbury, UK: Jam Book Publishing, pp. 50–59.

Saurine, A. 2008, 'Stephanie Rice Facebook Pictures Censored', *The Daily Telegraph*, 2 April. Online. Available http://www.dailytelegraph.com.au/news/rice-facebook-pics-censored/story-0–1111115947818 (accessed 2 July 2011).

Schechner, S. & Ovide, S. 2010, 'Record Draw for Super Bowl: An Audience of 106.5 Million Bucks Trend of Declining Viewership for Networks', *The Wall Street Journal: Media and Marketing*, 7 February. Online. Available http://online.wsj.com/article/SB10001424052748703615904575053300315837616.html (accessed 6 December 2010).

Schell, M.J. 1999, *Baseball's All-Time Best Hitters: How Statistics Can Level the Playing Field*, Princeton, NJ: Princeton University Press.

Scherer, J. 2007, 'Globalization, Promotional Culture and the Production/Consumption of Online Games: Engaging Adidas's "Beat Rugby" Campaign', *New Media & Society*, 9(3), pp. 475–96.

Scherer, J. & Rowe, D. (eds) 2012 forthcoming, *Sport, Public Broadcasting, and Cultural Citizenship: Signal Lost?*, New York: Routledge.

Scherer, J. & Whitson, D. 2009, 'Public Broadcasting, Sport, and Cultural Citizenship', *International Review for the Sociology of Sport*, 44(2/3), pp. 213–29.

Schimmel, K.S., Harrington, C.L. & Bielby, D.D. 2007, 'Keep Your Fans to Yourself: The Disjuncture between Sports Studies' and Pop Culture Studies' Perspectives on Fandom', *Sport in Society*, 10(4), pp. 580–600.

Schmitt, B., Rogers, D.L. & Vrotsos, K. 2004, *There's No Business That's Not Show Business: Marketing in an Experience Culture*, Upper Saddle River, NJ: Financial Times Press.

Schonfeld, E. 2009, 'Twitter Reaches 44.5 Million People Worldwide in June', *TechCrunch*, 3 August. Online. Available http://techcrunch.com/2009/08/03/twitter-reaches-445-million-people-worldwide-in-june-comscore/ (accessed 15 February 2010).

Schudson, M. 2008, *Why Democracies Need an Unlovable Press*, Cambridge, UK: Polity Press.

Scibilia, M. & Hutchins, B. 2012, 'High Stakes Television: Fan Engagement, Market Literacy and the Battle for Sports Content,' *Media International Australia*, No. 141, pp. 26–37.

Scott, A. 2007, '2020 Television,' *Inside Sport*, December, pp. 39–46.

Seidman, R. 2011, 'Super Bowl XLV on FOX Is Most-Watched Program in TV History', *Network TV Press Releases, TV Sports Ratings & News*, 7 February. Online. Available http://tvbythenumbers.zap2it.com/2011/02/07/super-bowl-xlv-on-fox-is-most-watched-program-in-tv-history/81751 (accessed 9 February 2011).

Sennett, R. 1998, *The Corrosion of Character: The Personal Consequences of Work in the New Capitalism*, New York: W.W. Norton.

Servon, L.J. & Pinkett, R.D. 2004, 'Narrowing the Digital Divide: The Potential and Limits of the US Community and Technology Movement', in M. Castells (ed), *The Network Society: A Cross-Cultural Perspective*, Cheltenham, UK: Edward Elgar, pp. 319–38.

Shirky, C. 2010, *Cognitive Surplus: Creativity and Generosity in a Connected Age*, New York: Penguin Press.

Silberman, L. 2009, 'Double Play: How Video Games Mediate Physical Performance for Elite Athletes', in N. Pope, K. Kuhn & J. Forster (eds), *Digital Sport For Performance Enhancement and Competitive Evolution,* Hershey, PA: Information Science Reference, pp. 167–77.

Silkstone, D. 2010, 'Scandal Playing Out Far from the Realm of Sport', *The Age*, 22 December. Online. Available http://www.theage.com.au/afl/afl-news/scandal-playing-out-far-from-the-realm-of-sport-20101221–194eq.html (accessed 22 December 2010).

Silverman, C. 2010, 'Inside the Social Media Strategy of the Winter Olympics Games', *Mediashift*, 12 February. Online. Available http://www.pbs.org/mediashift/2010/02/inside-the-social-media-strategy-of-the-winter-olympic-games043.html (accessed 15 February 2010).

Silverstone, R. 2007, *Media and Morality: On the Rise of the Mediapolis*, Cambridge, UK: Polity Press.

Sinclair, L. 2010, 'Cricket Australia Among Sports Losing Cash to Net Piracy', *The Australian*, 1 March. Online. Available http://www.theaustralian.com.au/business/media/cricker-australia-among-sports-losing-cash-to-net-piracy/story-e6frg996–1225835350611 (accessed 1 March 2010).

Singer, J.B. 2005, 'The Political J-Blogger: "Normalizing" a New Media Form to Fit Old Norms and Practices', *Journalism: Theory, Practice and Criticism*, 6(2), pp. 173–98.

Singer, J.B. 2011, 'Journalism in a Network', in M. Deuze (ed), *Managing Media Work*, Thousand Oaks, CA: Sage, pp. 103–09.

Sinnott, J. 2007, 'Fans Given Club Takeover Chance', *BBC Sport: Football*, 1 May. Online. Available http://news.bbc.co.uk/sport2/hi/football/6611729.stm (accessed 3 December 2007).

Skeels, M.M. & Grudin, J. 2009, 'When Social Networks Cross Boundaries: A Case Study of Workplace Use of Facebook and LinkedIn', in *Proceedings of Group'09*, Sanibel Island, Florida, pp. 95–104.

Smart, B. 2005, *The Sport Star: Modern Sport and the Cultural Economy of Sporting Celebrity*, London: Sage.

Smart, B. 2007, 'Not Playing Around: Global Capitalism, Modern Sport and Consumer Culture', *Global Networks*, 7(2), pp. 113–34.

Smith, M.D. 2008, 'Judo Olympian Ronda Rousey Uses Her Blog to Accuse an Official of Molesting Athletes', *AOL Fanhouse*, 25 June. Online. Available http://olympics.fanhouse.com/2008/06/25/judo-olympian-ronda-rousey-uses-her-blog-to-accuse-an-official-o/ (accessed 15 July 2008).

Smith, P. 2010, 'The Politics of Sports Rights: The Regulation of Television Sports Rights in the UK', *Convergence,* 16(3), pp. 316–33.

Smith, T. 2011, 'Global Web Index: Global State of Social Media in 2011', *Trendstream*, 15 February. Online. Available http://globalwebindex.net/thinking/the-global-state-of-social-media-in-2011/ (accessed 17 February 2011).

Snedden, M. 2011, 'CEO Column: One Million Fans Can't Be Wrong', *Twenty11: The Official Newsletter of the Rugby World Cup*, May. Online. Available http://www.rugbyworldcup.com/mediazone/news/newsid=2042880.html (accessed 2 June 2011).

Snickars, P. & Vonderau, P. (eds) 2009, *The YouTube Reader*, Stockholm: National Library of Sweden.

Song, F.W. 2010, 'Theorizing Web 2.0: A Cultural Perspective', *Information, Communication & Society*, 13(2), pp. 249–75.

Sparre, K. 2007a, 'Athletes Are Forbidden to Update Websites and Blogs from Pan Am Games', *Play the Game,* 23 February. Online. Available http://www.playthegame.org/news/detailed/athletes-are-forbidden-to-update-websites-and-blogs-from-pan-am-games-1133.html (accessed 25 February 2007).

Sparre, K. 2007b, 'Athletes at Pan Am Games May Update their Websites After All', *Play the Game*, 28 June. Online. Available http://www.playthegame.org/Home/News/Up_To_Date/Athletes_at_Pan_Am_Games_may_update_their_websites_after_all_21064.aspx (accessed 28 June 2007).

Spigel, L. & Olsson, J. (eds) 2004, *Television After TV: Essays on a Medium in Transition*, Durham, NC: Duke University Press.

Sport and Technology 2008, 'Comment—Looking Back, Part 2', February. Monthly Newsletter.

Sport Business 2008, 'Sport and Technology: The Conference 2008', Post Event Paper, 13 June.

Sport Business International 2008, 'Serie A', No. 141, August, p. 23.

Sport Business International 2011a, 'Social Streaming', No. 169, July, p. 20.

Sport Business International 2011b, 'Facebook Boost for UFC', No. 167, May, pp. 22–23.

Sport Business International 2011c, 'US Olympic Rights', No. 169, July, p. 9.

Sport Business International 2011d, 'Cunning Rebrand', No. 170, August, p. 23.

SportingPulse 2011, 'Partnerships'. Online. Available http://corp.sportingpulse.com/index.php?id=54 (accessed 20 April 2011).

Sports Geek 2010a, 'Digital and TV Rights—What To Do?' 19 April. Online. Available http://sportsgeek.com.au/web/digital-tv-rights-what-to-do/ (accessed 19 April 2010).

Sports Geek 2010b, 'A Look at the "Super Bowl Effect"', 18 February. Online. Available http://sportsgeek.com.au/social-media/a-look-at-the-super-bowl-effect/ (accessed 4 March 2010).

Sprouse, M. 2010, 'Fantasy Football is Not a Workplace Distraction', *Fantazzle Fantasy Sports*, 14 December.

Spurgeon, C. 2008, *Advertising and New Media*, London: Routledge.

Stauff, M. 2009, 'Sports on YouTube', in P. Snickars & P. Vonderau (eds), *The YouTube Reader*, Stockholm, Sweden: National Library of Sweden, pp. 236–52.

Stuart, K. 2010, 'Sports Sims: How They Become the Real Deal', *The Guardian*, 13 June. Online. Available http://www.guardian.co.uk/technology/2010/jun/13/sports-sims-motion-capture-technology (accessed 10 May 2011).

Sugden, J. 2002, 'Network Football', in J. Sugden & A. Tomlinson (eds), *Power Play: A Critical Sociology of Sport*, London: Routledge, pp. 61–80.

Sugden, J. & Tomlinson, A. 1998, *FIFA and the Contest for World Football: Who Rules the People's Game?* Cambridge, UK: Polity Press.

Sundaram, R. 2010, *Pirate Modernity: Delhi's Media Urbanism*, London: Routledge.

Surowiecki, J. 2005, *The Wisdom of Crowds*, New York: Anchor Books.

Sweney, M. 2011, 'Perform Digital Rights Group to Float on Stock Exchange', *The Guardian*, 10 March. Online. Available http://www.guardian.co.uk/media/2011/mar/10/perform-group-ipo-stock-exchange (accessed 12 March 2011).

Sydney Morning Herald 2011, 'Fairfax Media Breaks Ranks with Rugby's Top Body to Cover World Cup', 24 August. Online. Available http://www.smh.com.au/rugby-union/union-news/fairfax-media—breaks-ranks-with-rugbys-top-body-to—cover—world-cup-20110824–1j9sd.html (accessed 24 August 2011).

Taylor, D. 2011, 'Liverpool's Ryan Babel Faces FA Probe for Twitter Blast at Howard Webb', *The Guardian*, 9 January. Online. Available http://www.guardian.co.uk/football/2011/jan/09/ryan-babel-howard-webb-manchester-united-liverpool (accessed 16 January 2011).

Taylor, L. 2011, 'Clubs Should Serve the Fans, Not Pander to Fantasies of Democracy', *The Guardian*, 13 January. Online. Available http://www.guardian.co.uk/football/blog/2011/jan/13/football-fans-chairman-democracy (accessed 14 January 2011).

Taylor, N., Jenson, J. & de Castell, S. 2009, 'Cheerleaders/Booth Babes/Halo Hoes: Pro-Gaming, Gender and Jobs for the Boys', *Digital Creativity*, 20(4), pp. 239–52.

Taylor, T.L. 2006a, 'Does WoW Change Everything? How a PvP Server, Multinational Player Base, and Surveillance Mod Scene Caused Me Pause', *Games and Culture*, 1(4), pp. 318–37.

Taylor, T.L. 2006b, *Play Between Worlds: Exploring Online Game Culture*, Cambridge, MA: The MIT Press.

Telstra 2011, (Media Release) 'All AFL Matches Live on Mobiles, Tablets and Telstra T-Box', 28 April. Online. Available http://www.telstra.com.au/about-telstra/media-centre/announcements/all-afl-matches-live-on-mobiles-tablets-and-telstra-t-box.xml (accessed 5 June 2011).

Tennis Australia 2009, Submission to the Inquiry into the Reporting of Sports News and the Emergence of Digital Media, *Senate Standing Committee on Environment, Communications and the Arts*, Canberra: Parliament of Australia.

The Sports Factor 2007, 'My Football Club', *ABC Radio National*, 11 May. Online. Available http://www.abc.net.au/rn/sportsfactor/stories/2007/1920243.htm (accessed 2 October 2007).

The Sports Factor 2008, 'On Your Blogs, Get Set, Go! Athletes and the New Media', *ABC Radio National*, 7 March. Online. Available http://www.abc.net.au/rn/sportsfactor/stories/2008/2179195.htm (accessed 7 March 2008).

Theodoropoulou, V. 2007, 'The Anti-Fan Within the Fan: Awe and Envy in Sport Fandom', in J. Gray, C. Sandvoss & C. Harrington (eds), *Fandom: Identities and Communities in a Mediated World*, New York: New York University Press, pp. 316–27.

Thompson, J.B. 2000, *Political Scandal: Power and Visibility in the Media Age*, Cambridge, UK: Polity Press.

Thompson, J.B. 2005, 'The New Visibility', *Theory, Culture & Society*, 22(6), pp. 31–51.

Timmons, H. 2010, 'Google Sees a New Role for YouTube: An Outlet for Live Sports', *The New York Times*, 2 May. Online. Available http://www.nytimes.com/2010/05/03/business/media/03cricket.html (accessed 2 May 2010).

Tomlinson, A. & Young, C. (eds) 2006, *National Identity and Global Sports Events: Culture, Politics, and Spectacle in the Olympics and the Football World Cup*, New York: State University of New York Press.

Tomlinson, J. 2007, *The Culture of Speed: The Coming of Immediacy*, London: Sage.

Tulloch, J. & Jenkins, H. 1995, *Science Fiction Audiences: Watching Doctor Who and Star Trek*, London: Routledge.

Turner, G. 2009, 'Television and the Nation: Does This Matter Anymore?' in G. Turner & J. Tay (eds), *Television Studies After TV: Understanding Television in the Post-Broadcast Era*, London: Routledge, pp. 54–64.

Turner, G. & Tay, J. (eds) 2009, *Television Studies after TV: Understanding Television in the Post-Broadcast Era*, London: Routledge.

Tushnet, R. 2007, 'Copyright Law, Fan Practices, and the Rights of the Author', in J. Gray, C. Sandvoss & C. Harrington (eds), *Fandom: Identities and Communities in a Mediated World*, New York: New York University Press, pp. 60–71.

Tussey, E. 2009, 'Foam Finger Cubicle: Selling ESPN360 as Workspace Media', *FlowTV*, 10(10): http://flowtv.org/?p=4424 (accessed 18 October 2009).

Urry, J. 2007, *Mobilities*, Cambridge, UK: Polity Press.

Valtysson, B. 2010, 'Access Culture: Web 2.0 and Cultural Participation', *International Journal of Cultural Policy*, 16(2), pp. 200–14.

Van Dijck, J. 2009, 'Users Like You? Theorizing Agency in User-Generated Content', *Media, Culture & Society*, 31(1), pp. 41–58.

Van Dijck, J. & Nieborg, D. 2009, 'Wikinomics and its Discontents: A Critical Analysis of Web 2.0 Business Manifestos', *New Media & Society,* 11(5), pp. 855–74.

Van Grove, J. 2011, 'WordPress.com Blogs Garnered 23 Billion Pageviews in 2010', *Mashable*, 7 January. Online. Available http://mashable.com/2011/01/07/wordpress-blogs/ (accessed 7 January 2011).

Viocorp 2009, 'Australian Open—Wildcard Tournament', December. Online. Available http://www.viocorp.com/Showcase/december_showdown.html (accessed 20 January 2010).

Virilio, P. 1986, *Speed and Politics*, New York: Semiotext(e).

Virilio, P. 2001, 'Not Words But Visions! Interview with Nicholas Zurbrugg', in J. Armitage (ed), *Virilio Live: Selected Interviews*, London: Sage, pp. 154–63.

Virilio, P. 2007, *The Original Accident*, Cambridge, UK: Polity Press.

Wajcman, J., Bittman, M. & Brown, J. 2009, 'Intimate Connections: The Impact of the Mobile Phone on Work/Life Boundaries', in G. Goggin & L. Hjorth (eds), *Mobile Technologies: From Telecommunications to Media*, New York: Routledge, pp. 9–22.

Walter, B. 2010, 'Monaghan Faces Sack Over Mad Monday Dog Photo Disgrace', *Sydney Morning Herald*, 5 November. Online. Available http://www.smh.com. au/rugby-league/league-news/monaghan-faces-sack-over-mad-monday-dog-photo-disgrace-20101104–17fx1.html (accessed 5 November 2010).

Wann, D.L., Melnick, M.J., Russell, G.W. & Pease, D.G 2001, *Sports Fans: The Psychological and Social Impact of Spectators*, New York: Routledge.

Ware, W. 2008, 'One in 29,700', *MyFootballClub.co.uk*, 26 April. Online. Available http://members.myfootballclub.co.uk/article-33402# (accessed 26 April 2008).

Wark, M. 2007, *Gamer Theory*, Cambridge, MA: Harvard University Press.

Waters, R.L. 2003, '21st Century Corporate Mediathletics: How Did We Get to Slamball?' *Journal of Sports Law and Contemporary Problems*, 1(1), pp. 1–12.

Watts, R.B. 2008, 'The Florida Gator Nation Online', in L.W. Hugenberg, P.M. Haridakis & A.C. Earnheardt (eds), *Sports Mania: Essays on Fandom and the Media in the 21st Century*, North Carolina: McFarland and Co., pp. 243–56.

Weber, S. 1996, *Mass Mediauras: Form, Technics, Media*, Stanford, CA: Stanford University Press.

Wenger, E. 1998, *Communities of Practice: Learning, Media, Identity*, Cambridge, UK: Cambridge University Press.

Wenner, L.A. (ed) 1998, *MediaSport*, London: Routledge.

Whannel, G. 1992, *Fields in Vision: Television Sport and Cultural Transformation*, London: Routledge.

Whannel, G. 2002, *Media Sport Stars: Masculinities and Moralities*, London: Routledge.

What the Trend 2011, 'Twitter Trends'. Online. Available http://www.whatthetrend.com/ (accessed 17 January 2011).

White, D. 2009, 'Newcastle Pay Joey Barton £675,000 a Year for Image Rights', *The Telegraph*, 14 June. Online. Available http://www.telegraph.co.uk/sport/football/teams/newcastle-united/5526418/Newcastle-pay-Joey-Barton-675000-a-year-for-image-rights.html (accessed 23 November 2009).

Whitson, D. 1998, 'Circuits of Promotion: Media, Marketing and the Globalization of Sport', in L.A. Wenner (ed), *MediaSport*, London: Routledge, pp. 57–72.

Williams, R. 1974, *Television: Technology and Cultural Form*, London: Fontana/ Collins.

Wilner, B. 2009, 'The NFL on TV: Thriving Through the Downturn', *Sport Business International*, No. 147, July, pp. 20–21.

Wilner, B. 2010, 'NFL Fines Favre $50K for "Failure to Cooperate"', *Washington Times*, 29 December. Online. Available http://www.washingtontimes.com/news/2010/dec/29/nfl-fines-favre-50k-failure-cooperate/ (accessed 23 January 2011).

Wilson, B. 2007, 'New Media, Social Movements, and Global Sport Studies: A Revolutionary Moment and the Sociology of Sport', *Sociology of Sport Journal*, 24(4), pp. 457–77.

Wilson, W. 2007, 'All Together Now, Click: MLS Soccer Fans in Cyberspace', *Soccer & Society*, 8(2–3), pp. 381–98.

Winston, B. 1998, *Media Technology and Society. A History: From the Telegraph to the Internet*, London: Routledge.

Wolf, M.J. 1999, *The Entertainment Economy: The Mega-Media Forces that are Re-Shaping Our Lives*, New York: Penguin.

Woolgar, S. (ed) 2002, *Virtual Society? Technology, Cyberole, Reality*, Oxford: Oxford University Press.

WSC (When Saturday Comes) 2007, 'Gagged to Order', November. Online. Available http://www.wsc.co.uk/content/view/290/29/ (accessed 17 June 2008).

Xinhua 2008, 'IOC Official Praises China Anti-Piracy Efforts', *China Daily*, 22 August. Online. Available http://www.chinadaily.com.cn/bizchina/2008–08/22/content_6960971.htm (accessed 29 August 2008).

Yar, M. 2005, 'The Global "Epidemic" of Movie "Piracy": Crime-Wave or Social Construction?' *Media, Culture & Society*, 27(5), pp. 677–96.

Yar, M. 2008, 'The Rhetorics and Myths of Anti-Piracy Campaigns: Criminalization, Moral Pedagogy and Capitalist Property Relations in the Classroom', *New Media & Society*, 10(4), pp. 605–23.

Yeates, C. 2011, 'Old Media Powers Warned About Digital', *The Age*, 25 July. Online. Available http://www.theage.com.au/business/old-media-powers-warned-about-digital-content-20110724–1hvgp.html (accessed 25 July 2011).

YouTube 2010, 'The TechJournal.com—Olympic Twitter Tracker Visualizes Tweets'. Online. Available http://www.youtube.com/watch?v=DQazwDC7wBI&feature=mfu_in_order&list=UL (accessed 2 March 2010).

Zhang, L.L. 2006, 'Behind the "Great Firewall": Decoding China's Internet Media Policies from the Inside', *Convergence*, 12(3), pp. 271–91.

Index